◦A TIMELESS AFFAIR◦

•A TIMELESS AFFAIR•

THE LIFE OF ANITA McCORMICK BLAINE

⦿ ⦿ ⦿ GILBERT A. HARRISON ⦿ ⦿ ⦿

THE UNIVERSITY OF CHICAGO PRESS · CHICAGO & LONDON

GILBERT A. HARRISON was editor-in-chief of *The New Republic* from 1954 to 1974 and president of Liveright Publishing Company from 1969 to 1974. He edited *Gertrude Stein's America* (1965) and *Public Persons: Essays by Walter Lippmann* (1976) and wrote the introduction to *Letters of Alice B. Toklas* (1973).

The University of Chicago Press, Chicago 60637
The University of Chicago Press, Ltd., London
© 1979 by The University of Chicago
All rights reserved. Published 1979
Printed in the United States of America
83 82 81 80 79 5 4 3 2 1

Library of Congress Cataloging in Publication Data

Harrison, Gilbert A
    A timeless affair.

    Includes index.
    1. Blaine, Anita McCormick. 2. Social reformers—United States—Biography. 3. United States—Social conditions. I. Title.
HQ1413.B54H37   301.24′2′0924 [B]   79–15264
ISBN 0–226–31804–4

FOR NANCY

and

David, James, Joel, Eleanor

CONTENTS

ACKNOWLEDGMENTS

Without the assistance of Barbara Davis, this biography would not have been written. Mrs. Davis, then a graduate student at the University of Wisconsin, was employed in late 1970 to research the files of Anita McCormick Blaine at the State Historical Society of Wisconsin, to solicit information from those who had known Mrs. Blaine, and to organize the material so that a formal biography could someday be written. She had at her disposal in Madison, as had I, not only the extensive files kept by Anita Blaine but those of Anita's father, Cyrus Hall McCormick; her mother, Nettie Fowler McCormick; her three brothers, Cyrus, Jr., Harold, and Stanley; and her sister, Virginia. Also deposited with the Society are papers of the McCormick Company as well as records of the McCormick Biographical Association and the McCormick Historical Association. The comprehensiveness of the material is attested to in the *Guide to the McCormick Collection*, edited by Margaret R. Hafstad and published in 1973 by the State Historical Society of Wisconsin.

In 1974, having recently given up the editorship of *The New Republic*, I wrote the first of seven drafts of *A Timeless Affair*, finishing the manuscript in December 1978. I was aided by many private, family documents not yet in the McCormick Collection.

My indebtedness to Mrs. Davis and the Society in Wisconsin extends to the Chicago Historical Society; to the Library of Congress, for making available correspondence between Mrs. Blaine and Woodrow Wilson and Henry A. Wallace; and to individuals, not all of them still alive, whose recollections were helpful. They include Katharine Taylor, Charlotte Kuh, Joseph Faulkner, Harriet Welling, Richard and Phoebe Bentley, Lottie Haggerty, Hubert Will, Fowler McCormick, Reuel Denney, Harris Wofford, Cynthia Harris, John Blaine Lawrence, Eleanor Petersen, Sven Olafson, Tage Larsson, Anne De Mooy, Marie and Georgiana Ceder, A. J. G. Priest, William McCormick Blair, Stringfellow Barr, and, above all, my wife, Anne (Nancy) Blaine Harrison.

I

THE GENESIS OF FORTUNE

I

"All things are naked and opened," says the Apostle Paul, "unto the eyes of him with whom we have to do." But the flickering lantern of the human eye illuminates only fitfully. If we could see the wholeness of Anita McCormick Blaine by the light of the visible record of her eighty-eight years, all would be clear and distinct, for no paper was lost or discarded—no correspondence on public affairs, no penciled meditation or attempt to communicate with the dead, no observation on her remarkable family. The clues to her elusive nature lie in scores of file cabinets; yet the puzzle of her singularity remains.

The middle of five children born to Cyrus Hall McCormick, inventor of the reaper, and his wife, Nettie, Anita was raised amidst luxury that was saved from self-indulgence by the constraints of orthodox Presbyterianism. Her personality was paradoxical. She became both willful and dutiful, playful and serious, self-reliant and dependent. She sought the counsel of others, yet rejected whatever seemed incompatible with some hidden spring of feeling; broke free of the opinions of her class and age, yet so tenderly and unpretentiously there seemed to have been no break at all. To each personal encounter she brought an exciting promise of things to be learned, shared, done; and each new acquaintance went away wondering what chemistry or circumstance had formed her, had set her apart from her parents, brothers, sister, and from the "Chicago Medicis" among whom she grew up.

We see Anita first in 1871, when she is five, summering with her mother and her elder brother and sister at Richfield Springs, New York, the fashionable white-sulphur resort of the Northeast and rendezvous of prominent families who came to drink the mineral waters which reputedly cured rheumatism, gout, dyspepsia, catarrh, and "diseases of the blood."[1] It was a favorite spa of her father, then the sixty-two-year-old manufacturer of agricultural implements, and of his thirty-eight-year-old wife, who approved of its "wholesome" atmosphere. To the children, Richfield Springs was memorable for its "terrible smelling" bathhouse and the high, narrow iron tubs in which they were daily immersed by their governess.

By October, most of the visitors had departed, but Nettie McCormick lingered on with Cyrus, Jr. (twelve), Virginia (ten), and Anita, awaiting the return of Papa, who had gone to Chicago to settle some vexing dispute with his brother Leander over the management of the reaper company. The children entertained themselves playing croquet on the front lawn of their large, rented, red-brick house or walking (India rubbers over shoes) through the crimson and gold woods or inspecting a nearby hilltop that their father had recently purchased for a permanent summer residence. His wife, whose musings often took a melancholy turn, was especially solemn that autumn, for she had lost her blue-eyed infant daughter Alice some months earlier. She was anxious, too, over the silence from Chicago. There had been no word from her husband for several days, but no doubt she would soon have a reply to a telegram she had sent him, asking to be advised of his plans. The telegram had been carried to the village telegraph office by young Cyrus.

When the boy came racing back to the house, he was incoherent. After he had caught his breath, he explained that when he handed his mother's message over the counter, the telegraph operator stared at it, stared at the boy, and said, "Young man, I can't take that message, because there is no Chicago. There has been a great fire. The whole city was burned and is now burning!"

Nettie needed no further details. "We will take the first train home," she said promptly, and when her son asked how in the world they could do that, since the city was in flames, she replied, "We will go," whereupon the maids were instructed to pack. Later that day, word from Papa did get through from Chicago, telling them to stay where they were, that he was "safe and well." She ignored the instruction. "Perhaps he is having a hard time, and the first thing we have to do is to get there, and we will leave tomorrow afternoon at five o'clock."

On the following day, the family boarded the train, and after a brief pause in Detroit to deposit Anita and Virginia with a cousin, Nettie and her son reached Chicago, where they were met by an employee of the McCormick reaper company, who drove them in a carriage through the smoke-filled streets to the Caroline Court Hotel, on the as-yet-unscathed West Side, where mattresses had been spread on the floor to accommodate refugee guests. There they were joined by Papa, wearing a partly burned coat but with "spirit unbroken and courage unspent,"[2] Nettie reported to her daughters. He described how he had been forced to flee the Fremont Hotel and had hurried to the home of his brother Leander, who "seemed resting under the fatal delusion that their house could not burn"; he had urged him not to depend on the Chicago River for protection but to leave immediately, salvaging whatever he could. Nettie remarked that "everyone thought the fire would be arrested before reaching his home." Within hours, however, the flames, whipped by a twenty-mile-an-hour wind, had jumped the river and engulfed the North Side residential area. As a McCormick reaper salesman boasted to a customer in England, it was the "greatest fire of the age!"[3] Nothing could beat Chicago.

It had been a dry summer, thirty fires had broken out the first week of October, the firemen should have been prepared but were not, and, by the time the first company got to the burning stable behind the O'Leary house on DeKoven Street, it was too late. Within hours, a spectator noted, the city was a "sea of fire, the heavens all ablaze, the air filled with burning embers, the wind blowing fiercely and tossing firebrands in all directions, thousands upon thousands of people rushing frantically about, burned out of shelters, without food."[4] Warehouses, brothels, and saloons collapsed, along with the newly built Palmer House and the courthouse. Dazed men, women, and children crowded the streets that led to the lake. Every block had armed patrols, and looters were hung to lampposts. Having been released, a hundred and fifty prisoners pillaged the first jewelry store they came to. Department stores and private homes were broken into, and the scavengers, laden with goods, ran to the security of Lake Michigan. An hour of rain extinguished the fire but left the city in darkness and ninety thousand homeless. Fifty thousand army tents were pitched to house the poor.

For the first few days the McCormicks "just bumped around anywhere," young Cyrus recalled. He made trips to the Third Presby-

5

terian Church and stood in line for bread and blankets, which were being distributed by the army. The rich and the poor pondered their losses. "Men clasped each other's hand and said: 'the city of the West is dead,'" John Greenleaf Whittier wrote. But two days after the rain (11 October), the *Chicago Tribune* was back on the streets with the headline, "Cheer up! Chicago Shall Rise Again." And it did rise with a rapidity that astonished the world.*

About eighteen thousand buildings on two thousand acres of land had been leveled, among them the McCormick Reaping Machine Works. Virtually nothing was left of the three-story brick factory and several outbuildings, which had turned out over eight thousand reapers and mowers the preceding year. In addition, most of the stores and residences owned by Cyrus, Leander, and their two sisters had been destroyed. The widow of Cyrus's brother William was hardest hit, for all she possessed was the income on property, not the property itself, and there were no buildings to rent. The Republic Insurance Company, in which the McCormicks had invested heavily, was ruined and paid its investors twenty-five cents on the dollar. Cyrus estimated that he had lost $1,500,000, not including property rentals. Leander, wrote Nettie, felt "more heartsick over the loss of his comfortable house—stored with all comforts and supplies of various kinds—than over all else."

Cyrus McCormick's confidence in his destiny was not easily shaken. Until the fire, he had never had reason to doubt that since he was on God's side, God was on his. Had that fidelity not been demonstrated by the rise of a Virginia farm boy to one of the richest men in America? Now, however, he was troubled. Might the fire have been a sign that it was time to abandon the worldly struggle? For days he shied away from deciding whether to rebuild his reaper factory. And what if he did choose to begin again? What could be done about the scarcity of materials? Life was a battle, he had often told his wife, but was this battle worth fighting? He was rich enough; he could retire.

It was she, thinking of the children—particularly of Cyrus, Jr.— who took the lead. When Nettie and her husband drove to the still smoldering site and were asked by the workmen, "Shall we start the small engine for repairs, or the big engine for manufacturing?" hers

* Within a week after the fire, 5,457 temporary structures had been erected, and four weeks later 200 permanent buildings were under construction. Despite the destruction, Chicago's population was to jump from 300,000 in 1870 to a half million in 1880, and then to more than a million by 1900.

was the order to "start the big engine for manufacturing." Then, turning to Cyrus, she asked if that was not correct. "It is," he said, and by Halloween the ruins no longer presented "an aspect of wilderness." She would countenance no delay in constructing a new factory on the West Side, near the south branch of the Chicago River: "I constantly urge Mr. McC. to miss no opportunity to go forward *this year*—not to wait until *next year* to make the decision whether to build or not—*make it now*. He has told me lately that 'I have been urging him on with whip and spur' and that he 'makes the decision now to go on with the trade principally under my influence.'"

Under that whip and spur, a more modern, larger McCormick plant was in operation in seventeen months—four buildings heated by steam, lighted by gas, and protected from fire by every means then known. Reapers were soon being produced faster than ever, until the overexpansion of agriculture in the West and the fall in wheat prices brought on the panic of 1873 and a drop in McCormick sales.

After a few uncomfortable months at the Caroline Court Hotel, the family, now including Anita and Virginia, moved into a furnished house on Sheldon and Fulton streets, which unfortunately adjoined the tracks of the Chicago and North Western Railway. The air was thick with cinders and smoke, and Anita was kept indoors most of the day. Papa, wearing dust spectacles, rode his horse into town each morning to oversee the construction of the factory and of offices and residences on his extensive real estate holdings. Anita seldom saw him, and when she did, he was in no mood for talk or play. "Mr. Mc.C. asleep all the evening," Nettie wrote in her diary, "I left him on the sofa." She had had her way, and "the vital current was again in motion."

Anita Eugenie McCormick's birth in 1866 had been celebrated by fireworks, booming cannons, and parades, for it was the Fourth of July and patriotic fervor was high. The Civil War was fresh in the mind of every American, as was the assassination of President Lincoln the previous year. In a message to New York's Tammany Hall on the day Anita was born, President Andrew Johnson had pleaded for the "obliteration of . . . passions and prejudices [and] complete restoration of all the states to . . . Constitutional relations with the

Federal Government," and in his fight with abolitionist diehards over the treatment of former Confederate states, the new president had the sympathy of Virginian Cyrus McCormick. But restraint ran counter to the popular mood, and the atmosphere was acrid with the recriminations of Reconstruction politics. "Malice toward none" had been buried with Lincoln and would not be resurrected for decades. In the postwar New Order, the first commandment was to grab what one could and let one's neighbor fend for himself. The short-lived Johnson administration was to usher in the greedy, gaudy age of unrestrained free enterprise, and government would become an accomplice in corruption. Tweed's gang would steal a hundred million dollars from New York City; Jim Fisk and Jay Gould would loot the Erie Railroad, Cornelius Vanderbilt the New York Central. Collis P. Huntington would bribe the California legislature to promote his railroad interests, and John D. Rockefeller (whose daughter Edith was to marry one of Anita's brothers) would strong-arm his opponents to extend his oil empire. Industrialism was ready to roar, and New York and Chicago were its lustiest financial boosters. The times were tailored to entrepreneurial talent and drive, and the 1870s were to prove Cyrus McCormick's most prosperous years.

Shortly before Anita's birth, Nettie had moved her children, maids, governess, and baggage from a hotel in Manchester, Vermont, where they had gone for the summer, to a nearby private home. Perhaps as a result of these last-minute exertions the baby arrived a week early, with Papa away in New Hampshire at another mineral spa. Although he had admonished his wife to summon him in ample time, she had not, and he surmised that the neglect had been deliberate. "From a remark made in one of your letters, that you thought you should go through without drawing me off from the pursuit of my sound health," he wrote, "I now believe you have purposely kept me in the dark while I wrote you that I *must* be present." Still, when the news did reach him, he did not rush off to Manchester. "With your kind permission," he telegraphed Nettie, "I may remain a few days as there now seems no danger, and it may be better for me to do so. This affection on my feet is a very slow, a troublesome thing to get rid of, and must have careful attention." She replied tactfully that he should "remain and use the baths as long as you had intended"; he would soon see for himself that his new daughter was "not like other children but was of a far higher order of nature." And, she added, she would like to name the child Anita Eugenie, Anita after a woman they had met and liked during a trip to Europe, Eugenie after the popular empress of France.

By fall, the McCormicks had settled in a four-story, $80,000 residence at 40 Fifth Avenue in New York City, where Papa had important business connections. The property had a pleasant garden, a sunny dining room, in which the two older children recited Latin lessons to their tutor, and an impressive library for Papa—an altogether suitable home for a family with an established and envied position in finance and society. From it, Cyrus McCormick could oversee his investments in mines, railroads, and land companies, letting brother Leander manage the factory in Chicago. His real estate was now worth twice what he had paid for it; his annual income from rents alone was $95,000, and that was on top of his yearly reaper company earnings of another quarter-of-a-million dollars.

The house on Fifth Avenue quickly became a meeting place for Cyrus's eminent associates—Samuel J. Tilden, later governor of New York and candidate for president; Cyrus Field, who promoted the Atlantic cable; James Gordon Bennett, publisher of the *New York Herald*; and Horace Greeley, editor of the *New York Tribune*, who often dropped by for breakfast to escape his own tumultuous household. Nettie McCormick had her own circle, notably the ladies of New York's Southern Relief Society, whose sympathies accorded well with Cyrus's background. Her good friend from around the corner, Mary Mildred Sullivan, was one of that elite group of southerners who had been driven by the Civil War to seek security in a Northern city. Both families attended the Fifth Avenue Presbyterian Church, and George Sullivan, who was young Cyrus's age, was in and out of the McCormick house and often accompanied the McCormick governess on strolls down the Avenue with baby Anita.

If the fire of 1871 had not forced a choice between New York and Chicago, Cyrus might have stayed indefinitely in the East. But the reaper came first, and the reaper meant the Midwest. Anita would grow up knowing little about agriculture or the manufacturing that was the source of the McCormick fame and of her fortune, but it was with the invention of the reaper, more than thirty years before her birth, that the family story had begun.

Cyrus was the eldest son of an amiable Virginia farmer who was respected for his inventiveness but lacked that acumen and aggressiveness which carry a promising idea forward to a profit. In his blacksmith shop at Walnut Grove, Robert McCormick had tinkered with a threshing machine but had not developed it sufficiently to eliminate the back-breaking task of harvesting grain with a scythe or sickle. The McCormicks were sober, industrious, and God-fearing. Before breakfast, Cyrus and his smaller brothers cut wood or weeded the garden, and when they weren't busy with chores or instruction in letters and numbers, they prayed, the day beginning and ending with thanks to the Lord. Selections from the Bible and the Shorter Catechism had to be memorized, and on Sunday mornings as well as afternoons there was preaching at the Presbyterian Church. Cyrus's mother, Mary Ann Hall, was as ambitious as her husband was dreaming, believing that while piety was a duty, poverty was not. She took pride in fine clothes, in her carriage with its folding steps and spirited team of horses, and in her silver and furniture. In addition, she believed devoutly in learning, and after school her children were given supplemental tutoring by her or the pastor.

Although Robert McCormick's experiments with a reaper came to no fruition and the machine was left abandoned in a shed, the eldest son early acquired a firm grasp of the problems of mechanical grain harvesting. In 1831, at twenty-two, he had made a workable hillside plow and a mechanical harvester, still crude but capable of cutting six acres of oats. It was the first public appearance of the reaper which was to revolutionize farming by combining a "side draft" (the horse walking to the side of the machine, rather than in front of it); a horizontal knife at right angles close to the ground; a triangular divider which separated a swath from a standing crop; a row of projecting fingers, which held the straws vertical while the blades cut them; and finally a wheel revolving above the knife, bending the heads of grain toward the knife and, after they were cut, pushing them back onto the platform of the reaper.[5]

A foolhardy, ten-year venture in iron mining interrupted refinement of the reaper; so it was not until 1842 that Cyrus seriously tried to market it, selling six machines that year at $100 each, all of which were made in the Walnut Grove carpentry and blacksmith sheds. As sales expanded to the wheat fields of the Midwest, there were changes in structure and marketing and rivals contesting McCormick's supremacy; there were patent fights in the courts and countless problems as Cyrus sought the best way to mass-produce his product when demand for it outgrew the capacity of the Virginia shop. He tried subcontracting the work to manufacturers in Eastern cities, which led to confusion and inferior machines. Finally, in 1848, two years after his father's death, he made up his mind to move his entire operation to Chicago, where he could build his own factory near the nation's granary.*

Many other men that decade were pulling up stakes and setting out for the West with a scheme and little capital, drawn by the lure of wider opportunity or a pot of gold, but few had such spectacular success as the thirty-nine-year-old Cyrus, who, in short order, managed to borrow $25,000 from Chicago's most prominent citizen and its first mayor, William B. Ogden. In return Ogden was given a half-interest in the contemplated McCormick reaper works, which could have been the most rewarding investment he ever made, had he not, two years later, asked for repayment of his loan. He was promptly handed not $25,000 but $50,000, a handsome enough profit but a pittance compared to what he would have earned if he had retained his half-interest. Cyrus then invited his younger brothers, Leander and William, to join him, and by 1853, when their mother died, the McCormicks of Walnut Grove had all become Chicagoans.

Within five years, Cyrus McCormick was patronizing the best tailors in New York and London and was well known in Washington, where he lobbied for the extension of his patents, and in New York, where he dabbled in finance with the big money men. His commanding figure was likewise familiar in the Midwest, for he was his own salesman at displays of the reaper in farmers' fields and at county fairs. Traveling to and from these exhibitions, he carried on his business, jotting down figures on the backs of envelopes, along with Bible verses and lines from hymns, and devising strategies for outwitting his competitors. He wasted neither time nor paper, and like many men who deal boldly in large matters, he could be small about small change and suspicious if he thought he might be taken advantage of. Shortly after the birth of his first child, having hired a couple as coachman and cook, he required the husband to hand over his gold watch as surety that Cyrus would get back the money he had advanced for their fare to Chicago. He was already a very wealthy man when he persuaded his friend Potter Palmer of the Palmer House to furnish him meals at less than the printed menu price. Palmer agreed, with the qualification that the cut rate be "confined to yourself for the reason that $.75 does not pay me the actual cost of the dinners."[6] A McCormick employee risked reprimand if

* Before deciding to settle in Chicago in 1847, Cyrus had visited and considered Cleveland, Cincinnati, and St. Louis.

he wrote on correspondence paper heavier than necessary, thus requiring an extra stamp, or if he used a superfluous word in a telegram. From his employees McCormick demanded both thrift and respect. A black servant was instructed to use "proper and courteous language . . . which embraced the proper use of the word *Sir.*" At home, there had to be an economical planning of meals—so much mush for so much milk, so that there would be none of either left when breakfast was over.

It is testimony to her managerial ability and fortitude that as a bride of twenty-two, Nettie Fowler McCormick was able not only to cater to the imperious personal whims of this powerful man of forty-seven but to become an active ally in his business. Her sweet smile and sentimental address and her prim demeanor concealed a head for figures, a will as strong as his, and no reservations about her right to be heard. Three years after their marriage, observing that politics were then engrossing the thoughts of both sexes, Nettie wrote a friend, "And why not? As Madame DeStael wrote to Napoleon when rebuked by that imperial personage for engaging in political controversies, 'When women have their heads cut off, they have a right to ask *why.*' " In later years, there would be many differences of opinion between Anita and her mother, but never over a woman's right to speak up.

Nettie had come from Brownville, New York, a village on the Black River in that finger of land formed by the joining of the St. Lawrence River with Lake Ontario. Orphaned at an early age, she and her older brother Eldridge were taken in by grandparents, whose strict Methodism reinforced the young girl's faint morbidity and sorrowing unctuousness. Nettie's heart was torn by "the poor sailor far at sea" and "those who are turned out of house and home this stinging cold night." Her conscience was never at rest, the awareness of her imperfections ever present: "Another week is added to my life. Am I one week better? Am I better prepared to enter upon eternal life than one week ago?" She confessed that she was "apt to look on life very darkly" and imagined that this disposition was inherited; had not her grandmother met with a tear of pity "the widow's appeal and the orphan's desolate cry of anguish"?

She took long, solitary walks, often before dawn, and marveled at nature's "sweet spring . . . thy gentle showers and soft zephyrs, thy budding leaf and spring herb." All this went with an energetic practicality; she *"burned* to be great and good."

She had been educated above the standard for a girl of her day, and after three years at female seminaries and a term of teaching in the one-room school of Clayton, New York—a waterfront community on the St. Lawrence where nothing ever happened to interrupt "the monotonous thread of existence"—she had welcomed the chance to visit a cousin in Chicago, that booming community which was about to overtake Cincinnati and St. Louis as the most important center in the Midwest. The city did not disappoint her. When she first saw it in 1856, four miles of crowded wharves were lined with docks, warehouses, grain elevators, and also with packing plants, which dumped their stinking wastes into the river. But what vim! Weren't Chicagoans up and doing! Shipping twenty-one million bushels of wheat a year and already the world's biggest lumber market! Barges and other water transport competed with the newer railroads for the commercial trade. Ten trunk lines and eleven branch lines crisscrossed the city, ninety-six trains entering or leaving every day, and the population would triple in the 1850s to over a hundred thousand, almost half of them immigrants. What bustle and what opportunity! Moreover, unmarried women were scarce, not as in Clayton, New York. Why, there were often seven men for every girl at a social gathering.

Nettie skated at the Ogden ice rink near the lake, was escorted to dances sponsored by a fire company or a military lodge, and edified by lecture courses featuring Horace Greeley, Henry Ward Beecher, Susan B. Anthony, and Wendell B. Phillips. Mary McVickers made her weep as Little Eva in *Uncle Tom's Cabin*. At literary clubs, members read aloud from the latest Dickens novel or from some expurgated play. And there were private parties, a strenuous undertaking when custom required a hostess to deliver handwritten invitations in person and make all the food herself, except the ice cream. There were high teas with preserves, chicken salad, escalloped oysters, and fruitcakes, and evenings of square dancing with everyone home by midnight. Social distinctions were not then as rigid as they were to become a half-century later. A servant girl of good parentage might meet at one of the public dances, and marry, a lawyer or rising young businessman. "Basket charity" from the fortunate to the needy had not yet been institutionalized and carried no condescension. The tall prairie grass grew just outside the city limits, but the fashionable North and West sides boasted fine homes, shade trees, and gardens, and the courthouse and large hotels gave distinction to downtown. True, there was another Chicago—Kilgubbin, Conley's Patch, Hardscrabble—where the poor lived in hovels built on

13

stilts and were the first victims of fires, polluted water, the stench from the packing houses, and the damp air that hovered over the marshes. Unlike New England, the streets after a heavy rain were a sea of mud, and carts and coaches sank to their wheel hubs. Crime was increasing as fast as the population, and there were more saloons and brothels than churches. But that was the unpublicized and, to the young visitor from the East Coast, the seldom visible Chicago.

Nettie was introduced to Cyrus McCormick shortly after her arrival. Of course she had heard of him; who hadn't? Within a month he had proposed and had been told that she was leary of his "self-confidence that brooks no desire—a resolute determination to overcome every obstacle—a hardness and blindness of purpose that will not quit." She neither refused nor rejected him. He replied that she did him an injustice, that there was not "a man in the world who would strive more to please you than I should do—no one whose disposition and manner would be more under your control and influence than would be mine as your husband." Five months later, she accepted him. "I presume," he responded, "that I must expect to come in for my share of petticoat government, now."[7] He was not a man of wit.

Their wedding had to be postponed several times because of a reaper patent case pending in the courts, but when it occurred on 26 January 1858, the six-foot, forty-eight-year-old bridegroom—so a bridesmaid wrote friends in the East—was looking his best, "and the bride also, although the service tended to move Nettie to tears which gave her a pensive look."[8] The reception that evening at the home of Cyrus's brother William, was "the largest, and one of the most brilliant of the season and will be memorable in festive annals," according to the *Chicago Weekly Press* of 30 January, though Cyrus had worried that the house would not be large enough; it could accommodate no more than five hundred guests, and he wanted "a splendid affair," one on which he was prepared to spend "at least $500."[9]

Since Cyrus kept no journal, there is only Nettie's version of their early years together. Their honeymoon—a visit to Nettie's family in Clayton, New York—had been brief, and they had then moved to a hotel in Washington, where she saw little of her husband. While he was busy with his legal battles, Nettie drove about town with her cousin Ermina, shopped, listened to congressional debates, and was received by President Buchanan. By the end of 1858, they had rented a furnished house, the Maynard house on a corner of Lafayette Square, a block from the White House.

Nettie had promised herself to "always sympathize with my dear husband, I will support him, I will be his guardian angel, *do as he wishes*," which sounded "very *easy*, but it is *not* easy to be *real* good . . . to say the right thing in the right place." When the right thing to say did occur to her, he often was not in place to hear it. "I am alone all day as far as seeing and being on friendly intercourse with anybody," Nettie confessed to her journal. "I never speak to a soul from morning to night but my servants and my children." There came one disconsolate rainy day when she wept "*bitter* tears . . . how *my heart has ached.*" It all arose from a conversation before breakfast during which Cyrus had administered "a sharp rebuke." Having wept, she acted, writing a memorandum dated 13 May 1865 which read, "If either makes an abrupt reply or charge, the other is not to reply in the same strain but to direct the attention calmly to its spirit and effect, and to the real merits of the point involved." At her insistence, he initialed it.

Cyrus, Jr., called by his delighted father the "Young Reaper," was born 16 May 1859 in Washington, D.C., in the LaFayette Square house that Cyrus had rented while he awaited judgment by the Supreme Court on one of those frequent patent infringement suits. A week later, Papa was off to Indianapolis and the General Assembly of the Presbyterian Church, to which he took a proposal for a school in Chicago to train ministers throughout the Northwest in traditional doctrines. By fall, the McCormicks, including the "nice looking and very large" heir, were back in Chicago, caught up in controversies which only the Civil War would resolve.

An important terminus of the underground railway and a depot for supplies to "Free Soilers" in Kansas, Chicago was a cauldron of abolitionist agitation. Selected as the site of the Republican convention that would nominate Abraham Lincoln for the presidency, it was rapidly becoming uncomfortable for a Southerner like McCormick, who was on record as saying that "the Constitution sanctioned human bondage" and that "the Union should not be endangered by agitating the issue of immediate emancipation." The unpopularity of that view lost him the Democratic nomination for mayor of Chicago in 1860, a defeat which hurt his pride but earned him the congratulations of his wife, who thought he had escaped "a *great* bore"[10] and held that the Democratic party had been interested only in his money—an opinion that was shared by Cyrus's victorious rival, "Long John" Wentworth: "Whenever the Democrats wanted money in their campaigns, they would always try to get Cyrus in to bleed him."[11]*

To propagate his opinions on slavery, this "loyal son of the Old Dominion," as Cyrus referred to himself, purchased and combined two Chicago newspapers, used the merged daily *Chicago Times* to promote the presidential candidacy of Stephen A. Douglas, and was thereupon attacked as a "rebel" and "slave driver" by the pro-Lincoln *Chicago Daily Tribune* (12 February 1861), the daughter of whose owner, Joseph Medill, would later marry a nephew of Cyrus and bring that newspaper into the McCormick family. A McCormick-inspired editorial appeal in the *Chicago Times* for peace and compromise triggered threats against the paper and its owner by antislavery mobs, and, by late April 1861, popular passions had become so intimidating that Cyrus felt compelled to issue a temporizing statement as a signed editorial in the *Chicago Times:* "Born and reared in the South, I would disgrace my manhood did I not say that my heart sickens at the prospect of the conflict which must ensue . . . [but] though a native of the South, I am a citizen of Illinois, and of the United States, and as such shall bear true allegiance to the Government." The statement did not appease his critics; the attacks mounted, and a year later Cyrus fled to England, taking his entire family, which now included a second child, Mary Virginia. Until the summer of 1864, he carried on his business as best he could from abroad, observing with "deepest concern the progress of events at home" and urging a policy of "stop the war, declare an armistice —call a convention and consider terms of peace."[12] On their return, undaunted, Cyrus again ran for public office and again was defeated, this time as Democratic candidate for Congress in the First District of Illinois. "Poor white trash," the Republican *Tribune* called him, "a better friend of slavery than the slaveholders themselves." Once more Cyrus retreated, this time to New York, where he was joined by Nettie, Cyrus, Jr., Mary Virginia, and the newly arrived baby Robert.

Almost immediately, the children came down with scarlet fever, and on 6 January 1865, fifteen-month-old Robert died. Nettie was sure she had been responsible, and all her lacerating guilt rose to the

* According to one of Cyrus McCormick's biographers, Herbert N. Casson, a clergyman once asked the inventor what glory he could hope to get out of politics, to which Cyrus replied, "I am in politics because I cannot help it. There are certain principles that I have got to stand by, and I am obliged to go into politics to defend them."

surface. "Oh that I had done this or that," she cried. "I am all the time thinking how I could have saved him. . . . Oh God, I could not have been smitten in a spot so sensitive—Oh that I could feel right —Oh that I could repent—Oh that I knew the right way to feel. God is punishing me for my sin, my procrastination, my slothfulness." Hours on end, she prayed for guidance on how to protect her children—"not their *bodies* alone, but what impressions to make upon their minds, and *how* to make them." How could she give them "hearts to answer back with sincere response when the cords of feelings are touched," how was she to "keep the pure pages of youth *unsullied?*"

She was haunted by the dangers to virginal innocence. "Dear Child," she was to counsel Virginia (no longer called Mary Virginia) on the child's thirteenth birthday, "the sweetest thing about a woman is her tenderness and purity." Sex was never to be mentioned. She was equally obsessed by the hazards to sheer survival. When the children went out to play, they were dressed so warmly that the slightest exertion left them drenched in sweat. At the first sign of a sniffle or an ache, a child was put to bed and kept there for days. When they were no longer children, their mother's letters would chase them across the country, admonishing them to wear rubbers over their shoes, avoid drafts, eat properly—always full of "health and business," Virginia complained. And poor Virginia, who was to live most of her life in the shadow of mental illness, wanted so much more from Mama: "Oh! won't you *please* put something very private in your next letter," she wrote in May 1865, "I want a letter from you *all my own!* Make it a regular *love letter.*" A year after that plea and eighteen months after Robert's death, Anita was born.

The months after Anita's birth, first in Vermont, then in New York, were as restful as any Nettie had known since her marriage. The baby was "just as good as any baby was, she sleeps and grows," and Nettie wanted nothing more than to stay put, at which point Papa decided they would all go to Europe. She did all she could to dissuade him. She said that constant travel was harmful to children, that she would not leave them, that he would have to go alone. He bent but did not yield, merely changing their steamer reservations to a later date. She nevertheless continued to hold out "a most persistent opposition," and then, two days before the scheduled sailing, abruptly gave in, having persuaded herself that despite her "misgivings as to the effect of the undertaking on the baby," perhaps the sea voyage would be "sanguine" for the children's delicate constitutions. At the very last moment, however, she again changed her mind. Because he demanded it, she would accompany her husband, but the little ones would be left with the Luther Wrights of Oswego, New York, who had fresh vegetables and "a cow for baby's nourishment."

The Wrights sent Nettie frequent reports describing one-year-old Anita's "cunning little ways," of her learning to walk and to say "bow wow," and after each letter Nettie renewed her appeal to Cyrus to cut their trip short; she longed to hear the children's "sweet voices and to have them about me." Well, he had urged her to bring them along in the first place, he replied. They were away nearly a year, during which Nettie had a miscarriage, and when the family was finally reunited in New York, in March 1868, Anita did not recognize her mother.

Still smarting from his political repudiation in Illinois, Cyrus seemed content to remain in the East. "Chicago," he wrote, "while a great city and with a great future before it, had lost much of its interest for me by means of the radical rule there."[13] Their house on Fifth Avenue was commodious, and New York was a convenient base from which to fight his legal battles. From there also he could exert his considerable leverage on the church, helping to preserve Presbyterianism from the modernists. Early on, anticipating that the slavery issue would split his denomination and incite the reformers to further mischief, he had taken steps to minimize the damage by underwriting two religious newspapers, a succession of churches, and a Presbyterian Seminary dedicated to strengthening conservative theology in the Midwest, all with Nettie's approval. He had stood valiantly, she wrote him proudly, "against the fanatical tide."

When the 1871 fire brought the McCormicks back to Chicago permanently, Cyrus had seen immediately that no one but he had the money, energy, and interest to save his seminary and a favored Presbyterian newspaper from bankruptcy. Having rescued them, he was given control over them and used them to further the cause of Southern reinstatement into the Presbyterian Church. Tempers in the country had begun to cool, the fundamentalists and modernists would compromise their differences, and the seminary would settle down to years of steady growth, aided by his further gifts of houses for the faculty and a student dormitory. Old grudges were being washed away by the postwar wave of new opportunities. The Chicago fire itself wiped out some of the personal bitterness against McCormick. It was a time to pull together, there was a city to be rebuilt, and for Cyrus more money and perhaps even a political career still to be made. When a splinter Republican convention nominated his old friend Horace Greeley for president in 1872, Cyrus again plunged into politics. He was present at the Democratic convention in Baltimore, which endorsed Greeley on the first ballot; served on the Democratic National Committee; was chairman of the Illinois State Committee; and was considered, but not chosen, as a candidate for governor, state senator, even vice president. At sixty-three, he even found time to father another child.

With the birth of Harold Fowler in 1872, eight-year-old Anita was no longer the youngest, and she adopted the infant as her special charge. He would always be her pet and she his defender and comforter. She could not have foreseen the responsibilities she would later have to assume for Harold, or for the last of the McCormick children, Stanley, who arrived in 1874.

Nettie was thirty-nine when Cyrus, sixty-five, was at last prepared to build a permanent home on Chicago's North Side for his wife of sixteen years and his five children. Having been so long delayed, however, the house was too important an undertaking to hurry, and Anita was thirteen before the Rush Street residence was completed. Meanwhile, she was entered at the Misses Grant's Seminary, for which she was expected to feel grateful: some girls, she was reminded, were sent to public school as punishment for their frivolity. Her timetable, drawn up by her mother, was as regular as a railroad's—up at seven, dressed by seven-thirty, downstairs by eight for half-an-hour of piano practice followed by another hour at the piano after breakfast, study in her room until lunch at one, unless she was required to be at school, in which case she attended classes at Misses Grant's in the morning and worked at home in the afternoon. Then a walk or drive before six-thirty dinner and bed at quarter of nine. The demands did not seem too exacting to Anita, and since she "very early manifested a beautiful repose and an acceptance of things as they came along," according to Nettie, as well as "an intelligent homey-sweetness," discipline was light. The younger boys were not quite so accepting, and when their tomfoolery got out of hand, Mama's slipper was applied to their bottoms.

The children could not remember when their home was not a port of call for seminarians, ministers of the gospel, and especially missionaries from far-off lands. "All praise to these dear workers who have patiently, by years of fidelity, won their way to the hearts of these darkened races," said Nettie. Dwight L. Moody, evangelist and YMCA leader, was a frequent visitor. Although Anita came to question his theology, as a girl she loved "the invigoration of his presence as he blew in, his religion a gorgeous, happy thing." Family attendance had been compulsory at Moody's Chicago crusade the winter of 1866, Papa rousing them before dawn, so they would be sure of securing seats near the platform in the tabernacle. Being only six months old, Anita was left home, but it was not long before she joined the others on their walks each Sunday (the carriage was not driven on the Sabbath) to services at Fourth Presbyterian. How pleased Mama was to record three-year-old Anita's words: "I will say my prayers, God bless papa, mama, sister and brother. I love dolly—dolly loves God." After early-morning family prayers in the library, there was Sunday school, and after supper came evening services. Play was prohibited. One would have said it was not a playful house on any day, and the young McCormicks' circle of acquaintances was narrowly circumscribed. They were never permitted to associate either with the children of Chicago's more worldly upper class or with the lower orders. Anita's companions were her cousins Anna Chapman and Lucy McCormick.

This not too unhappy routine continued uninterrupted until just after Anita's twelfth birthday in 1878 (it was the year Nettie gave up making entries in her journal), when Cyrus notified his wife that he planned to be present at his reaper display at the Paris Exposition that July and wished his family to be with him. The familiar tug-of-war was resumed; Nettie prayed for light and again, not surprisingly, was guided along the path her husband had marked out. They left for Europe in installments—Cyrus, Jr., first, then Mama with the younger children, and finally Papa. While the two Cyruses demonstrated the wonders of the reaper in Holland, Nettie and Virginia took an "air cure" on the "gentler slopes" of the Swiss Alps, the three smaller ones having been deposited in England at Ramsgate, to be looked after by Harriot Hammond, sister of Nettie's New York friend, Mildred Sullivan. The selection of "Missy" Hammond was to prove fortuitous. Although paid for her services, she was not a governess, was treated as a friend of the family, and became Anita's most valued confidante.

The child of wealthy, slave-owning parents, Missy had been raised by an aunt and uncle in Virginia, turned to school teaching after the Civil War and then came to live with her sister in New York, where Nettie met her and occasionally recruited her as a convenient foster mother. She had been born with a compound spinal curvature, and though "affliction so great as hers could not escape notice," one of her students commented, "the beauty of her countenance, the exhalted expression of her clear, brown eyes, the shapely mouth and hands . . . all made of her an impressive personality. Never twenty-four hours without pain, her classroom duties must have been more taxing than we knew, for except a slight hesitancy of manner, over in a flash, there was no hint of stifled agony, no curtailment of her vivid interest, no interrupted thought, no withdrawing from the subject at hand."[14]

That summer of 1878 in England with Missy, Harold, and Stanley was a "delicious time" for Anita; such a "splendid sensation," she wrote, to be ducked under the sea waves by "a strong *stout* bathing woman"; such fun to watch her brothers "digging in the sand with such a lot of healthy dirt on them." And English history seemed so romantic when one could see the Dover cliffs, "on which those *brave* Britons came to defend their country against the Romans."

In August, the exciting word reached Ramsgate that Papa's reaper had won the Grand Prize for agricultural machinery, to be awarded 21 October, and Missy was instructed to bring the children to Paris for the festivities. They arrived in time to see Papa made an officer in the Legion of Honor and to watch a brilliant procession, led by the Prince of Wales, file into the Palace of Industry for the ceremonies at which the inventor received his gold medal. The most dazzling event, however, came that evening, when Nettie, Virginia, and Anita (Papa chose not to attend) stepped into a carriage outside their hotel near the Tuileries and were driven to the Versailles Palace and the Grand Fete, for which twenty-five thousand invitations had been issued. Nettie found the "mass of human beings" appalling, but Anita was ecstatic. It was three in the morning before they left the palace and located their carriage, which lost its way. They ended up walking to their hotel, where they were told their rooms had been rented to someone else, and it took two hours to find other accommodations. To Nettie, the assemblage had been nothing but "a well-dressed mob"; to the twelve-year-old daughter the evening had been a fairy tale: "The lovely palace behind us, the lights and the splendid gates before. . . . In the beautiful heavens was the new moon, the crescent with Venus near it, artlessly placed there by Nature. . . . The air was so bracing and fresh that though tired, it aroused me so that I did not like to approach the hotel." After a supper of bread and wine, Anita went to sleep on a mattress on the

21

floor. It was "the first ball sister and I had ever been to," she recalled touchingly.

Within twenty-four hours, Nettie's exasperation with the mob and Anita's exhilaration and even Papa's pleasure in his medal were forgotten. Cyrus developed a massive suppurating abscess on the back of his neck, and the headache, fever, and loss of appetite became so severe that his life seemed threatened. The French physician whom Nettie frantically consulted took drastic action, reported with a shudder by Anita in her diary: "Dr. Guyon with an iron, flat and round at the top, like a finger, ran the iron—heated to a white heat—through the carbuncle, and then crossed it two or three times. Oh!! It was frightful!!! The pain was something *horrible*!!! because they gave him no chloroform. Papa bore the pain without a *murmur* or a sign and he moved not a muscle." Convalescence was protracted and Cyrus was not a patient sufferer. During fits of irritability, he fired his nurses, found fault with the surgeon's bill, and constantly demanded to know when he would be allowed to travel. The slowness of the recovery was especially provoking to him because his partnership agreement with brother Leander and Leander's son Hall was being challenged in Chicago, and echoes of family combat were reverberating across the Atlantic.

Ever since Cyrus had brought his brothers West to help run the reaper factory, Leander in charge of manufacturing and William in charge of business administration, the two younger McCormicks had resented Cyrus's getting most of the money and all the glory, and they the work. Both men became wealthy through their investments in Chicago real estate but nonetheless felt that the inventor had taken too large a share for himself. Indisputably, Cyrus had done well. Twelve years after his move to Chicago, he was earning an annual income of $231,667—most of it from buildings, land, gold, grain, pig iron, and wood. The first of many family contracts had been negotiated in 1859, under which Leander and William, each with a salary of $5,000 a year, were in addition to have one-fourth of the reaper company's profits, the capital to manufacture the machines being supplied by Cyrus. By the time of William's death in 1865, Cyrus was worth $4 million, and his wealth would more than double by 1884. The discrepancy in family fortunes was bound to create tension.

The long-distance bargaining between Paris and Chicago in 1878 had been primarily over a demand from Leander that his son Hall become an equal partner in the firm. Cyrus, suspecting them both of trying to take over, had refused. Anyway, he was grooming his eldest son for eventual presidency of the company. Nothing, however, could be settled until Papa was well enough to travel.

Cyrus, Jr., had left Paris for his second year at Princeton, but the remaining family was immobilized, with Nettie hovering over an irritable husband who could not abide noise and could barely tolerate a French doctor. Virginia, now a beautiful young woman of eighteen, spent her days sitting for a portrait by the renowned Cabanel, taking riding lessons, or escorting Harold and Stanley on walks along the Paris boulevards. Anita, at that awkward age when she thought herself "big as a hogshead" and a "top-heavy windmill," was sent a short distance away to further her education. A French convent being out of the question for a McCormick and secular French instruction seeming no safer, Nettie had settled on a respectable Englishwoman who ran a pension boarding school at Neuilly, at which the older ladies knitted in the evenings, while someone read aloud in French. "Rather lonesome," Anita confessed, although there were compensations—strolls through the countryside, large slices of bread with butter and brown sugar, a "perfectly splendid" dog who conceived a particular fondness for her, and horse-drawn streetcars which she rode twice a week on trips to Paris for music lessons. She was the school's only boarder.

From Neuilly, she wrote her mother of her first menstrual flow and had a reply, headed "Burn This!" instructing her how to pass the napkin "between the limbs" and how to make hot-whiskey-water in case of cramps: *Do not walk tomorrow.* A commiserating note from Virginia was enclosed: "Poor child, I know all about it as I was so when I was thirteen."

At last Papa was able to be moved, and in May 1879 Anita bid farewell to Neuilly. The dozens of bags and trunks were packed, and the McCormicks headed for Chicago and their long-awaited house on Rush Street, under construction for three years but which they were not to occupy for another few months. All the children except Cyrus, Jr., spent the intervening weeks until Thanksgiving on the East Coast with Missy, and when they finally did enter their new home, they found it filled with clouds of dust from the floorlaying, the smell of paint, and the noise of hammering, sawing, and burglar alarms being tested. "It has taken some little time," Missy reported to her sister in New York, "to fall into a

state of chronic chaos, without showing some little worriment." The gas fixtures having not yet been installed, Anita practiced piano by candlelight. The little boys amused themselves by tumbling into a heating vent while craning their necks to see the dining room ceiling, and Nettie rushed about superintending the workmen, making sure that tin cuttings were packed around the foundation walls of the stable to keep out rats, and measuring the bathtubs for their depth.

Of late French renaissance inspiration, the house had been designed by the noted architectural firm of Cudell and Blumenthal and was made of Lake Superior brownstone. Avoiding the gingerbread intricacies then fashionable, it had straight, simple lines, a high mansard roof topped by a mansard cupola, and iron grillwork accented by bull's-eye windows and "rusticated" stonework. Windows on the lower floor were bordered by intricate ornamentation, banded columns, garlands, and medallions. A matched pair of zinc lions, couchant, guarded the entrance. Approaching the house, one climbed several stone steps to reach a massive doorway which opened onto a wide hall set off by a fireplace with brass appointments, bronze statuary, and frescoed oak walls. The first floor rooms were paneled in different woods, the reception hall in gilded maple adorned with salmon-pink hangings embroidered in blue. In the large drawing room, decorated in satinwood and rosewood, the furniture was Louis XVI and the ceiling painted in soft tones with sky, flowers, and birds. Here, three cherished family portraits by Cabanel were hung and glass and porcelain displayed in the cabinets, notably the prized Sèvres vase given Cyrus at the Paris Exposition. Across the hall were Papa's office and library, the latter in ebony inlaid with silver. Sets of bound books chosen in New York and London were preserved in locked cases, the keys to which were so massive that few troubled to use them. The dining room was a showpiece of mahogany set off by an elaborate wainscoting and panels of antique tapestry, its ceiling depicting the emblem of the French Legion of Honor and a reaper sheathed with grain, beehives, and the names Pomona, Flora, Ceres, and Diana. The same coat of arms appeared over the fireplace. A hydraulic elevator led to the second floor, where bathrooms, closets, dressing rooms and bedrooms were all connected, handy for games of tag or hide and seek. The nursery and school rooms had Mother Goose drawings on the walls and tiles around the fireplace illustrating Bible stories. A third-floor ballroom was complete with stage and a private theater seating two hundred persons. There were walk-in vaults for linen and silver, a cubicle for

the telephone, and electric burglar alarms attached to each ground floor window. The barn for horses, cow, and pony was steam-heated. Reported to have cost $175,000, the house was described by the once hostile *Tribune* as "the chief of the many private residences which have made Chicago noted as the city where not only solidity and wealth but genuine taste in art prevails." Some thought it second only to Potter Palmer's castle on Lake Shore Drive. The interior decoration was largely the work of Marcotte of New York and Paris, who had also done the home of Marshall Field.

At last, after twenty-two years of marriage, Nettie had the home she wanted and that would be hers for the next forty-three years. But its comforts came too late for Cyrus. A weakness he fought against but could not shake off foreshadowed the end of his career. He disapproved of weakness, he hated idleness, he chafed under the restrictions imposed on him. He was not a homebody. He had been proud of his family but too occupied for any intimacy with his children; he never said "*anything* loving to me," Virginia had lamented. He kissed them in the morning and at night, if he was there, and was gratifyingly astonished when the younger boys jumped out at him from their favorite hiding places, or when they got under the buffet table and growled at him; that always got a "big fine laugh." But they regarded him less as a loving parent, one of the boys thought in retrospect, than as "the great power, the forceful character, the invincible, and the unyielding foe of whatever was opposed to him." Qualities that had made him so successful—tenacity, competitiveness, relentless attention to detail and an imposing physical presence—were ones to respect, but they did not engender affection. He was quick to anger, at times ungovernable, and then his voice would rise to a squeaky high pitch and the children knew it was time to get out of the way. A personal word from Papa was so rare it was cause for rejoicing, and when he telegraphed "love and kisses" on Anita's sixteenth birthday, it pleased her far more than his present of a cart and pony.*

It was only toward the end, with his illness and growing dependence, that a subtle change came about in his relationship with

---

* Asked by an interviewer in 1933 whether his father had been "demonstrative," Cyrus, Jr., replied, "He never did such a thing as taking us to a show or any amusement. He was one of the strongest characters I have ever known—he knew nothing about amusements. He never played—except athletic games. He never had any pet horse. He had one horse, Napoleon, after the fire. He was very fond of that horse, but he wasn't fond enough to go and feed him or pet him."

Anita, and she treasured the memory of it—his "pleased surprise" when she read to him and her "proud sense of happiness!" She learned to play billiards "quite passably" so that he could "still have his game in the evening," and as he became feebler, her desire to serve him mounted. She vowed she would do "all I can to contribute to his happiness." Later, gazing at his picture and "all the wealth of expression of his face," she would remember not the combative energy but the "child-like helpless, appealing expression that used to come into his face . . . an expression of the softness and sweetness of his character." She remembered that when she had gone into his sickroom to tell him she was to have an examination in school that day, "he was so anxious about it and the moment I got home would inquire—and when I got my papers back, with high marks, he was so pleased and asked me to read him my logic paper in which I had nearly one hundred." Still, when she dared confide to him that she didn't like funerals and that she never expected to make any money, he upbraided her, and "it was very hard, and I couldn't do too much to make it right—but when the tears would come to his eyes as I caressed him, or when he would take my hand and press it, then I knew how he loved me." Thus, she made her peace with him.

Cyrus's infirmities were further evidence to Nettie that we are put on earth to serve and suffer, and she accepted them as she had her own affliction, deafness, which was only partially alleviated by the use of a long ear trumpet. Her hearing had grown progressively worse, and by the 1880s all verbal communication had to be filtered through a tube held to her ear. With its imperfect assistance, she judged the worthiness of missionary appeals, soothed Cyrus, supervised the servants, admonished the children, directed dinner conversation, and gave orders on business matters with which her husband could no longer competently deal. The importance of her contribution to his financial affairs while he lived is difficult to assess. Her own opinion was that she was "helping him constantly," as she had told twelve-year-old Cyrus, Jr., and that "he couldn't get on in his business without me." Long after his death, the eldest son having succeeded his father as president of the harvester company, Nettie went on thinking it her right and duty to inquire into the smallest details of management and manufacturing, such as the hardness of the wood used in crating, and as an aged lady she would appear in the factory from time to time, walking from department to department, greeting employees and asking questions about their work.

But she veered from smothering concern to forgetfulness. In the former mood, she would check her children's wraps, their lessons, and especially their diet, for she was always on the watch for incipient illness and had a sizable stock of home diagnoses and prescriptions. "Poor Anita," she wrote Cyrus, Jr., when he was twenty-three, "has been *very ill* with *liver congested* by eating candy. Cyrus, when the liver becomes charged with bile, look out for trouble. The liver *should not* be charged with bile. It should unload bile, and is trying to, in Anita's case."* She was an absentminded manager, haphazardly pulling the children up short one moment and giving them free rein the next. As her husband's condition worsened, however, she was obliged to entrust more of their care to servants, and her mind, Harold said, seemed to be "moving around—distant, somewhere." They saw her at morning prayers, or when she scooped one of them up on her lap for Bible reading, or when they misbehaved and she shut them in a dark closet to do penance. When it occurred to her, she wanted to know what they were up to, but, rather than asking directly, she peeked out at them from a window or through a crack in a curtain. Unlike her husband, she preferred indirection and evasion to confrontation, even, Anita came to believe, when a straightforward exchange would have been healthier. Laughter embarrassed her, irony escaped her, and time-wasting angered her. So that Anita would be reminded of her slowness in reaching the breakfast table, the child was obliged to record how long it took to brush her teeth and to dress each morning.

A teetotaller, Nettie found it prudent to ignore the hot rum toddies her husband had been accustomed to having in his private dressing room, but when Anita was old enough to order "Shandy-gaff" (half beer and half ginger ale), Mama was "aghast" at her daughter's "sportiness." She required her undergraduate eldest son to read his Bible in Princeton at exactly 8:15 each morning, so that they both would be in touch with the Lord's word at the same hour. This preoccupation with moral edification was not confined to her family. When a girl who had lost her mother became engaged to a senior at the McCormick Theological Seminary, Nettie gave a luncheon at Rush Street in her honor, during which she led the young guest to the automatic elevator, shut the door, drew her down on the seat, and said that she must warn the bride-to-be of the "pitfalls

* In a note written in 1889, Anita (she is twenty-three) says that "Mama has come with renewed ideas about my rest. She has talked with Dr. Brown about me and he has an opinion about my nervous condition. He has seen that my 'cerebration' was too acute or intense or something— and he expressed the opinion that I needed six or eight weeks of perfect rest (shall I ever want to hear the word again?). He has gotten Mama quite disturbed on the subject. . . . I just wish she would come to some definite ideas on her own."

between her eager feet." Having done so, she brought the bemused girl back to the other guests. The picture the children eventually formed of their mother was of someone "carrying heavy weights along," which was not unlike the picture Nettie had of herself— someone burdened "with duties that seem like a millstone hanging on my neck." In her mid-twenties, she had given up normal sleeping habits and adopted her husband's—an early evening nap and work until two or three in the morning. Anita thought it was "too bad" that Mama had to spend so much time on such matters as oversee-ing contracts for the building of Seminary dormitories. "It makes me feel a positive grudge," she wrote Nettie in 1886, "against these things and people that keep you from me. . . . Yes, I grudge even Seminary dormitories, your time that you might spend in the coun-try and with us."

The truth was that Nettie embraced her burdens as an aspirant to sainthood might welcome the rack. Yet her daily duties were not as onerous as she imagined—"a visitor to dinner, three people on business . . . a telegram from Papa that needs attention, a letter on business to send . . . then a few clothes to send away to persons who need them now if they need them at all, and then some attention to the children." She was frequently at odds with her husband over his "habit of business, always and at all times and at all places," which she said left "little room for any family life, such as I see it in well-regulated families; or for good sleeping, or eating in quiet— or with any regularity of the family having any regard for meeting each other at any regular times around the family board." Yet he was not wholly to blame for the household irregularity. Nettie would pick up a project, lose interest, drop it, and pick up another. She kept visitors waiting for hours, dithered over minor decisions, and was rarely on time. Plans for tutoring the boys or for Anita's edu-cation were constantly being altered. "You do not seem to realize," Anita once wrote her mother, "that this year and the next are the most important of my school life. I have just nicely caught up with what I missed by being late. . . . Take me out now from these classes and I should be just one year more behind." Moreover, it was "per-fectly absurd" to insist on Anita's seeing a doctor; she was "per-fectly well and all that, taking plenty of exercise, keeping regular hours, and not studying too hard at all!"

Not until she was in her fifties could Anita admit that her mother had had "a real disregard for the rights of—I would say almost any-one, but especially any child who would be present." Cyrus, Harold, and Stanley briefly escaped the maternal meddling when they went to Princeton, and it had to be said that they owed that escape to her, for Nettie believed as firmly in a college education for her boys as she did in their working thereafter for the reaper company. She had overcome her husband's fear that college would "effeminate" young Cyrus, though she herself was not without misgivings about sending her boy east "like a lamb among wolves to that most dangerous and gilded pathway to destruction." Happily, the dutiful eldest son came through unscathed. Apprenticed to his father at twenty, nominal head of the company at twenty-five, he was the model heir—respectable, reserved, a bit pompous, and given to writing light verse set to pleasant tunes.

But the destiny of young ladies in the 1880s did not include a college degree or a career. Nettie's daughters had only to learn the feminine graces and the social obligations proper to their station and their Christian inheritance.

Two years older than Anita, Virginia in her teens was an acknowledged beauty, an accomplished pianist, and with "something so earnest," her mother remarked, "an affection so persistent, a fountain so full and gushing, that to resist it is impossible." It was too gushing. Virginia's good-nights were as ardent as a lover's parting, kisses and hugs so fierce that Mama could not disengage herself without force. The ardor showed itself, Nettie noted, "in the direction of not being satisfied when arranging anything about her until it is done in her own way and time, which is sometimes inconveniently long." In her teens, Virginia was given to hysterical prayer, bouts of weeping, shortness of breath, insomnia, and sleepwalking, diagnosed as neurasthenia or poor posture or consumption, and by her twenties she was wandering from one resort to another in search of health, with no marked benefit. She developed a disquieting habit of suddenly appearing at odd hours at the doorstep of family or friends and requesting that everyone come with her to Sunday school. Proud of her wealth and position, scorning her social inferiors, at sixteen she had addressed an indignant letter to her mother because the governess had had "breakfast yesterday with Papa, and nothing was said about it. These people are so hard to deal with whom you can't treat as *servants* exactly, any more than as equals!" She was to break down completely after her father's death in 1884, and an endless search would begin for some regimen that might help her regain her sanity, or at least screen her from anything which might upset her precarious hold on reality. It was a search for which Anita was to take major responsibility.

To Anita's displeasure, little Harold and Stanley were run in tandem, though they were very different. Harold was robust, happy-go-lucky, excellent at sports, uninterested in study. He could wheedle

his way out of any awkwardness, held no grudges, whistled beauti-
fully, was keen about tennis, and grew into a "thorough boy," whom
Anita endearingly called just "a little fresh." His younger brother
was cast in a finer, more fragile mold, and his interests ran toward
the creative and reflective. Friends thought that his chiseled features
and tall, slender frame gave him a certain "artistic" look. Nevertheless, like Harold, Stanley was slated for the reaper organization and
never managed to carry his point that another career might be more
congenial. Cyrus, Jr., having blazed the trail, the two younger brothers were to go to Princeton on 12 February 1892, where they were
to pray, or so they wrote their mother, that they might "do always
what is right and leave college as much a Christian as we entered
it, taking as our example our dear Father." They were given the only
room on campus available to freshmen, for it had not gone unnoticed that they were McCormicks, that their elder brother was a
Princeton trustee, and that the president of the university was a familiar guest at the Rush Street house.

When they were younger, and in their mother's absence, the boys
had been looked after by Anita, who was charged to report whether
they had got up at seven, said their prayers, eaten properly, and
reached school on time. Those absences were like a holiday for
the children; everything was "so homelike," sixteen-year-old Anita
thought, with the boys sliding across highly polished floors using
pieces of carpets as skates, "their shouts of glee" ringing out. Life on
Rush Street could be light-hearted. Indeed, young Cyrus's twenty-
first birthday in 1880 seemed to Anita "recherché in the extreme"
and "the event in society here this year." Three hundred and fifty
guests filled the house for a musicale; the singing was "simply
charming."

That year had been good all around. Cyrus, Sr., had been elected
president of the Society of Virginia, and his family had gone to the
Palmer House to applaud his tribute to Southern Womanhood. ("Can
any of us forget how the mother was enthroned in the true Virginia
homestead, and with what untiring, loving tact and sagacity she
swayed her scepter . . . ?" etc.) Then, not long after, on Papa's
seventy-second birthday, there was a "gorgeous" dinner at which
they "drank to Papa's health," Anita wrote, and to Mama's happiness. "Then a house guest called out 'to the beauties of St. Louis and
Jamestown let us drink.' After that 'to the beaux of Chicago' without
going into particulars." In "capital spirits," they "repaired to the
billiard room, and were a divided family, mother and father versus
daughter and son. It was nip and tuck all the way—*very exciting.*"

One visualizes that brightly lit room in 1881, warm against the cold wind of a Chicago February. One sees each McCormick in turn walking around the billiard table, animated by the champagne and Papa's unaccustomed liveliness. Even Mama gets into the spirit of the evening, cheering a good shot, and Anita, flushed with the thrill of participating in the grown-ups' game, encouraged by a dapper older brother. The butler stands by, ready to send for more wine or something tasty.

Although Cyrus was to live three more years, that birthday party was his last joyous celebration. The McCormick works, more prosperous than ever, were sending fifty-five thousand reapers a year to farmers throughout the world, but without his supervision. At the summer home which he had eventually built at Richfield Springs, Anita pushed his wheelchair around the grounds so that he could survey the rose bushes, vines, and trees, and his favorite *arbor vitae* hedge. He watched as others played croquet, and once, when he could not bear to see his daughter losing a game, he took over Anita's ball, making shots from his chair, and came ahead to win.

The eczema that troubled him sporadically became worse. (A famous Chicago physician prescribed local applications of cranberry.) Each morning, Cyrus, Jr., went to the factory with a heart "heavy as stone"; Virginia "gave way to grief." The younger children were not told how desperate the illness was, though they saw how Papa winced when his valet lifted his stiff legs or moved him from his bed. Anita brought him roses, rubbed his hands, stroked his burning forehead, and told him of her wish to travel to Europe after her graduation from the Misses Kirkland Academy, so that she could "study and learn to play the piano well and sing, and then come home and be such a pleasure" to him. He nodded, giving her "the high sign as if to say I'll be seeing you," and that wordless exchange formed itself into one of her most poignant recollections, proof that she was special to him, and that despite his tempers and his absences, he cherished her.[15]

At six in the morning on 11 May 1884, Anita was awakened by her mother and told to get up, because "Papa may be with us for sometime in body, but not in mind." She dressed, went to his room and found him "shouting out, as if calling for someone." Cyrus, Jr., asked if he would have prayers as usual, to which he replied, "Oh yes—oh yes." They tried to start a hymn, and while they struggled with the tune, his voice sang out. Anita bathed his eyes and felt sure that he recognized her from the way he gripped her hands. He spoke his last that night—"I know of no better place to die than in harness," according to one account. Another thought he said, "Classification of patents . . . reaper—reaper all over the world"; still another remembered the words, "Nothing now but heaven." "There was a death-like stillness," Anita wrote in her diary, "broken occasionally by the reading of a verse from Scripture. The gas had been lit a little all night, but about five o'clock we began to see the dawn through the shutters. Oh, I shall never lose the impression produced upon me when the cold, gray dawn filled the room, and the twittering of the sparrows outside the windows was heard—while inside all was still and calm, and a life was ebbing away to eternity! At seven o'clock and ten minutes, Papa breathed his last. We knelt by his bedside while brother prayed to our Heavenly Father . . . knowing it was *well* with him, but feeling, oh, so desolate."

The factory employees sent a replica of the reaper, made of white flowers, with the main wheel broken. Four hundred workers walked in a double line past the coffin. The Rush Street house was "empty and strange" to Anita. Schooling, piano practice, all those newly acquired graces had been for Papa's benefit. Now they meant nothing. Two weeks after the funeral, she dreamed that she was standing in the door of the room where his body lay. She turned toward the bed, "when lo! Papa opened his eyes and held out his arms to me! I shall never forget the feeling of unalloyed joy I felt as I ran to him and felt him clasp me in his arms. 'My dear child,' he said as he held me there. 'I have been conscious this whole time and that tells you the whole story.' 'Oh my Father,' I said, 'how terrible! But oh I love you *so much*, and that tells you my whole story.' " She awoke with the most "vivid sense of his face and all about him, and the great love in his voice when he spoke to me."

The tributes to his "grand character, his noble deeds, his qualities of perseverance, untiring energy, integrity, justice" left her cold. Her forthcoming diploma, so valued while Papa was alive, was a piece of paper. She was within two months of her eighteenth birthday and would have dropped out of school if it had not been for the school's insistence that she finish. The topic she had had in mind for her graduation essay, "The Comparative Effect on the Mind of Mathematics and Literature," had become "perfectly impossible," and she chose instead "a kind of resume of the Moral philosophy." It got no further than, "Some things are right, others are wrong, and the right are praiseworthy, the wrong blameworthy." She knew that she had not done herself justice. She didn't care. She graduated, wishing that "the thing had never been spoken of." She was "perfectly desolate. . . . He was my father and he is gone."

II

LOVE

II

Had she been worthy of his love? Would she be worthy of the love
of God? She could not doubt that Papa had gone on to happiness
everlasting, but she was left to answer for her own life. She thought
back to the days before her confirmation in the Fourth Presbyterian
Church four years before, of how she had stood anxiously in the
hallway outside the library, wanting a word with the minister when
he emerged from a conference with Papa, needing to ask why she
should be confirmed and whether she was good enough to become
a certified Christian. It was not a subject she had felt free to discuss
with her father. The library door had opened, Dr. Herrick Johnson
stepped into the hallway, came toward her, took her hand, and in
response to her earnest question replied, "You must be confirmed a
Christian because Jesus loves you." The answer had seen her through
confirmation; love given must be returned. "I have been thinking
seriously over this 13th birthday," Anita had written in a formal
note to her mother: "I feel that in the thirteen years I have lived, I
have not learned all I should have learned. Whenever I get angry
with Harold or Stanley or have said anything bad to sister, I find
the best way to get over it is to go and lock myself up in my little
room and tell it all to Jesus." Dr. Johnson had been so kind, spoken
so gently of their Lord. "Oh Mama! I do think now that I *have* given
myself into His hands entirely. Sometimes I think I am deceiving
myself, but it cannot *be*, and I do pray for a right spirit and to be

35

convinced that I am saved by the Grace of God." And yet, it was so hard to remember little things, "such as never to put a wet towel on the wash stand for it will take off the varnish. It is those things I forget. How did you do it when you were little?"

But the doubts of adolescence are compensated for by the vitality of its hopes and by its susceptibility to beauty. That summer, rowing on the lake, when Anita heard a band on shore playing "Safe in the Arms of Jesus" and "Shall We Gather at the River," she looked into "the deep water, and then up into the stormy heavens," and she thought how great and infinite He was, "for He had made them all." Then she was sure that Jesus did love her and vowed she would share that love.*

At fourteen, she had attended missionary meetings at which papers were read on the castes of India and the decrease of idolatry and had listened to the "very delightful" sermons of Herrick Johnson, who made the seemingly incompatible principles of free will and predestination as clear as a "beautiful geometrical proposition." She did wonder whether it was the minister's "lovely way and lovely character that I want to follow and please more than the Lord." If so, it would be "dreadful." She took to heart the parable of the talents: "It says in the Bible 'whom the Lord loveth, he chasteneth,' and I had sometimes thought, well, the Lord can't love me very much for *I* never had any real trouble. But last night . . . I thought how ungrateful I had been to distrust the Lord because He has been so good as to withhold trouble from me for some time." Following her mother's example, she longed to spread the word, to tell those "who do not know the Savior's love how much they miss." She began teaching a children's Sunday school class, where Bible lessons were brought "down to their little comprehensions by using simple language and illustrations." That was not enough, however; it required too little of her. She wanted to "bring Jesus' love to the poor people." But how? The way will be found, Nettie said, and it was.

Walking down Huron Street near Clark with her cousin Lucy McCormick, Anita had passed some shabby dwellings and stopped to stare at them. They resumed their walk, Anita silent. The bell of duty had rung. She would come back and inquire whether the children in those poor homes went to Sunday school. At church the fol-

* "I think I am like you in my enjoyment of Nature—just Nature," Anita wrote her mother in 1883. "Nature as seen especially in the sky—I love the sky—but also in the mountains and fields, in the trees and flowers. And the contemplation of these things always calms and softens me."

lowing Wednesday night, Dr. Johnson spoke movingly of the sending out of the seventy (in the tenth chapter of Luke) and of the spirit in which they went—in obedience, faith, joy, and humility, and how they feared not, "because Jesus watched them and enfolded them in his love, as he does all His workers." The way had been made clear. Friday afternoon, Anita and Lucy boldly knocked on the door of one of the tenement houses. A woman appeared. Anita asked if the little girl they had seen enter the house attended Sunday school. No, she did not. "The house was very small indeed," Anita told her mother "but very neat, and the woman seemed very good. She hesitated about letting her child go to Sunday school with us—said she didn't know what her husband would say—that the child was not 'fixed up' to go." The girls departed and the following day bought goods for a dress, each paying half. Nettie let her seamstress cut out the lining. Monday, they again called, hoping to bring the little girl to Rush Street for a fitting, "never dreaming of a refusal." To their dismay, "the woman wouldn't think of it," and Anita concluded that the mother wouldn't let "Francy" go out with strangers, "though we had told her who we were." They left but returned with the seamstress in tow, and "it all came about so nicely." The seamstress entered first, "and when we arrived, she had talked to the woman and told her all about us. Then she said she had asked her husband and he said it would be alright. I suppose he knew Papa's name. So the little girl had the dress and is going."

It was Anita's initial venture in philanthropy, and her audacity seems astonishing, an early manifestation of an indestructible confidence in straightforward dealing and in the magic of the McCormick name. Her elder brother had said, "It isn't done," but she and Lucy had done it.

Anyway, she was beginning to have her own ideas about what was and was not "done." The Misses Kirkland's Academy was teaching her geometry ("perfectly fascinating"), natural philosophy ("very nice indeed and growing much harder"), Latin ("the stupidest thing on this earth"), but the school routine seemed to her "a regular treadmill." Why should her teachers expect her always to defer to their superior judgment, never encouraging her to argue a point, since that would be "unbecoming." Why did they expect her to repress "all undue ecstasy and excitement?" With whom *could* she let go? If only one were able to raise "real" questions with someone. The friends her own age were not much help. Cousin Lucy and Bessie King were nice. They pulled candy, lunched at each other's houses, had their tintypes taken, or went to the opera to applaud the arias of *Lohengrin*. One could discuss with them the finer points of social deportment, but not the "big questions." Only in the summer, when the McCormicks set out for Richfield Springs, did her spirits soar, routine was discarded, and the Misses Kirkland's Academy then was as remote as the Himalayas. Here, Anita could wander happily through the woods, unsupervised, or engage in exciting carriage races with the driver of the Tally-Ho from Cooperstown. And if Mama ordered Swedish exercises and the swallowing of sulphur water, that could be put up with.

It should be understood that the McCormicks, for all their wealth and prominence, were not "in society" or the Chicago whirl of fashionable entertainment. Perhaps they felt above it. Nonetheless, they were too conventional to disregard the social proprieties. Cyrus, Jr., gave select dinners at Rush Street at which Anita had opportunities to observe company manners—some of which struck her as foolish as the academic routine at the Misses Kirkland's Academy. When she once addressed a guest by his first name, she had been given a "reproving look or word." She was admonished to sit straight in a chair, keep her knees together (crossing the ankles was permissible), not to stare or slouch or interrupt. She learned. "Tomorrow night, brother is going to have four young men to dine with him. Fancy me at the head of the table surrounded by five men! I suppose its good practice and I'm getting hardened to it."* Mama was gratified by her progress.

But her window on the world was still shuttered, and she would hardly have recognized the Chicago of the 1880s as portrayed by the local novelist Henry B. Fuller, who was not much older than she: "All the unclassifiable riff-raff that is spawned by a great city leered from corners, or slouched along the edge of the gutters, or stood in dark doorways, or sold impossible rubbish in impossible dialects wherever the public indulgence permitted a foothold."[1] Rush Street was an enclave, mindful of course that the poor are with us and have a claim on Christian benevolence—so long as they congregate elsewhere, behave themselves, and do not ask one to examine too closely the causes of their poverty. The labor strife which rocked Chicago in Anita's teens was seldom mentioned at home, and when it was, it was derided. "Yesterday," Virginia informed her mother, "*seven-*

* Anita was "quite astonished to find myself entertaining these boys [at a New Year's Day reception in 1880] and also Paul Blatchford, whom I had to entertain alone." "You know," she told her sister, "how hard it is for me to talk to anyone."

teen police at the rolling mills dispersed 7,000 cowards, just by frightening them with their pistols which they shot over their heads! Why the mob is composed chiefly of half-grown *boys!* Firm resistance, will, I feel, surely quell them entirely." Anita could not have written anything so heartless, yet her knowledge of city affairs or the larger events of public life was slight. She saw the Republican national convention held in Chicago in 1880, at which James Garfield had been nominated after so many ballots divided between Ulysses Grant and James G. Blaine, as mere theater: "The delegates all got up and crowded around Garfield, and the roof was nearly carried off with cheers and the noise, when suddenly the band struck up, 'Rally Round the Flag Boys,' and everyone in the house began to sing at the top of their voices. Oh it was grand! So exciting! I wouldn't have missed it for the world." In the uproar following the shooting of Garfield, fifteen-year-old Anita could only echo her father's outrage at the prospect of Chester Arthur and his Stalwart faction taking power. It was Papa's "private idea" that if the president should die, "the Republicans and Democrats should join forces in a common cause, demand Arthur's resignation, and if he refused, 'kick him out,' and Conkling with him." Papa was her authority on politics.

After reform movements had become more stylish, Anita was to study the evils of industrialization and to count among her acquaintances some of the most perceptive social reformers of the day—Jane Addams, Jacob Riis, John Dewey, Graham Taylor, Raymond Robins, Louise DeKoven Bowen. But that was not to happen until long after her father's death.

A cluster of strikes, followed by labor disputes at the reaper factory, had culminated in the Haymarket Riot on 4 May 1886, during which a bomb exploded in the midst of a mass meeting near the McCormick works, killing police and several civilians. It was never proved who threw the bomb, but respectable folk thought they knew. A fiery editorial in the Chicago *Arbeiter Zeitung* had called for revenge by the workers: "They killed six of your brothers at McCormick this afternoon. They killed the poor wretches because they, like you, have the courage to disobey the supreme will of the bosses. . . . We call you to arms."[2] Family correspondence barely alludes to the tragedy, and when six "radicals and anarchists" were arrested, tried, and sentenced to death for the murders, Nettie's complacent comment to young Cyrus was that they had "together done what we could to uphold liberality and fairness in our dealings with the laboring classes so far as our men are concerned, and where the issue is one of principle, we have been unwilling to surrender, whatever might be the cost." Mother and son thought alike when property was at stake, and in that year property seemed threatened by populism and panic. A socialist, Eugene Debs, had just been elected to the Indiana legislature. How long before the hired would be telling the hirer how to run his business! Writing from Chicago to the Republican leader James Gillespie Blaine (Anita's future father-in-law) in December 1886, Blaine's son Walker had advised a public statement on the labor question—"a rather ticklish subject, for I can see that out here the Capitalists are greatly alarmed and very sensitive. The large vote of [Henry] George, the in-many-ways indefensible action of Knights of Labor in strikes, etc. have alarmed owners of manufactures and employers of labor. There is a consequent danger that they would, i.e. Capitalists, support [Grover] Cleveland, believing in his conservatism." Commissioner Theodore Roosevelt of New York roared that he would like to lead his city police against the Chicago agitators![3]

Rather than accede to the demands of McCormick workers for an eight-hour day and a cancellation of wage cuts,* Cyrus, Jr., after conferring with his mother, had shut down the reaper plant, throwing fourteen hundred men out of work, and had refused to dismiss five nonunion workers on the grounds that he had the "right to employ and discharge whom and as many" as he pleased. When the factory reopened, it was under the protection of uniformed police, detectives, and imported scabs, plus a complement of Pinkerton guards.[4] "To do *justly* does not mean to make hasty concessions under compulsion," Nettie had advised. When the strike failed and the men had returned to their jobs, she demanded to know what her son had conceded: "If reports are correct, what you have done prepares the way for repetition [of] some trouble." Yes, he admitted, he had given way on some points, but he reminded her that the

* In his study of labor-management relations at the McCormick works, Robert Ozanne wrote that young Cyrus had "little understanding of the issues or possible consequences. Nothing at Princeton or in his four years as understudy to his father had given him any insight into the feelings of the 1400 men who labored in his factory.

strike had saved the company about $40,000, through lower wages paid before the lockout. She nevertheless told her son that the course he had pursued "was all a miscalculation of what a man can do with employees."

Neither of them thought to discuss the labor disputes with Anita. A proper lady in her twenties was not to bother her head about workers, wages, and profits. Nor did Anita ask to be consulted. She was content to take what the good Lord and the harvester company provided, meanwhile exhorting herself to "walk humbly each day in the path which is before me, seeing in every worry overlooked, every unkind word or act forgiven, every temper subdued and impatience checked, every loving and tender encouragement and help given, a service to the Savior." Her duty was to balance her personal moral ledger; business bookkeeping was the province of her brothers and mother. The year of the Haymarket riot, Anita, in a lengthy, revealing letter to her mother, showed how preoccupied she was with the interior life and the struggle for personal perfection. "Life is a problem I for one have not fathomed. . . . Is it end enough just to try to round and broaden ourselves as much as possible, and develop our faculties to their highest extent? . . . I do a little at one thing, and a little at another, but perfect myself in nothing; nor am I essential—even beneficial—to anyone in any way. I could drop out of the universe and no one fare the worse."

Within the family, Anita could not fail to observe that Nettie's grasp of affairs was not steady and that she was becoming increasingly erratic. Not wishing to blame her mother, Anita blamed herself for the oddities she could not ignore and for the impatience she felt, and she redoubled her reassurances: "I *love* you, *love* you, *love* you and long to help you." Only to herself could she acknowledge that "selfish or self-righteous self-denial is, I am sorry to say, quite common," and that "some people are hypocritical enough to pride themselves on their humility and blow their trumpets while they sit in 'sack cloth and ashes.'" The allusion to her mother was obvious and disturbing, and by her seventeenth birthday, Anita's divided feelings had become so distressing that she vowed there would never again be "a difference between my Mother and my self about a dress! or any other strife! or indeed anything. Her views must be mine, and if I differ, mine must be sacrificed at any cost. If ever again any occasion should arise, let me fly to my room and pray and compose myself until I remember that a perfect understanding between us should not be sacrificed for any ordinary thing." The promise was sincere but impossible to keep.* Blind love enslaves, and if she was not to abdicate the sovereignty of her own judgment Anita had to come to terms with her mother's faults and vagaries. For instance, Nettie had to be almost physically prevented from digging by the hour in old trunks, sorting out materials for a memorial volume on her husband. When Anita asked her elder brother how they might deal with the problem, he advised letting Mama "do what she wishes done, *in her way.*" It was an evasion, not a solution. Nettie *had* to be protected from such destructive impulses as the compact she made with Harold and Stanley, offering them rewards for obeying her. Didn't Cyrus understand, Anita asked, that bargains of this kind encouraged the boys in "the ruinous way of fawning and cajoling and being hypocritical," turning them away from "the only true refinement which comes from a kind heart?" And how could it be right to require the governess to sleep in the same room with the boys? Didn't everyone need "a retiring place where he can recruit his forces—mental, physical, and moral?" She found it painful to ask these questions of her mother, for any questions were "an implied criticism, and I cannot seem to do that." Occasionally, Nettie could be brought "to take a certain position of firmness or leniency," but "all the persuasion in the world won't make a person hold to any course that is not dictated by their own reason," Anita concluded, "and we can't stand in anyone else's shoes for them, can we?"

It was a makeshift defense against family friction and served well enough when the issue was the discipline of small boys. It did not work when the stakes were higher; then Anita could not stand aside. Most importantly, her mother could not be allowed to do as she wished about sister Virginia, which was to pretend that all was well. Unless Nettie could be brought to face frankly the mental instability of her oldest daughter, mother as well as daughter might well slip totally out of control.

Virginia had been courted by several men, whose suits had been discouraged after anguished family counsels, and in the spring of 1885, "considerably agitated," she had finally been taken to Boston for medical consultation. So that Nettie, Anita, and the younger

* Although Anita never stopped trying. On her twenty-fifth birthday, she is writing that "it is bootless for me to say, as I feel out of the depths of my heart, that I long to undo all the pain I have ever given you and multiply a thousandfold the pleasure I may have given you—for forgiveness is in the very essence of your sweet love, and of that I lay hold and am happy to be forgiven and loved still."

boys could be near the patient, they rented a house in Marian, Massachusetts. When the consultation led to no firm conclusions, Nettie insisted that Virginia be brought back to Rush Street, where she became worse, refusing to see anyone, locking herself in her room in the day, and wandering about at night with a lamp, pounding on doors and climbing out of windows to walk on the roof. Each irrational episode reduced Nettie to fits of weeping and praying, and everyone, including Missy and the doctors, urged her to separate Anita and Virginia if she did not want to risk having two sick daughters on her hands. It took months to persuade her even to consider placing Virginia under some confinement, a decision Anita by now thought inevitable, though horrible: "When I think of Sissie's life—wrecked—and the possibility she possessed for a high and useful and happy one all gone—unless God should see fit to lift this cloud, it seems to me I could die for her."

Heretofore, the family had succeeded in hushing up the truth, but if Virginia was to be sent away, Chicago was bound to hear of it, and think the worst. "How studiously we have guarded her ailment from the ears of everyone," Anita wrote Missy. "They have, I think, only thought her peculiar and perhaps morbid. . . . Oh, may God direct these physicians to do and say the right things!"

What made it doubly difficult for the doctors to do the right things was Nettie's inconstancy and interference. Virginia's brief stays in two hospitals were interspersed with visits home or journeys with Mama, which benefited neither of them. Dissatisfied when a course of treatment produced no improvement, Nettie would reach for some new diagnosis—delusional insanity, original paranoia, dementia with delusions and maniacal episodes—and some new physician. One recommended travel, another stricter discipline, another gardening. Convinced that her mother's vacillation was imperiling any chance of recovery, Anita privately advised one doctor that "if he thought his orders were important, he should have insisted that Mrs. McCormick follow them, and not leave the onus of taking action upon her." Virginia, Anita was now convinced, had to be removed from those who, loving her, were tempted to cater to her irrational whims. Back and forth it went, Nettie consenting to a separation, then reneging. To give up those occasional visits seemed like consigning her daughter to strangers and admitting that she would never again be well. And after all, wasn't home the safest place for a troubled child?

Face-to-face with her sister's breakdown and her mother's disinclination to "say or come to a conclusion," Anita anguished over why she had "to worry and think over such things," why she couldn't be "happy and light-hearted and have no care." But the spells of self-pity were short-lived and followed by self-reproach for being "selfish through and through." She prayed for light on the conflict "between Christian resignation and wicked discontent—between disinterested love and mean selfish complaining."

Only with Missy, the "hunch back with the most lovely expression in her face," could she communicate in their "unspeakable heart language" her anxieties and disappointments. What, for example, of her own suitors? How was she to handle them? There was that agreeable young gentleman who had been astonished that a young lady could discuss philosophy: "I told him," Anita wrote Missy, "I supposed he knew we had minds—what did he imagine we thought about?" And how tiresome "to have all of the sudden and queer things you do put down to the score of . . . 'oh, it is just McCormicks.' " Did they expect her to model herself on the book of etiquette she had been given to read—"to exhale a subtle magnetism, purely spiritual?" She couldn't do it; anyhow, it was wrong "to try to pattern yourself on the rest of the world." One had to search for one's own way; then could one walk "on holy ground."

There came moments, in her early twenties, when this conviction that each must be free to find his own truth was overshadowed by the doctrine of predestination taught her as a child, and then Anita would ask herself whether her every step was "ordered by as divine a law as that which brings the wind to carry the leaves away." An unsettling doctrine, for if true, how could we "measure the results of our mistakes and transgressions," and were errors as inexorable as the divine law was good? The questions themselves induced depression, when "the dark side of everything comes out in bold relief, things seem hopeless, my own endeavors seem fruitless, life appears short and fleeting, and my own self utterly miserable, and worthless." Rush Street was then a "gloomy place"; a thousand things made her sad—"so many regrets, so many longings that may never be fulfilled, so many dissatisfactions." She felt like "just lying down to sleep, or even to die, if I could get away from everything." She found little satisfaction in social gatherings. This "meeting and passing place we call society" was only the "ups and downs of everyday affairs." One was still alone, and there was no one with whom to enter "the inmost sanctuary."

She supposed that a condition of love was that "we bear one another's burdens," but with whom and when was she to share her deepest feelings? At twenty-two she had read widely, from *Mrs.*

Henderson's Dinner Giving to Plato's Dialogues, Matthew Arnold, George Eliot, Emerson, Carlyle, Macaulay, and Ruskin. She was familiar with *Gems from Sacred Minds* as well as the poetry of the Brownings, Milton, Tennyson, Wordsworth, Byron, Keats, and Longfellow. What was she to do with such knowledge? Men could "make for themselves a definite aim and object—and say thus and thus I wish to do with my life—and so live to that end." Her vocation was to live "just as we are placed, with perfect contentment, instead of making circumstances. . . . We cannot carve out our path, but must take it as it is."[5]

In those low moments, she exaggerated. None of her brothers had been free to choose a career. Still, she was more right than wrong. The rules of the game prescribed that she write grammatically and neatly, play the piano or sing, dance and dress elegantly, speak French and German "sufficiently for society purposes" (so read the contemporary book of manners), and demonstrate "a modest self-control" that would "conceal especially strong dislikes and preferences." The summit of perfection was to become "queen over some household over which she hopes to reign."[6] Before acquiring the skills of the drawing room and ballroom, she was supposed to appear only at children's parties or intimate family gatherings, although that rule had been broken when Anita helped entertain her brothers' bachelor friends or stood by her mother's side on New Year's Day, when Chicago gentlemen paid formal afternoon calls on ladies who greeted them in their best evening gowns and served them from gorgeously laden tables. Not until her official presentation to society five months before her twenty-first birthday could Anita look forward to parties just for her and her friends, to membership in one of the local literary societies, and to acknowledged suitors, of whom she would have quite a few.

She was, by the eve of her coming out in 1887, a tall, brown-eyed, attractive brunette with an oval face, high forehead, straight nose, and small mouth above a pointed chin. She dressed only in black, gray, or white, since the family was still in mourning for Papa. The preparations for her presentation to society were not as elaborate as those for Queen Victoria, who that year was celebrating her golden jubilee, but when the McCormicks set out to impress, they knew how. The gas had been lit all afternoon in the house, for it was February. A profusion of flowers adorned the drawing room, where Anita in white gloves and white crepe, cut V-shaped at the neck, received with mother, Cyrus, Jr., and several assisting ladies. In the background, musicians played softly as the stream of those Nettie called "our dear 500 guests" passed by. Forty young people remained for dinner in the library and dancing until eleven in the upstairs ballroom, where Johnnie Hand, who played for Chicago's first families, led the band. Nettie found it "terribly fatiguing" and, thinking of poor Virginia, would have "turned away gladly and shut myself up with tears." But the young guests thought the music was "capital and the floor excellent and the dancing therefore splendid."

Having "come out," Anita was now entitled to attend the Bachelors and Benedicts dance on New Year's Eve, a grand assembly ball in January, and small dinners at Rush Street supervised by Nettie and solemnized by the elder brother's respectable presence at the head of the table. Each dinner menu was filed. There were clams followed by asparagus soup, iced salmon with mayonnaise and iced asparagus, frogs' legs "à la poulette," roast squabs on toast, new potatoes, and beans. An interval of punch (orange and pineapple sherbet in Jamaica rum) preceded broiled woodcock, peas, and tomato salad. Dessert began with individual ices, then came strawberries, and finally, for the eleventh course, coffee in the drawing room. Claret, sherry, and apollinaris water helped wash it down. At more intimate family gatherings, McCormick, Adams, and Shields cousins met for a lighter supper and an evening of singing with Anita at the piano. There were also daytime luncheons for female friends, teas and ambles with a new collie puppy along Lake Shore Drive. Lawn tennis was popular, and Anita—"a nice healthy, calisthenic girl" according to one friend—played in a white and gray striped wool dress. It was all quite enjoyable and diverting.

More enjoyable was the new club for young ladies of the North Side, organized by Chicago's *grandes dames*. Men's clubs had been the vogue since the 1880s, though there were still wives who refused to let their husbands join them, but by 1888 numerous women's clubs were testifying to the new freedoms. Anita and her young friends were not sure what they wanted to do with their group, but they were convinced they could do better than their mothers, who belonged to the exclusive Fortnightly Club. Anita was elected treasurer and had the honor of proposing to call the new organization the Friday Club, the name Blue Stockings having been rejected. Its object, they decided, would be "literary and artistic improvement"—for instance, a talk on "Some Tendencies of Modern Luxuries" by Mrs. Potter Palmer, a review of "The History of Society in our National Capital" by Mrs. Reginald DeKoven, and a lecture on "The True Spirit of Etiquette."

In retrospect, the Friday Club seems a modest assertion of feminine emancipation; yet its members saw themselves as pioneers, moving from Victorian domesticity toward social and intellectual endeavors created by them for their own pleasure and edification. And, indeed, the club played an important role in the education of respectable women for participation in public life. If the programs sometimes produced a soporific afternoon,* the members nevertheless believed, as Anita said, that they were "fighting superstition, knocking down the barriers that trammel and separate us, giving the light of loving kindness to each other and to all, doing our little best—a joyous, growing, living, rising band, with ever-widening horizon, enriching life."

A Miss McCormick of an age to attend balls and join clubs was likewise ready for the Grand Tour, and though she regretted parting with her "only daughter companion," Nettie fell in with Anita's plan for a five-month trip to Scandinavia and Russia with her friend Bessie King, cousin Lucy McCormick, and Missy. The foursome went first to England. In a letter to her mother from London, Anita described sitting in Lady Peel's box in the House of Commons, in company with Mrs. Gladstone, whose husband had resigned as prime minister the year before—"a sweet looking old lady with white hair and a kind expression. . . . [She] was dressed oddly and carried a bouquet of country flowers. But the moment Gladstone seemed absorbed in what was going on, she was all attention. . . . He leaned forward, his elbows on his knees and hands working nervously and his eyes intently watching each speaker alternately. And while we were wondering what was going on in that brain, he rose to speak. He seemed very feeble. And his presence was more significant than I had imagined, and his voice at first shook—*but*, as he warmed up to the subject [the Irish crimes bill] and showed such a comprehensive grasp of the subject the others had been beating around the bush, we realized that this was a different article from anything we had heard before."

Anita and her traveling companions then took the boat to Norway to fish for cod at midnight and to climb the cliffs of the North Cape. From there they journeyed south in horse-drawn carts, passing glaciers, waterfalls, tiny villages, one-room huts of cowherds, the only smudge on the landscape being a party of Germans—"atro-

---

* In Anita's absence in 1887, her friend Bessie King let her know that the club was still dragging "its slow length along. . . . After one of Mrs. [Handlin's?] soliloquies [we had] a discussion. As usual, when she paused for a reply, a deathly stillness reigned with an occasional cough that made the silence more intense. What a brilliant set we all are, to be sure."

cious, wretched people" who had "taken all the rooms and eaten all the best food at every inn." Anita's feelings about Russia were ambivalent. She was moved to tears in Moscow by a boys' choir but appalled by the "dirt and degradation" of the streets. An hour's train ride brought them to a monastery where, Anita wrote her mother, "the scum of all Russia went the rounds with us, much to our disgust." All her instincts rebelled at the sight of the "wretched pilgrims and their narrow-minded priests, steeped in their ignorance" and enduring such a "dark and cheerless existence." No doubt, she wrote, "some of the excess devotion we see is sincere—they are an emotional people. But I do not believe it influences their lives. And it seems such a terrible imposition on them by the priests and such a fearful extortion of their pittances, even from the depths of poverty, to deck shrines already loaded with jewels. . . . It is a mockery of religion." She was "almost ready to cry, away with *all* forms."

And on that Protestant note, she left Russia for Paris and home, finding it as she had left it, with nothing to engage fully her mind or heart.

Yet the Chicago to which Anita returned in October 1887 was stirring. Hull House and the high tide of municipal reform were a few years off, but women had begun to venture out of the snug harbors of kitchen and church. In the summer of 1890, earnest young ladies thrilled to the gesture of a judge's daughter who worked for two weeks in a stuffy tailor shop, so that a working girl could have a vacation, and Anita found her way into this awakening concern through the Howe Street Mission, where poor girls with little education came in the evenings and Sundays to learn sewing or cooking, or to listen to an uplifting book read aloud by a genteel volunteer. Nettie thought highly of the mission, for it was said to bring girls off the streets and out of the gin palaces and dance halls of the tenement district; to Anita, the shopgirls with their velvet hats, feathers, and gold chains were something altogether strange, "entirely respectful in manner" but rather like lower-class characters in a Dickens novel. She could barely understand them. They spoke so oddly, many in halting English. And a few were black!

Until she had visited acquaintances of the McCormicks in Virginia when she was nineteen, Anita had never been near blacks.

They were unseen in her parents' home, where the menial work was done by girls from immigrant Scandinavian families. The trip south had been a revelation, and Anita romanticized it—so "touching" to hear the Negroes sing at their work in a tobacco factory, their rich voices blending in perfect harmony as they sang, "I will sing de beauty of de Lord, we will dwell wid him foreber." Wasn't it blessed, she had written her mother, "that they have their religion?—exaggerated and emotional as it is. And must there not be much that is innately good, where there is so much music, and so much fervor?" The South, she told Missy, was definitely "a field for missionary labour," and Missy, born and raised in pre–Civil War Virginia, replied that she was "so glad" her darling's interest in the Negro had been aroused, for the black man would never rise without the aid of "all the good and intelligent in the classes now so far above him." It was the duty of whites, she reminded Anita, to give their black brethren "a pride of race. . . . To do this without involving a social relation, is indeed the most difficult problem that the South has to face; but we should face it voluntarily, not be driven grudgingly."

Hindsight rejects that patronizing homily, but it was said at a time when Jim Crow laws, first in the South and later in the North, were wiping out freedoms blacks had won during Reconstruction, and for a southerner in the 1880s, Missy's attitude was rather advanced. At any rate, Anita adopted it as her own. Years afterward, when she had met W. E. du Bois and had Booker T. Washington to tea ("very inspiring and helpful and uplifting"), had given money and her prestige to the National Association for the Advancement of Colored People and had helped Jane Addams raise funds to defend blacks arrested during the Chicago race riots of 1919, she saw the race problem from a different perspective. Even then, however, Anita accepted the refusal of a Lake Forest country club to house a Negro member of a conference she had planned. She regretted the discrimination but made no fight of it, merely arranging for his housing elsewhere.

But we must return to the Howe Street Mission and to Anita's involvement with it in the year of her coming out. The enthusiasm was short-lived. The girls were bored by her instruction; she felt "so useless." Perhaps if she had her own club, managed her way, the response might be more positive. At any rate, it seemed worth finding out. And so in the winter of 1888 she rented a flat not far from the Howe Street Mission, hired a "very destitute and worthy" widow to live in it and keep it clean, and with financial help from Nettie furnished it as a meeting place for girls who wanted to learn

49

"practical cooking and dressmaking, with some reading and music."
At the start there was one weekly meeting, but Anita was anxious
to keep the club open every evening and put it to more use by adding a library.

Having been warned that the girls must be given a part in running
and supporting the club if they were not to feel like charity cases,
she tried delegating responsibility. The apathy was as deadly as
ever; the girls could only be aroused to take what she gave. But if
she stopped giving, she wrote Missy, the club "would sink out of
existence and perhaps leave hardly a ripple." She carried on for a
year before closing the club for lack of interest, having "only succeeded in gaining experience for myself." Worst of all, she didn't
understand why she had failed: "I feel so incompetent to do it right,
and I feel somehow as if it should be different—though I don't know
how." Whatever the reasons for the failure, it had a lasting effect on
its sponsor. It taught Anita that she was not cut out to be a social
worker or to run a settlement house.

What ought she now to do with her time, she asked Missy de-
spairingly. She ought to think more of the "social claims and pleasures" appropriate to her upbringing, Missy replied, and to put the
failure behind her. It was all she could think of to comfort a dis-
heartened idealist, and Anita followed the advice, though in a rather
unorthodox manner. A memorable leap year dance at Rush Street
was held in 1888 at which the customary relation between the sexes
was reversed, ladies taking the male role and doing "a thousand
little things that were funny and mannish, without," Anita hastened
to assure Missy, "being in the least bold." Such a lark for the ladies
to wander about unescorted and empty-handed (the men had to
carry the fans and bouquets), picking partners at will and deposit-
ing them "in the nearest chair" when they tired of them! The men
retaliated by coyly saying they were engaged when asked to dance.
Yes, the social game could be diverting. In January of 1889, taking
her first turn at the lecturn of the Friday Club, Anita ventured some
teasing of Chicago society, comparing it to a stage: "The play is
called Commerce, and the youngest actors are brought on in the
guise of autumn wares—to be disposed of before the spring—while
the older actors are arranged in various groups, all laughing and
clapping. There are some trafficking with visits—others with wedding gifts and Christmas presents—all favors bought and sold on
the grand commercial principle of equivalents with the small coin of
effort." But she could not end the talk without making the moral
point directly. The effect of the game was belittling, and "any pos-

sible benefit which might come simply from the mutual currents of influence and sympathy between people is lost." The speech was a hit, Nettie reporting that "some of the literary ladies here said it was brilliant."

A party at Rush Street for the clerks of the harvester company climaxed the social season that year. It was a "rare spree," Anita wrote in her journal, the clerks and their wives so "funny and stiff," the McCormicks trying to thaw them out by calling for a "good old" Virginia reel, and Anita dancing a polka with an elderly gentleman who assured her he hadn't taken a step for eighty years. She was "never more amused." Full accounts of such festivities were sent to sister Virginia, now guarded by nurses and servants in whose custody she traveled from one to another of various properties bought for her—an estate in New York, an Adirondacks camp, a house on the beach.

And how much fun it was when the family escaped from Chicago to "rough it" on an island the McCormicks owned near Iron River, Wisconsin—except that a series of incidents the spring of 1888 nearly put them all off the outdoor life. Harold, chopping wood, lost control of his ax and sliced Anita in the neck just in back of her ear. "I don't know just *how* it happened," Anita wrote Missy, "for I didn't like even to refer to it to him. And of course no one saw. The axe head did not come off, and the cut was downwards about one inch deep." Cyrus was sent on a twelve-mile journey by horseback to collect the nearest doctor, who put in five stitches by lamplight at two in the morning. While Anita was still immobile, a guest got a fearful chill and became delirious. Nettie, who tried to serve as nurse, was too deaf to hear the patient's complaints, and then the maid took sick, and when all the campers were well enough to travel, they had to endure a five-hour trip to the train station in a lumber wagon—a bandaged Anita lying in the bottom of the wagon—"over a road of perpetual bumps and jolts." They missed their train and spent the next twenty-four hours in a log cabin, "the first ladies that had ever been in it," the wife of the woodsman told them.

It should be mentioned that the event which had brought the harvester clerks to dance the Virginia reel at Rush Street was Cyrus's engagement to Harriet Bradley Hammond, a docile girl who lived near the McCormicks with her aunt, Mrs. Stickney. One might suppose that the gift of a compliant daughter-in-law would have pleased Nettie; on the contrary, she was crushed. She liked Hattie well enough (there was, after all, nothing to be said against her), but it was tormenting to accept "anyone being dearer to my boy than I

51

am." She sought to stifle her regrets as "unworthy," to be "silent as to any trials I have to carry," but it was an audible silence. First, she objected to their marrying in California; any place west of the Rockies was unthinkable. Then, in an about-face, she decided that California was the perfect setting and they would all go, but she would go first, taking Stanley along to help her establish a new household on the West Coast for Virginia. Off she went to inspect real estate, leaving Anita to arrange for a special railroad car to transport the Chicago guests across the country to Monterey.

When the wedding was over, Anita wanted to sleep for a year. It was deeper than physical exhaustion. "The central fact that pierces keenly when other things fail to," she wrote Missy from California, was that she was "so alone" and didn't know whether she would "always feel this way," or whether it was "merely a transition and I shall grow by and by to take things more calmly—accepting the half portions and not longing for the intensities of life."

Nettie was too absorbed in her own remorse at losing a son to notice her daughter's lassitude. "How strangely wedding bells and funeral notes are blended in this world," Nettie had written Cyrus's bachelor friend George Sullivan after the ceremony, and how she prayed that George's "dear mother may never have to feel just as I did then."

Two weeks after her return to Chicago, Anita fell in love.

Emmons Blaine was not what Nettie had had in mind for a son-in-law. He was rather portly, had a mustached chipmunk face, had come to Chicago in 1880 as an administrator for railroads, was ten years older than Anita, prematurely gray, not pious, not a Democrat, and not wealthy, although his mother regarded him as a "thorough businessman, a discreet counselor"; and he was said by a friend to be "the most sunny tempered, the gentlest, the kindest man I have ever known, who was strong." He was not handsome, but he had winning ways. He could make Anita laugh, and he adored her.

It had been rumored in a Philadelphia newspaper that young Mr. Blaine would become the son-in-law of Joseph Medill, editor and publisher of the *Chicago Tribune*, but Philadelphia erred. That he came of an eminent family was incontestable. Emmons's father, James Gillespie Blaine, had been nominated by the Republicans for the presidency, served as a representative and senator from Maine, as speaker of the House of Representatives in 1860 and 1861, and was to be secretary of state under presidents James Garfield and Benjamin Harrison. The elder Blaine had well-connected acquaintances in finance whose fortunes were far larger than his but whose interests he was not disinclined to advance. The Blaines lived well, if not luxuriously.

Emmons's mother, Harriet Stanwood Blaine, was cheerfully devoted to her energetic husband and their six children and thrived on "the envelopes in the gravy, the spattered table linen, the uncertainty of meals."[7] Before her marriage she had been a teacher. All the children in this lively, affectionate family had gone to boarding school, Emmons to Andover and Harvard.

Amiable, fond of food and billiards, young Blaine quickly became "one of the principal young men in society," according to Anita, who first met him when she was fifteen when he had come to Rush Street for dinner. She had thought him "very nice."

Before Emmons's appearance in Chicago, the paths of the Democratic McCormicks and the Republican Blaines had crossed only once. Nettie had had tea with Emmons's mother in 1883, when Mrs. Blaine visited Chicago, which she found "interesting." At one luncheon given in her honor, she wrote her children, "All the ladies, save your humble servant wore very large solitaire diamond earrings, so that they were hard to tell apart. There was one who did not have them at first, but she soon remembered the deficiency, and going to the telephone, which was in the front hall, she telephoned her maid, who soon brought them, and my one landmark was obliterated." Still, they were "real ladies," and Mrs. Blaine didn't see "what there is in Chicago to apologize about."[8]

After Anita's coming out in 1887, Emmons had shown up at dinners and dances at which she was present, although her diary mentions him with no marked favor; he was one of several young men who showered her with courtesies. She had already had proposals of marriage, the first when she was seventeen. "Sir," she had admonished that suitor, "in returning your letter to you, I can but express my amazement that you should have so written to me. . . . I consider it wholly inexcusable that you should have made such an advance to me. Permit me to say that your pardon can only be granted on the ground that I shall never again be interrupted by any repetition of any such sentiment on your part toward me." He was not heard of again. George Sullivan, her elder brother's boyhood companion, had cherished Anita as the "dearest object of his life," but the affection was not reciprocated. Then, shortly before her nineteenth birthday, a Mr. Forsythe, whom she had met during a springtime trip to Atlantic City, had asked for her hand. "Why can't men be satisfied to be friends?" Anita wrote Missy, having turned him down, "and what is there about poor little me that calls forth such sentiment?" She was embarrassed by these avowals, a bit ashamed that she could not return the love that was laid at her feet, and she prayed that she might "so live that anyone who is so unfortunate as to give me unrequited affections may find himself strengthened and helped on in the struggles of life by having known my friendship, and that his ideal of womanhood, instead of being debased, may be elevated." The last suitor she had rejected was a stockbroker who never married and named Anita as a beneficiary in his will.

Anyway, she mused in her diary, why did people think matrimony was "such a desirable thing in itself?" Wasn't it often "a perfect Hades?" Far better to live alone, "unless there be a mutual fount of absolute love that makes anything easy and home a heaven"; anything less would be spiritual suicide. The "calm mutual satisfaction" of most marriages (was she thinking of her elder brother's?) had no appeal, unsanctified as such unions were by "a love that exists by the necessity of two natures which must cling together regardless of circumstances."

When did she begin to think that she could find this total communion with Emmons Blaine? She afterwards hinted that a "seed of love" had been dropped very early into her heart, but in fact the attachment took root only when her mother took alarm and Emmons persisted. He sent her notes and flowers. He served as her guide to the Republican national convention in Chicago in 1888 and was amused at how little she was impressed by politicians. "Such a dilatory body of men," Anita had commented. "If they had been women and had delayed so, no end of fun would have been poked at them." She had had a close-up view of the convention proceedings, for Emmons's father, nominated four years earlier and defeated in that election by Grover Cleveland, again aspired to be the Republican candidate. The votes, however, were with Benjamin Harrison, and Senator Blaine finally withdrew with a tacit understanding that he would be appointed secretary of state.

Once his convention duties were over, Emmons turned his full attention to Miss McCormick, appearing unbidden that summer at Richfield Springs, where he got a chilly reception from Nettie. He was not discouraged. His "pride was up," he said; he was "a good

The McCormick reaper factory (1867) before the fire

Nettie Fowler McCormick, 1862

Cyrus's mother,
Mary Ann Hall McCormick

Anita's birthplace, Manchester, Vermont

The Robert McCormick farm in Walnut Grove, Virginia, where the reaper was invented

Cyrus Hall McCormick, shortly after his marriage

Nettie, 1870

Anita, four years old

Sister Virginia, before her breakdown

Anita and her mother, 1880–81

Cyrus, with sons Stanley and Harold

The McCormick mansion, 675 Rush Street, Chicago

Anita and Stanley

Anita, just before her coming out

Virginia and Anita

Schoolboys—Stanley and Harold   Anita and Cyrus, 1887

The McCormick mansion, interior

Chicago tennis party, about 1885 (Anita far right, second row)

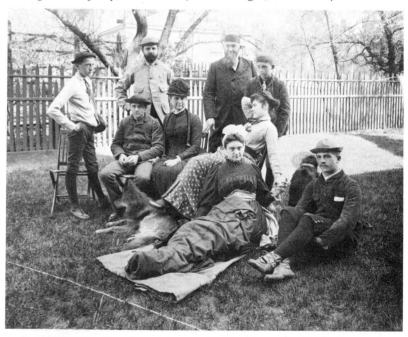

Anita and friends. Standing, left to right: Ned Ryerson, Cyrus, Jr.,
Dr. William C. Gray, Stanley. Seated, left to right: Harold, Nettie,
Miss Roberts. Seated on the ground: Anita, John Ryerson

Anita in her Paris wedding gown

Mrs. Cyrus Hall McCormick
requests your presence
at the marriage of her daughter,
Anita,
to
Mr. Emmons Blaine,
on Thursday, September twenty-sixth,
at twelve o'clock.
Presbyterian Church,
Richfield Springs, New York.

Richfield Springs, at the time of Anita's earliest visits

Mother and son

Emmons and Em

Emmons, Jr., a year after his father's death, in Lakewood, New Jersey

Em in New Mexico, with the foreman of Stanley's ranch

Em with his tutor Alan Eaton
(also Anita's secretary), 1906

"The Rev."—William B. Lusk

Henry B. Favill   Em

Mr. and Mrs. James G. Blaine, on their visit with Andrew Carnegie at Carnegie's castle in Scotland, 1887. Carnegie, holding his bowler, stands behind Harriet Blaine; James is second to the right

The Paris Exposition—Nettie and Cyrus, Jr.

Anita

Mother and daughter

Anita with Em

Cyrus, Jr., Anita, and Nettie

101 East Erie– the home of Mrs. Emmons Blaine

Tea with Mama

Mama's
eightieth
birthday

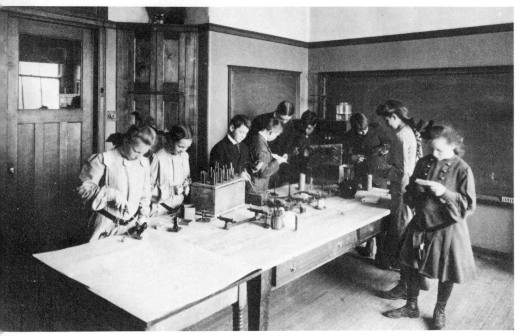

Educational experiment–the University of Chicago "Lab School"

Homes of the poor—Anita at work
for the City Homes Association

Cyrus Bentley, about 1924

John Dewey

Flora Cooke

"The Colonel"
Francis M.
Parker

Cousin Carrie McCormick

Mrs. Harold Fowler McCormick
(Edith Rockefeller)

Stanley and Katherine in Geneva,
on their honeymoon

The happy days—Stanley   Mathilde McCormick

Muriel and Fowler McCormick, 1903

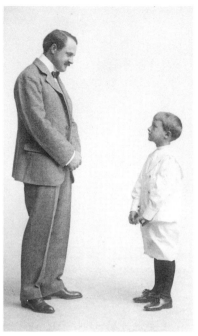

Adah McCormick at the time of her marriage to Harold   Harold and son Fowler, 1905

The Blaine home at Bar Harbor. Front row, left to right:
James G. Blaine, Jr., Mrs. Henry Cabot Lodge, President Benjamin Harrison,
Harriet (Mrs. James G.) Blaine, James G. Blaine, Harriet Blaine Beale

Margaret Blaine Damrosch   Walter Damrosch

Ganna Walska

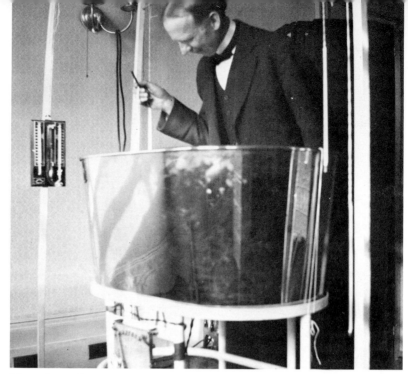

Nancy's incubator at 101 East Erie

Anita with her granddaughter

Clark Lawrence

Em as a young man

Eleanor and Em

Four generations — Anita, Nettie, Eleanor, and Nancy

Nancy

John Blaine Lawrence

Nancy

Anita and Nancy in 1953, with the first great-grandchild, David Blaine Harrison

Sir Oliver Lodge with Anita at his home in Salisbury

The inveterate writer

At home at 101

Henry Wallace in 1943 at the
Blackstone Hotel, Chicago

Coming down the stair with Eleanor – Anita at her eightieth birthday party

deal of a Yankee, and could not bear to be defeated!" He had tried to "shake this thing off—it would not be shaken off." He had written Anita some weeks before that "unless you and I get better acquainted I have little happiness to look forward to. . . . I cannot shut my eyes to the fact my future is largely in your hands." But he was up against another Yankee. Nettie was no readier than he to be beaten, and if he had not been so skillful at tactical retreats, she might have won. When she suggested that her daughter give dinner parties to which Emmons not be invited and that he be excluded from all the festivities of Cyrus's impending marriage, he said nothing. But the day Anita returned to Chicago from Richfield Springs, roses and a note awaited her. He would have brought them himself, he wrote, "but I'm afraid I couldn't get in."

Suddenly, matters took an unanticipated turn. He showed up at the house later that week, was admitted, declared his love, and almost before they had a chance to realize what had happened between them, he was "snatched away" for a confrontation with Mama, who recorded what followed.

"You were surprised yourself when you had found you had succeeded in winning her love, were you not?" Nettie asked.

"Well, I meant to try hard."

She asked him to leave the house.

At three that afternoon, he reappeared, and the two of them went at it again, with Nettie on the offensive.

"You are a man of the world," she said. "You are a club man, and that means satisfaction in the life that goes on at the club. Neither her father nor her brother cared for club life, so going to the club would be a new thing in my daughter's life."

"I go to clubs," he replied, "because I have no home, not because I prefer that life. I know what you think. You think I am an irreligious man."

"I am not bringing up the question of your religious life. I do not care to meddle with the religious life of anyone."

He thanked her for that. If, after three months without seeing him or hearing from him, Anita remained of the same mind, would she then give them her blessing?

"I think," Nettie answered, "you may safely trust me to act right at the expiration of three months." But she promised nothing.

"My happiness lies in Anita's happiness, and she could not be happy without her mother's blessing. I want to ask you to be very kind to . . ."

"Why of course I will be kind to my own child."

"But I mean you can wound her deeply through assaults on me."

"You can trust me for that."

"I shall be very tender for her," Emmons said. And with that, Nettie rose and extended her hand. He refused to shake it; she quit the room, leaving him with Cyrus. Emmons apologized, left, and turned up the next morning.

Having so recently surrendered her eldest son to Harriet Hammond, albeit with a "struggle to subdue a feeling in my heart that I must face the hard fact that another had the right to first place in that dear boy's heart," Nettie did not want to give up her daughter, not yet, and not to Mr. Blaine. "Some days ago," she wrote her friend Mary Mildred Sullivan in May 1889, "I began a note to tell you our reason for wishing so much to see your dear sister, Miss Hammond. In my attempts I got as far as 'Dear Mildred'—and beyond that, my pen would not move! Suddenly the thing you dreaded seems impending—and that my child (whose indifference for all these years has come to make me feel that she would never look at anyone with more than a friendly regard) was in danger. . . . Many people came, she seemed indifferent to all. How could I suppose that this one would fare differently? On May 7 was the first I knew of anything serious in this matter! And we were so stunned, surprised and saddened that we all wished for dear Miss H. and telegraphed her asking her to come. She came, and it has been such a comfort! She has been so kind through it all—herself carrying a thorn in the heart! She advised us to think all the good of him that is possible, and learn all that we can about him that we can!"

Missy, a woman of delicate perception, maneuvered for delay, advised Nettie to be patient, and hired "a juvenile Swede" to give Anita a "regular overhaul every morning as part of a program to regain physical and emotional health." Anita allowed herself to be rubbed and pummeled, but what good did they think massages would accomplish, she asked Missy? Couldn't Mama see that she was "beyond all human help but love," that her spirit was breaking, that the freshness of her love was being "brushed away in the very bloom?" "It is but the fight, dear, that we all have to make," Missy answered solemnly, and Anita cried, "but must I fight so always?"

She turned for support to Emmons, her "strong oak," but he too counseled forebearance; they would be "all the happier" having overcome obstacles; they must accept Nettie's latest request that her daughter "be left for a short space, entirely free from the urgent influences that beset a girl's heart in the presence of the lover, so that her feelings may have time to find their true equipoise." Time would not change her feelings, Anita replied; nor would she settle for any halfhearted approval of Emmons. Mama must give her "hearty consent. . . . Satisfy yourself as to what is in him, my life is involved in this decision."

Shortly before Anita's twenty-third birthday, Nettie, in one of her sudden reversals, gave in. "A door in Anita's heart is opened that can never be shut," she wrote in her journal, "and whatever change may come over *him, she* will never change . . . and now my place is by *her* side, to share with her this lot, in adversity or prosperity. Her life and happiness are staked upon it, and I have no *possible choice* but to fall in with it, and as Missy H. said, make all things as happy as I can, and like what he likes, no matter how great my sense of her superiority over him."* Having so decided, she took Anita on her lap, handed her a sealed package which Emmons had left, containing his picture and a note, and said that "from this time on, your cause is to be my cause, and I will go with you no matter where that will lead, so great a thing it seems to me to secure your happiness." Anita wept: "Oh Mama, how good you are." They joked about the picture, Nettie pretending she could not part with it: "It is mine, too, and dear to me. You must promise to give it back to me when you have the original!" Then they telegraphed Emmons, summoning him to Rush Street for a family conference.

Anita celebrated by writing a poem:

One morn I woke to calm and smiling skies.
A radiance as of heaven met my eyes—
The seed of love had blossomed to a flower.
Its fragrance filled my life. It was a light
Of lustrous depth that made all else seem night.
Words cannot tell the rapture of that hour.

Ere long the sunny skies are overcast—
The rose bud faints and falters in the blast—
Hot winds and fiercest gales in contest close
To drain its life—but power in it lie,

* Anita was unsure why "the barriers broke down." "I can't tell just what changed Mama at the last," she noted in her journal. "It had been gradual, I think, and she said she had been purposing to give [Emmons] to me on a month from the day, if she could do so heartily."

That could at need a stormy world defy.
   The bud but opens to a full-blown rose.

Wear it, beloved—hold it close to thee.
   So shall it find its regal destiny,
And fadeless til eternity be thine.
   And when we too have done with life on earth,
My love—my rose—transformed in heavenly birth,
   Will share with thee that timeless life divine.

He gave Anita a ruby flanked by two diamonds, and she was "so glad his taste was . . . a little different from all the world's." She seemed to be drifting into a faraway land that only two could enter, and yet how wonderful that theirs was not "that narrowing love that shuts out all other objects and inevitably dwarfs life." She was eager to embrace Emmons's family, whom she had not met, and proposed inviting them to Richfield Springs, where the McCormicks would soon be vacationing; but to her surprise, Missy urged that she steer clear of the Blaines until after the wedding. Rumors were afloat which she feared might cause awkwardness. James G. Blaine was said to have committed certain injudicious acts during his political career and had countenanced conniving and dishonesty, and although the allegations were not proved, they had made a "sufficiently forceable" impression on Missy so that she advised caution. "You alone, my dear," she wrote, "can weld these two family circles into harmony. You must go slowly in this work—and have no steps to retrace." She might as well have counseled the sun not to rise. Nothing could cloud the rightness of Anita's choice, nothing but Emmons himself.

And what of her lover? Was his commitment as unqualified as hers? If he were not to find his true delight in her, she would "wither up and die, only I couldn't die soon enough." She confessed that she had come away from one of their talks "feeling as though we did not perfectly know each other. . . . Truth is, Emmons, I am altogether intense by nature. My feelings are my whole life, and all my feelings center in you—and therefore I am expecting you to know me as you only can after long knowledge—and when I find your heart not keeping absolute pace with mine, it hurts." Perhaps she wearied him "by the very intensity of my loving." Was there, could there be "a shadow of a doubt about our future in your mind; tell me before I mar your life. Anything would be preferable to me to giving you my life to burden you." Alone, she pondered the falsity of "a chivalry that makes a man act at any point with greater feeling than he possesses—or without a feeling that he should have so to act." She even considered postponing the wedding, until word came of the death of Kate Fowler, her Uncle Eldridge's second wife, a young woman and married only two years. There would be no further delay.

A date in late September was set, and an exuberant about-to-be bridegroom sent word to a friend in Baltimore: "I am lucky, awfully lucky, don't care for anything else in the world, I am in that state of exalted beatitude." The secretary of state extended a "cordial and affectionate welcome" to his prospective daughter-in-law and assured her that Emmons was "the truest of sons and the most manly of men" and would prove "the most affectionate, most loyal and most devoted of husbands." Mrs. Blaine thanked Anita for "giving Emmons his heart's desire"; in so doing, she had given his mother "a great happiness, and at my age there are few who can confer this boon upon me." And finally, Emmons's favorite sister, another Harriet, came to Richfield Springs. "Anita has been playing the most beautiful soft music ever since we came in from church," she reported to her family, "and has made me more conscious of being happy than I am able to put into words. . . . I have fallen in love with Anita. She is everything one could ask, and thank heavens! sees the funny side of things. She and Monsy are pretty cunning together. They never spoon but are together all the time and take each other in a very natural and unembarrassing manner. Most of the time they sit and laugh. Stanley told me that 'Anita was gayer than she used to be and it seemed to change people to be engaged.' The wedding is spoken of constantly and Anita says they try to speak of it before her mother as if it were nothing more than a lawn party."

There were moments at Richfield Springs that summer when Anita and Emmons were just as glad that Mama was hard of hearing, but when her ear trumpet did take it in that they intended to be married in September, she put her foot down. It was much too soon; Cyrus and his bride were in Europe and could not possibly return by then; anyhow, preparations for a proper Chicago wedding could not be completed in a few months. Well, why have it in Chicago, Anita asked? She'd much prefer a simple ceremony in Richfield Springs, removed from "all the disagreeable accompaniments of a city wedding, which seems like nothing but a show." Cyrus and Harriet would have to get back as best they could. Nettie held out briefly, then surrendered, and there were hugs and kisses and general jubilation. But as 26 September drew closer, Nettie's agitation revived and she was overcome by melancholy: "To feel that soon Anita's things will all be gathered together, how can I say it—to take away! I have just got to stop and sit down and cry until I am almost blind." She fussed over floral arrangements, the invitation list, the decorations, Anita's dress and appearance; and Anita, unable to take any of it seriously, told Emmons that "Mama was trying to make me believe this afternoon you would love me better if I would try, by following her wise injunctions, to preserve my exceedingly small portion of good looks. I told her if I felt as she did, I would take poison and be done with it. She sagely replied that some day I would 'see things differently'—which I hope I never might. Sometimes I have thought Mama had a streak of romance in her—but I verily believe that she has grown so practical that she is loath to believe in absolute love."

In Paris, Cyrus's wife was visiting fitting rooms, hurrying them along to finish Anita's wedding dress of white satin draped with Valencienne lace. Missy shopped in New York for gowns and lingerie. Nettie demanded periodic reports from the furniture maker ("the carving in the bedstead is the most *exquisite* piece of work I have seen in a long time, it has taken two weeks to carve each panel"). Dr. Herrick Johnson of Fourth Presbyterian was invited to officiate, flowers and food were ordered, the small church in Richfield Springs reserved, Anita's music teacher engaged to play the organ, and the manager of the Richfield Springs House persuaded to keep his hotel open to accommodate out-of-town guests. In deference to Virginia, who could only sit on the sidelines, there would be no bridesmaids.

In the midst of the preparations, Nettie raised a delicate question. After their marriage, who would manage Anita's considerable fortune? Nettie thought that "some control of her property is pleasant to a lady if her taste lies in the direction of business affairs," and that her daughters (this was written in 1885) "*ought* to have considerable to say about their own property. They might want to do good with some of their money. . . . And yet, I don't want the care of it to bear so heavily upon them as to be a toil to them, as it might be without a helper." Unless other arrangements were agreed to, her husband would control Anita's fortune, and while they had no reason to distrust Emmons's probity or competence, Nettie pointed out, Papa would have wanted ironclad financial protection for his daughter. A trust document was thereupon drawn up, giving Cyrus, Jr., and Anita's uncle Eldridge Fowler complete authority over her property; she would get only the income. The resignation of control was irrevocable for her McCormick company stock, which accounted for most of her wealth, although she could, if she wished, take charge of her other properties after ten years. Emmons discretely kept out of the discussions, but the arrangement was not as customary as Anita had been led to believe. She unhesitatingly signed the necessary papers, thinking only of his "waiting for me and loving me." The one transaction that she initiated and carried through on her own before the marriage, her first gift on a grand scale, was the establishment of a trust fund for "precious" Missy, who accepted it under protest and swore she would give the income to charity.

The uniting of one of America's richest families and one of its best known was national news. Reporters rang the Rush Street doorbell, clamoring for details, and were sent away empty-handed. Refused a photograph of the bride, the newspapers published a drawing which Nettie called "an atrocious charicature." Speculative columns described the trousseau and the wedding gifts, the *Richfield Springs Mercury* reporting several silver pieces, including a repoussé tea set from Nettie, pitchers and bouillon cups from the Blaines, a fruit dish from Virginia, and flatware from Cyrus, Jr. Emmons was said to have given Anita a diamond brooch which could be worn as a pendant. There was mention of a gold-back toilet set, a gold belt, a "rare Chinese smelling bottle," and a large bronze bust of Felix Mendelssohn from Andrew Carnegie. One journalist quoted an anonymous source who claimed to have seen thousands of dollars' worth of imported lace and dozens of pairs of white silk stockings, some embroidered in silver or gold. Lily-scented sachets imported from Holland and encased in monogrammed and lace-edged satin bags allegedly sweetened Anita's trunks, in which were packed a new winter opera cloak of heavy white silk embroidered with gold and "lined from top to toe with the long silky hair of the Persian lamb." Another paper reported that her dresses were laid inside an antique Venetian chest which Anita had picked up during one of her shopping excursions to the Continent. Several claimed that she had gone to Paris to be measured and fitted for her new wardrobe. Declining to join in such speculation, the *New York Times* noted that only intimate friends, previously sworn to secrecy, had been permitted to see the gifts and the trousseau, and that the servants had proved unbribable.

Residents of Richfield Springs decorated their streets and buildings with flags and lanterns. A prenuptial reception and luncheon was given by the McCormicks in honor of the secretary of state, at which another romantic event was announced, the engagement of Emmons's sister Margaret to Walter Damrosch, the New York composer and conductor. And on a rainy 26 September 1889, in the small, red-brick Presbyterian church adorned with Abyssinian banana trees and rare palms and a screen of smilax covering the upper walls, Anita and Emmons were married. Emmons's "I do" was heard only by those in the front rows; she responded in a clear, strong voice. She would always remember, she later told him, "the perfect exhilaration of going in to you by that music, the utter solemnity and deep meaning of every word, the picture of you engraven on my mind forever, and then the going out with you, with a sense of gladness and lightness and possession." They ran through the rain to their carriage and were driven to Clayton Lodge for the reception, where the florist's triumph was a canopy of orchids and rare roses under which the newlyweds stood to receive two hundred guests. The caterer's masterpiece, "Salmon à la Emmons" and boned turkey "à la Anita," graced a long table. The salmon rested on an oval of white confection mounted over a white grotto, under which, in a miniature lake, a Cupid bestrode a swan and a boatman rode his tiny skiff. Real fish swam in the pond. The boned turkey was quite as elaborate, the head, wings, and breasts of pheasants decorating mounds of meat; it, too, was mounted on a confection platform under which, reported the *Richfield Springs Mercury*, was a log cabin; "a pretty sugar milkmaid was standing by a sugar cow, and a sheep gamboled nearby, while a spring of water flowed from the ferns and shrubs at the foot of the tree into a little watering trough." Throughout the reception, an orchestra on the porch "discoursed delightful music."

The guests cheered the departing couple, and Nettie wept as Anita and Emmons boarded a private railway car for their honeymoon journey to the Blaine family cottage in Maine. His generous tips assured them privacy. "The country never looked better," Anita merrily wrote her mother, "the cook turned out to be *Cordon Bleu*, what more could two happy people ask."

From the front windows of the Blaine cottage in Bar Harbor, the honeymooners looked out on the dense pine woods of Mount Desert Island's upper road. A broad veranda commanded a splendid panorama—a sloping lawn and the waters of Frenchman Bay. On sunny days, and there were some in late September, tiny islands glowed like sapphires, and when it stormed the pines danced in the wind and huge birch logs were thrown on the fire in the living room. The wedding seemed to Anita "ages gone by . . . a prehistoric age." Each moment took them "a new step into our happiness together." They "lazed away" the mornings, "looking at each other and occasionally at the view."

Emmons proved the kindest of husbands, solicitous not only of his wife's desires but of her mother's. Before leaving Chicago, he had been given briefings by Nettie on what he could expect. They included a clinical description of her daughter's physiology, and when Anita's menstrual period began the day after the wedding, he was prepared. He made her stay in bed late, breakfasted at her side, and afterward sent Nettie the full report she had requested. "It was very hard for her, but the innate dignity of her character carried her through that trial and left her composed and serene at the end. . . . You may imagine what a relief it is to me to be able to tell you that I do not believe there is any room for anxiety at all."

Anita also had had instructions. It was essential to avoid "maternal relations" until she had recovered from the wedding and the preceding months of emotional strain, and under no conditions was she to forget that abstinence was advisable during the ten days following menstruation.

October passed quickly, and in November the newlyweds journeyed to Baltimore, where Emmons had a new and higher position with the railroads. It was lovely to be in charge, even of a rented house! There were groceries to be ordered, linen to be sent out for washing, a place chosen for the larder, servants to hire, nooks and crannies to explore, boxes in the basement to be opened and each gift put in its place. Anita dashed about Baltimore buying oyster plates, soup plates, dessert plates, and platters, proudly telling her husband that although her purchases were of the best quality, she had not exceeded his budgeted limit. When they were settled in, Nettie was invited to come for Christmas, so that she might see for herself how efficiently her daughter could manage. Mama came, murmured her approval, was enchanted at being taken to dinner at the secretary of state's house in Washington, where President Harrison was among the guests, and now, Nettie said, Anita must return the favor and pay a short visit to Chicago.

Anita suspected at the time that she was pregnant, but at Emmons's urging chose to say nothing to her mother. Though she went reluctantly, once there she admitted to enjoying the "whirling winter activities" of her old friends. And yet, she wrote her husband, "I seem to have gotten a weight in my life that has gone down deep and made these things of necessity take the surface, and I turn from them to the deep real life we live together, with such a peace and joy." He wrote that he was lonely and missed her. She replied that away from him, "life seems only half lived. . . . A yearning comes over me, something that I couldn't express, that must be felt to be understood—a longing to be one with you my darling in my mind's life, which is my real life."

Baltimore had the advantage of being little more than an hour's train ride from her in-laws, and Anita and Emmons paid frequent visits to the Blaines in Washington. They were present at a merry house-warming on Lafayette Square, at which Walter Damrosch christened the piano and Emmons's mother took them on an inspection tour of the house, relating how the son of Francis Scott Key had been shot down on the steps by a jealous husband, and how an assassin had attacked secretary of state Seward in the upstairs bedroom the night Lincoln was killed. "You know," Harriet Blaine laughed, "the house is cursed"—a prophetic remark, for during an influenza epidemic which struck Washington that winter of 1900, the eldest Blaine son, Walker, died of pneumonia. Emmons, who was present, telegraphed Anita, who came immediately and "spent the day till four, when I brought my tired boy home to rest—he had been doing everything for everybody." Not long after, the second Blaine child, Alice, contracted the same illness and died. The parents "seem not to know where to turn," Anita wrote Nettie; they were "perfectly stricken."

The week Walker was buried, however, there was joyous news for the Blaines—Anita and Emmons announced that a grandchild would arrive in August. There was so much to be done—summer clothes to be let out, stores toured for infant wear, a list of "things you think are necessary" obtained from Mama, little French night-gowns ordered from Marshall Field and Company. In late June, with Anita seven months pregnant, they fled the stupefying Baltimore heat for the bracing air of Bar Harbor, stopping in New York only long enough to greet Nettie before her departure for Europe with Harold and Stanley. The rendezvous was brief, but Anita felt for the first time that her mother and Emmons had come "very near to each other," which gave her "much joy." Nettie's thank-you letter for the "procession of comforts" she had found in her cabin reached them in Maine: "the choice books, the fine wine to cheer the meals, and the between-meals, the clams, so grateful to the palate here, the helps to warm clothing—the pungent ginger for a relish . . . and then your lovely flowers—roses, sweet peas, pinks—a large boxful."

In Bar Harbor they picked wild flowers and found a path through the rocks to a view of the sea. In the evenings, Emmons read while Anita sewed or filled the pages of a journal with her meditations, summed up in the resolve "not to act in reference to what another will feel, but to act from within!" And if things went amiss, "not to pull away" but to "sail right in and look hard and understand the facts of ourselves as far as we can see them." She thought of "the deep waters and great happiness" she and Emmons shared and how it would "go through the years increasing in depth." On her twenty-fourth birthday Emmons's gift was a tiny heart made of diamonds, which she wore next to a crown of diamonds he had given her the year before—symbolic pins, the first for their union, the second for the "truest crown of our love [which] will come a little later."

In his more casual way, Emmons was as happy as she. Before leaving Baltimore, he had resigned from the West Virginia Central Railroad (from which he had received a salary of $8,000 a year) and was looking forward to a larger opportunity as assistant general manager of the Baltimore and Ohio Line, headquartered in Chicago, and to temporary residence in the McCormick house on Rush Street, which they would have to themselves the rest of the year. Nettie intended to remain in Europe through the summer and to spend the winter in New York, where Harold and Stanley would attend an exclusive private school, along with John Rockefeller, Jr., and several other boys from comparable backgrounds.

From England in July came "four lovely combination underwear which I have set my heart upon your wearing in latitudes where a low temperature prevails." "Dearie," Nettie wrote, "how I wish I were there to thoroughly rub olive oil upon all the muscles that are to be called upon to yield at the proper time. True, Nature does her part well, but she can be *mightily helped*." Mama hoped that Nature would give the baby "the boon of his own natural food—its fountain being in his mother's breast." And Anita must not be put off "by the hurt of Baby's drawing it, you must try to stand it." The letter ended with the familiar injunction: "Please Darling, burn this as soon as you have read it."

By mid-August, Missy Hammond, a nurse, and an out-of-town doctor were in attendance. "Now if you were only here," Anita wrote her mother, "you would not see the frightened child I expected to be, but your own child the same as ever, waiting for her little one with absolute calmness and happiness. I can never be able to tell you what peace comes to me from being in this home of all my girlhood now. . . . I did not realize what a blessing it would be." On the afternoon of 29 August, Anita took a carriage drive with Emmons, beat the doctor at a game of backgammon, dined with friends, showed them the baby clothes, and before retiring felt a slight pain, as though she had "eaten a green apple." Each instant of the ensuing drama was recorded by Missy for the benefit of the absent Nettie: "At about a quarter to five o'clock this morning, Emmons knocked at my door and asked me to bring some cracked ice and give it to Anita. I quickly got it and upon entering found darling Anita in bed, her back supported by Emmons, and the doctor holding both of her hands in his. The darling had been suffering ever since 12:30. I can never tell you the innate sweetness, dignity and strength of character in those trying hours. Emmons was *all in all* to her. . . . At last, when the doctor knew the time was at hand, Emmons left the room, and with the nurse holding one hand and I the other, she unconscious from the chloroform, the dear baby-boy 'came into this land of ours.' His first cry awakened her. She says it was like calling her from death to life."

The nine-pound baby was carried to the nursery by Missy, Emmons returned to the bedroom with a reviving glass of whiskey and water and whispered, "Nitzy, it's a boy!" and minutes later the child, washed and oiled and wrapped in flannel, was placed in his mother's arms and she could "look at his darling funny little face." Anita then dictated a message to Virginia, so that it could be dated the baby's birthday, after which she had brown bread, toast, milk, and sleep. Her feelings about the baby were best expressed long after, in a style all her own, in a letter to her granddaughter: "He on that morning coming out of the body of me—all because the love of one for another—How mysterious! And he starting a new existence—all his own—we all belonging in different ways to it—all his own—How mysterious! And all of it—the whole world of it—belonging to each of us and to all as we lay hold of it and give him to it."

Emmons fit the fatherly role to perfection, talking to his son "as if already they were boon companions entirely appreciating and understanding each other," Missy said. Possible names were debated, Emmons suggesting McCormick—"a very jolly name," Harriet Blaine commented, "and Mac is a good abbreviation," but whatever the boy's name, she wrote her brother, he ought to be "as near perfection as our sinful race has yet attained to. Perhaps I am prejudiced a little, but you and Anita seem to me to combine about all the virtues with just as few faults as would serve to anchor you to earth."

Secluded in Virginia's old suite, quiet as a saint's sanctuary, Anita was permitted after seven days to receive visitors. Throughout the week, flowers, telegrams, and enough hand-knit blankets for ten infants had been handed to the butler at the front door. Nettie, back from her travels, gave her first grandchild an expensive baby carriage and was delighted that the father wished to name his son after her husband. Emmons refrained from telling her that James, not McCormick, had been his first choice, and that he had been dissuaded by James G. Blaine, who wrote that "if you do not name him Emmons Blaine, Jr., it will be wise to name him for your wife's father—C. McCormick B. My reason for speaking is that possibly you may be thinking of me in connection with the matter. Great as would be the honor, I beg to impress upon you the belief which must sincerely hold, that one of the suggestions that I have made would be better—and that I could have and would have not the slightest possible feeling except one of warm approval." He asked Emmons not to "let Mother know I have written you on the subject."

Having satisfied herself that mother and child were well, Nettie returned to New York to be with Harold and Stanley, and Anita and Emmons were free to arrange the Rush Street household to suit their convenience. Except for a rash which appeared soon after his birth, the baby was healthy ("eats like an ocean voyager," Emmons wrote Mrs. James G. Blaine), and Anita continued to nurse him, marveling at how quickly this tiny creature had become indispensable; it was "almost painful to be bound up in the happiness of anyone as we in his." Her engrossing aim now was "to order his life aright."

The year 1891 passed calmly—spring at Virginia Beach, where Missy joined them; summer with three servants in a rented cottage at Bar Harbor, near the Blaines. On his first birthday, the baby had a bite of cake and the juice from a piece of steak, and seeing him at the table with "his mouth and hands all brown with beef juice," Anita imagined him old enough to rifle the pantry. She was eager not to lose any memory of his childhood and requested her mother to put on paper "all the impressions you think of in his first year. I want something that will tell of the baby when I am eighty and he, fifty-six."

In the fall, something occurred which made her fear for the baby's life. Stomach attacks which had begun in late summer had by October become menacing, and it was several weeks before he was pronounced out of danger. Haggard from day and night nursing, Anita thought that she had never before realized "how much of our life is lodged in him," and she redoubled surveillance of his diet.

Sunday school classes, the education of working-class girls and the Friday Club were now like toys stored in the attic. She observed her boy by the hour, astonished at each new task mastered and praying that God would grant her "the right kind of love and wisdom." Recalling her own childhood, she worried that she might possess him too greedily, influencing him so strongly as to "spoil his life with any wrong expression of it." But after discussing her worries with Emmons, she concluded that they "may be spared that fault. He is not ours to possess and make what we wish. He is his own and God's, ours to help and to enjoy." She tried to read the baby's feelings in his eyes and to put herself in his place, and when he said "No-No" to something that was offered him, she examined her assumption that he was simply being contrary and needed discipline. Perhaps the adults around him did not comprehend what he meant; even a baby had a right to his preferences, "particularly as his grasp of the material world is new." Wouldn't it be wiser "to *positively* encourage him in his justifiable 'No-No'—to go the whole length and show that we not only understand his wish but sympathize in it, and so disarm it of self-will? So, he will appreciate that his 'No-No' is not always disregarded and not always wrong, that there are differences, and later, it will have much force when he is *not* allowed to differ, from the fact that he is sympathized with and encouraged in a difference whenever possible."

This scrutiny of every baby gesture for its secret and perhaps profound message was something Emmons contentedly left to his wife. They were living what he called a "Darby and Joan life," altogether satisfactory, indeed nearly perfect. He saw no point in turning over each stone to examine its underside. He had been promoted to vice-president of the Baltimore and Ohio, had financial security, social standing, a son, and a wife with "depths of sweetness and nobleness that I did not know." The amenities of Rush Street were agreeable; he was amused at the butler's passing after-dinner tonic as if it were a delicious liqueur. They went to the opening ball of the 1891 season. They dined with the Cyrus McCormicks, and after dinner he played the drums and Anita the piano. They spoke of building their own home, to be ready in time for the World's Columbian Exposition in Chicago in 1893. There would be numerous out-of-town guests Emmons hoped to entertain. Missy later recalled that Emmons, referring to the "gaieties of the North Side," had said, "We're not in it." She mentioned his "quiet little fun as he spoke of the great scope of the intended 'Congress' [Exposition] and the hordes of women from Western towns, bent on 'culture,' who would swoop down on the city. He went from grave to gay, and from sentiment to humor, in the whole talk, so that it was delightful."

The first sign of stress between Emmons and Anita appeared when Emmons became ill in February 1892 of an undiagnosed intestinal ailment. Heretofore, Anita had leaned on him as her "sturdy oak." Now, the dependence was reversed. "We are learning much," he said, but his illness made him tense and fretful and the hours of nursing wore Anita down. They journeyed to Washington for his convalescence, leaving the baby in Nettie's care, but his recovery was halting. He found that he could not summon up the energy to deal with his wife's emotions; the demands of absolute love were fatiguing. In a letter to his mother in October 1896 Emmons had referred to "my unimpassioned self." Anita thought she understood why he was irritated but could not help imagining that he didn't love her as he once had. "I talk to him about the baby and fancy he is displeased. I have gone through a great deal of struggle and great suffering," she wrote on the back of an envelope, which she then hid. "I have by selfishness made Emmons very unhappy—have made him feel outraged, and when we talked it over I even then fell to blaming Emmons for not turning around and applying himself to comforting and helping me." He was not outraged, he told her, simply weary; he needed peace and quiet. Then, "seeing him a little better," Anita would again try to "make him talk about these fancies of mine, til he, with splitting head and depressed about his health, and more depressed by my doubting him, can't stand it longer."

In the past, she had accepted blame for upsetting her mother; she accepted it now for upsetting her husband. "Do I want the Angel Gabriel," she asked herself, "and do I want him wedded to a reed?" She accused herself of being "entirely selfish—permeated with it— from the beginning of life almost til now. . . . Oh God, help me to live in others and out of myself." She had to find the strength for them both. "Is he to have it all, or are we to go through this difficult life side by side, each helping each in the best way, and each bearing for each. . . . Let me give out more true love to the one I would rather make happy than anyone else in the world."

He was sufficiently well to attend the Republican national convention in Minneapolis that June, drawn by paternal rather than party loyalty. "When men grow old," he had said to Missy, "they take different views of things—the vista broadens. They see all sides, they cease to be partisan working for a party, they work for

69

their country and the race." Still, Emmons had been his father's chief aide since the death of Walker and was needed for a poorly organized, last-ditch effort to capture the presidential nomination, or at least to block Benjamin Harrison's bid for renomination. Emmons sat in on all the caucuses and buttonholed delegates, but the only result were noisy demonstrations for Blaine, "the Plumed Knight," not votes. The defeat of his father came with "crushing force," the *Chicago Herald* reported, and Emmons arrived home dispirited and worn out.

He complained the next day of the intestinal pains he had had earlier. Doctors were again summoned, diagnosed "colic," and administered cathartics. He got up for several hours and reclined on a sofa in the upstairs sitting room, covered with Nettie's white wool shawl, and she, thinking it would distract him, brought one of her visiting missionaries to the sitting room to discourse on his work and pressed Emmons for his opinion of its worth. Yes, he told Nettie wearily, "it was a good thing to contribute," whereupon she wrote the expected check. He joked about one of Nettie's favorite diseases: "I know now what cholera morbus is, for I have gone through it this last twenty-four hours." Anita came into the room smiling and he reached out his hand for hers. He went downstairs for lunch that noon, but the nausea and pain returned, and by evening he was running a temperature of 105 degrees. Anita telegraphed her father-in-law. A surgical operation was hastily planned and abandoned. Emmons died the next day of "ptomaine intoxication with uraemia as a fatal complication."

The chimes of St. James Presbyterian Church tolled, servants were dispatched to inform relatives, and reporters who had been hovering about the house were admitted to hear a statement by the doctors. The press had been asked to delay publication of the story until the secretary of state could be located, but it leaked out, and the Blaines, who learned of their son's death from the newspapers, reached Chicago two days later, accompanied by Harriet and their only surviving son, Jamie. The funeral service was simple. Emmons, as Cyrus, Jr., put it, was "a Christian outside of the Church." The *Chicago Herald* paid its respects by observing that Emmons had been "a strong favorite with clubmen, as with his business associates."[9]*

They had seen "the dawn of life," Anita was to write after nearly a half century had passed. "It grew into morning, so clear, so fair.

* His estate was valued at $80,000.

70

We looked ahead in life and the only question that I could ask was whether I was good enough to belong to him. But that question couldn't live in his sunshine. When our boy came, it seemed that no brighter sun could shine on earth than shone on us. And then with one swift stroke, life separated us and left me holding on and gazing into it with belief and conviction that we were not separated at all. I faced it only in the thought that he still lived." She was twenty-six.

IIII

EDUCATION OF A SON AND CITY

III

The days were like unnumbered blank pages, and Anita in her grief thought endlessly, futilely, of things that had been said or left unsaid. She was torn by regrets, preoccupied by the past, and only vaguely aware that the nation at that moment was in the grip of the worse industrial depression since the 1870s. Wages and prices had collapsed, banks were failing, there were strikes and soup kitchens blocks from Rush Street, and debates raged over Free Silver. But the world's clamor was shut out. She wandered from room to room, picking things up, putting them down. "No Calvinistic devil could invent it worse," she wrote in her diary. Again and again she returned to the question: what would Emmons have wanted her to do? She willed to see with his eyes, to be his agent, and fastened finally on the thought that Emmons would have wished her to be near his despondent parents. Secretary Blaine, seriously ill with Bright's disease, had resigned from President Harrison's cabinet, and her place was surely at his side. Nettie was of a different opinion, but having made up her mind, Anita went with her baby to Bar Harbor. After spending several days in the Blaine house, she moved into a separate cottage nearby, one with a wide porch on which the child could play on sunny days.

She should not have come, for she was closeted with memories she could not escape—her honeymoon, the happy weeks of 1890 waiting for the baby, the summer of his first birthday. "Trying to make a life and finding it difficult," she sent bewildered letters to her family begging for guidance and apologizing for burdening them. "I really am upset and don't know what to do," she wrote Cyrus's wife. "I am so at sea. I am ashamed of my weakness—but I cannot think it all out again."

On 30 August 1892, the baby's second birthday, she was still in Bar Harbor and chose that day for his christening at Stanwood, the Blaine summer home. The boy had never been formally named; Anita now settled on Emmons, Jr. He was taken to the Blaine house, where the paternal grandparents, Nettie told Cyrus, "received these two dear ones with hearts too full for words." A few friends, invited because of their closeness to Emmons, assembled in the drawing room and at once Anita entered with the child in her arms, his father's pearl pinned to his white dress. "How sad a figure it was," Nettie wrote—"these two standing there, the mother there alone to accept for this dear child the promises and obligations implied in baptism." The ailing grandfather, "who had through the ceremony seemed almost overwhelmed with emotion and was leaning with head bowed on the mantel," brought out a tiny silver-encased book with a clasp and had all the witnesses inscribe their names.[1]

Before leaving Bar Harbor, Nettie made the strongest case she could for Anita's return to Chicago; it was not right for a widow of twenty-six with a small child to live apart from her family. Anita was in no mood to argue; yet she held back, saying she feared the effect of a bitter Midwest winter on little Em's health. And there were the Blaines to consider. If she remained on the East Coast, she could see them more often. All she wanted was "to live Emmons' life" and the life he would have her live, and that meant being "as much to his mother and father as I can." She decided to rent a house in Lakewood, New Jersey.

Then, in the middle of January, in the midst of packing, Anita received word of James G. Blaine's death in Washington, three days before his sixty-third birthday. She unpacked, all resolution dead, and with no purpose on earth but to "make me ready for what is coming after." She was immobilized, physically and spiritually.

On the first anniversary of Emmons's death she was still in Maine, searching through drawers for something of his to hold, to look at, to read. If she could just have a sight or sound of him. "To be so cut off from you is terrible," she wrote, "and forever in this life. Such volumes I would have to say to you if I could see you, and yet all would be understood without a word." She had "tried so hard to do all things just as you would have me. I have lived lives since then.

I have lived them for you. I am so changed, so different—all yours—ten-thousandfold yours. If we could but now have life again, I could be so much more to you. You would not let me say it, Sweet, but I could. I have gone through fires. If you could take me now, I believe I should be purer and more worthy of you."

She came upon a sketch of his "dear face" and tried to imagine that he was in a "far country and we were separated only for a time —even so long as it might be, and is that not so?" "Must we not believe that we still continue after this earth?" she wrote. "If I could but know. If I could but talk to you about it my beloved one. I am heartsick for you. There is no one, no not one that knows my heart, that knows our heart. There is no one who can rest my heart of its ache. I give of myself to my baby and to others. I give for you, but oh I need refreshment. I need you. I grow so restless. It is all work, effort. My wellspring is gone. I am trying so hard to make a life. I believe the power will come, but sometimes I think not—the power to make interests for themselves and for the baby. He does not figure as a spur to my doings. I know not how that will be. But I must not revolve my life about him, it would be bad for him. What can I do? All my interests were so centered in you—all my doings took life from your interest in them. I will try, but I faint when I think that such a substitute is what my precious must have instead of the wealth he had in you."

Her plan to winter in New Jersey was abandoned. Instead, she and Em hid away in the vacation home of her childhood in Richfield Springs. Then, as spring and summer drifted by, life raised its head, her depression began to lift, and when the days turned cooler she was ready to fall in with her mother's plea that they come back to Chicago for good.

The streets of the city which greeted Anita in 1893 were crowded with jobless men and homeless families, and all the talk was of hard times. A stock market crash in May 1893 had triggered an economic depression that was to carry through for five years. Governor Altgeld of Illinois, speaking to workingmen on Labor Day of that year, warned that they faced "a long dark day" of "suffering and distress." Chicago newspapers carried the report that saloonkeepers were giving free lunches to sixty thousand men a day. Mayor Carter Harrison estimated there were two hundred thousand unemployed in the city after the closing of the Columbian Exposition. By mid-1894, 154 railroads were in receivership. A strike against the railroads led that year by Eugene Debs had failed, and Debs and three of his colleagues were jailed on conviction of conspiracy.

On the day Anita returned, Samuel Gompers, Henry George, and Clarence Darrow had just addressed a meeting of twenty-five thousand people on the lakefront and demanded a public works program, promptly dismissed by the *Chicago Tribune* as impractical. Nettie may not have sympathized with what Gompers, George, and Darrow were preaching, but she understood hunger and homelessness. Her benevolent impulses were aroused; it was no time, she told Anita, to brood over personal tragedies. They must show themselves to be Christian by helping the unfortunate poor. What was meant by help is illustrated in a lengthy account published that December in the *Chicago Record* under the heading "Visited by Fairies."[2]

"Fairies," the story opened, "are not all in the storybooks, at least that is the opinion of twelve-hundred boys and girls who live in the little wooden buildings sprinkled along California Avenue. . . . They are all pupils in the Hammond School, and their fathers and mothers are having a hard struggle this winter to keep coal in the bin and food in the cupboard, to say nothing of buying shoes and jackets for the children. Last week, principal H. F. Tibbets told his pupils that fairies were going to provide such a Christmas celebration as they never have before seen in their lives."

When the glad day arrived, the account continued, "there on the platform stood the big Christmas tree ablaze with lights and sparkling with colored ornaments of glass. At the top glowed a silver star. Oranges, candy and packages of food were banked in prodigal heaps about the base of the tree. The room had been festooned with wreaths and drapings of evergreen, and the stage was gay with bright-colored flags." Tibbets then told the children how the fairies had brought the gifts and provided the feast and, as he spoke, he pointed to Mrs. Emmons Blaine, who sat at the piano. "She is the fairy," he said. Three cheers were given, followed by a shout of joy: "Tears sprang into Mrs. Blaine's eyes. She was making the children happy, bringing sunlight into their clouded lives."

On the platform sat Mrs. James G. Blaine, Miss Harriet Blaine, and Nettie. The boys and girls were served ice cream, which many of them had never tasted before. Each received an orange, a bag of candy and a box of lunch. One hundred and twenty-five sacks of provisions, including turkeys and a large amount of groceries, were given to families in the neighborhood "whose worthiness was vouched for by Principal Tibbets." Not a few of the little ones—and the oldest was not more than fourteen—"came up timidly with an orange in each hand to thank the 'fairies' for the gifts."

It was after nightfall before the patronesses entered their waiting carriages and were whisked away, "followed by the enthusiastic cheers of one-hundred small boys grouped on the sidewalks."

The panic of 1893 notwithstanding, Chicago that year had set out to dazzle the world with the grandest show ever imagined—the World's Columbian Exposition, which opened on the first of May and would attract twenty-one million awed visitors before it closed. It was not to be missed, Anita wrote Missy; she must come and stay in the house Anita had rented on Walton Street so that they could enjoy this magnificence together.

The publicists had not exaggerated. On a 550-acre stretch of lake-shore swamp and sandbars, a "white city" had been constructed—plaster palaces, walks, fountains, and pools. Strolling through the grounds arm in arm, Anita and Missy saw the Sèvres porcelains, the Gobelin tapestries, the long-distance telephone to New York, the nine thousand paintings, the map of the United States made of pickles, "little Egypt" dancing the hootchy-kootchy, and of course the McCormick Company's exhibit of a gold- and silver-plated reaper. And at night the most magical sight of all—the fairground ablaze with electric lights.

The long talks with Missy were salutary, and for the first time since Emmons's death, Anita began to put her mind to the future, and particularly to building a home, as her husband had wanted.

There were two possible locations—the Lake Shore or the area where she had grown up. The latter meant a house on a McCormick lot across the street from her mother, near Cyrus, several other relatives, and many of her childhood friends. The attraction of the Lake Shore property was its very distance from family, and in considering it Anita admitted to a "blind wish to get out of the way—and out of the neighborhood—and a feeling that I should be more myself and more use consequently to them all and everyone, if I were in a freer sort of atmosphere." On the other hand, a major reason for returning to Chicago had been her mother's need of her, and if she built on the Lake Shore, she would "always be thinking about Mama without such an easy way of seeing her."

The decision was predictable, and in July, 1894, a contract was signed for construction of a house for Mrs. Emmons Blaine at 101 East Erie at an underestimated cost of $62,011. Her front door would henceforth be less than fifty yards from Nettie's.

When it was too late, Anita acknowledged that her choice had been unwise. Proximity put affection to exhausting tests. Overdoing the elder brother role, Cyrus, a block away, too often volunteered his opinion on the rearing of Em, which angered her: let Cyrus do better with his own son, who was Em's age and something of a bully. Nettie, rattling around with a company of servants in her vast house, dropped by 101 at inopportune moments, often accompanied by a missionary. After having listened politely to one of those earnest evangelists recounting the saving of some native population from damnation, Anita confessed that she "would have done better to be further away in distance, for I was so very far away inside from the general family life that my mother was conducting."

She let no one speak to Em about his father, not wanting his recollections, or hers, to be crowded out or colored by the impressions of others. When he was four, he was taken to the cemetery, and when he asked "where Dada?" she answered that "we don't see people after they're gone to heaven, so we put their name on a stone in this garden to let people remember them." She shunned public tributes to Emmons, rebuffing a Chicago publisher who commissioned biographies for pay. She did, however, send $10,000 in her husband's name in 1893 to the public library in Augusta, Maine, and three years later donated an organ to the Presbyterian church in Richfield Springs, "placed here to the memory of Emmons Blaine by his wife Anita McCormick Blaine and in commemoration of their marriage in this church, September 26, 1889." At the dedication, Walter Damrosch played the organ, and as they "came out of that door into the quiet, calm winter evening," Missy Hammond recalled, "we brought with us a stronger and more comforting reassurance of the reality—the power—of the 'things unseen.' " That "reality" would engross Anita for the next fifty years.

Em's health was her most pressing concern and here her zeal matched her mother's. Thermometers were installed throughout the house, and he was not allowed to enter a room until it was the right temperature. During cold weather, his clothes were checked and double-checked to insure their snugness. His digestion was easily upset; when he threw up at suppertime, she wondered that she ever lost sight "for an instant of the fact that every fatigue or anything goes to his stomach." Daily cold baths were instituted, he was fed bland foods, his bowel movements were recorded. Any hint of indisposition drove her to reexamine his routine: "Illness comes, you try to find out the causes and cures, conditions are against. You see, but you can't make circumstances right—or else, you find by not seeing it straight, you have injured the case—ill results—and you must bear it." Meanwhile, she was constantly being told what to do by health-conscious Nettie, by her brothers, her cousins, her in-laws —"so surrounded by so many people who love my boy and want to advise me about him, that it is very important for me, standing alone in responsibility about him to follow a consistent course with confidence." One doctor admonished her for being "too methodical about all his daily life and doings, watching too closely for every little sign of something wrong." Her sister-in-law Harriet thought it necessary to remind Anita that Em had "ancestors and circumstances to account for him as well as you, and if you eat your heart out about what is best for him anymore, I shall eat mine from sympathy."

However unwarranted by the state of medical science in the early nineteen hundreds, Anita's respect for physicians was unshakable, and if the opinion of one was desirable, that of a second seemed more so.

How she came to consult Dr. Henry Baird Favill about Em's health is unrecorded, but their meeting had profound consequences for them both. A newcomer from Madison, Wisconsin, who had quickly built up a large and influential Chicago practice in internal medicine,* Favill was to become a trusted counselor who, from the start, was as interested in the mother as he was in the son. Improper feeding during the baby's first year, he told Anita, had resulted in "very greatly impoverished nutrition" followed by several years of overfeeding. Given a regular regimen, Em's lack of stamina, headaches, occasional stomach pains, and vomiting would disappear as the boy grew up, but if she was overanxious, there would be vacillation in discipline, and vacillation made Em more irritable and headstrong.

Pages of her journal at this stage were devoted to what limits she ought to set on her son's freedom. She accepted Dr. Favill's warning that she must deal firmly with him, and yet avoid imposing too rigid a set of rules. "Don't ever get allied or given over to any set of ideas to the extent of making him feel it impossible to place the opposite before you," she noted in her private journal. "Or, more rightly, don't ever do so in a way to make them feel that. Hang on to the tentativity of all found truth. Balance it like a compass needle, ever ready to free itself, if shackled, and turn to its pole—the Absolute." Above all, she must not forget that each soul must "take and absorb and live out what he can—and grow."

Although Anita had been assured by Dr. Frank Billings, when Em was three years old, that he was "a very vigorous boy, both mentally and physically," that opinion was not wholly endorsed by Dr.

* Favill also held the chair of medicine in the Chicago Policlinic, an adjunct chair of medicine at Rush Medical College, from which latter he was promoted in 1898 to the Ingals Professorship of Preventive Medicine and Therapeutics, and in 1906 to the chair of clinical medicine.

Favill, who doubted the boy's "ability to take unusual strain, either mental or physical." At any rate, Anita was constantly on the alert to any sign of his becoming overtired. Considering the possibility of summer camp for him when he was six, she wrote the camp director that she did not think she could send him away from her for the whole summer, "both because I could not bear to miss so much and also because I must keep track, more or less, of how things go physically with him." In her absence, Anita was sent daily reports by Em's nurse on his bowel movements. From Maine in 1907, Anita would write her mother of Em's "slight cold—which then I felt I must see through for fear it might come into one of his things. . . . I had timely doses for him and I was so glad I was here."

Early on, Anita recognized that her standards tempted Em to deceive her. His diet was restricted, and as he began to play with other children in their homes, he would be given something he knew his mother did not want him to eat, or asked to join in games she would have thought too strenuous. It was hard for him to say no and harder to tell his mother that he had not said no. She never punished him physically for these lapses. They talked over what he had done and why, and because it was simpler and because he loved her, he would unconditionally accept her judgment, unconsciously imitating his Uncle Cyrus, who had thought that the best way to handle Nettie was to do things *her* way. But uncritical acceptance was not what Anita sought. "Why should a child do so and so?" she asked herself. "Because its mother will be displeased otherwise? Because something will happen otherwise? No a thousand times. Because it is right." She resolved that she would not read too much into any one falsehood and avoid "too great dominating of my thoughts . . . my full analysis on every point." Besides, Em might be right and she wrong. "Is any lie so bad as a possible true one?—one that from outward signs might be so, but which twists falsely the intent?" If he ordered everyone about in the house, so that she was "ready to go and live in a two-room farmhouse and keep it, in order to have a life where things can't be done all and solely for him," was it not because she was spoiling him? Perhaps she should dismiss the servants, dress and feed him herself, and then go out and do other work, so that he could "lay hold more of the reality of life." That was not a thought that would have occurred to her mother or to her elder brother, nor did she act on it.

She wanted to give Em a sense of modesty, but without the tormenting guilt which had darkened Stanley's childhood. At eight, the boy was instructed that nature "has to have a way to rid itself of waste, and those parts of the body that attend to it are kept as private and out of the way as possible" and that those who did otherwise were "not nice people." She was determined that he have the facts about sex, and from her, and yet her own reticence often blocked the way. Although she adored being embraced by him, when he was three and a half she told him it was "unmanly" to ask her for a hug in public. She took every opportunity to impress upon him that since men are stronger than women, they should "wait on them and do for them and take care of them."

At six, he was curious about how cats got kittens and she carefully noted in her journal the conversation which ensued:

"Oh they just get them."

"Yes, but how?"

"Just as hens get their little chickens and birds their little birds—they just lay them."

"Do they come in an egg?"

"No, I don't think there is any eggshell around them, but it's all the same, they are very little."

At which he began speculating on the size of newborn kittens and the subject of their origin was passed over.

It seemed to Anita that a proper beginning had been made in that interchange. Her answers had come "as I had always planned they should, with truth and simplicity. If I had not answered it would have become a point of more thought. If I had put mystery, mystery would have hung about it. If I had said I didn't know, he would have wanted to go to someone who did. And if I had fabricated, someday there would have been an end to his confidence in his mother." But inevitably, the question arose again, and more pointedly. Where did babies come from? Well, their bodies grew in their mother's hearts, a reply she thought had "dropped into his consciousness like a dewdrop into a rose." She then took him to the Art Institute, so that he could observe nude statues; he walked by them unseeing. He was ten when, hearing that an older cousin was pregnant, he asked how people knew what week babies were coming. She had told him before, she said, babies came "right in the mother's heart—and so when the little life comes, then the mother feels it, and so she knows. You know all life comes that way, one life from another, and that we call the mother's life."

"And the father's too?"

"Yes, from the father too, though not in the same way. The father takes care of the life. You see this is the most precious sacred thing in the world, and some people think that little children are not able to take care of such a precious truth, so they tell them fairy tales about it."

That silenced him until a few months before his eleventh birthday, when he and his mother were in the bathroom, he in the tub, she washing her face at the sink. Rather musingly, he observed that "ladies always sit down when they p.p., don't they?" She went on washing her hands, wanting not to let this chance slip by, and then she turned to him, knowing "beyond reasoning, beyond doubt, beyond stopping," what she must do.

"You know why women always sit instead of stand for their p.p.?"

"Because their trousers, I mean their dresses, don't open in front?"

"No. That's true, but they don't have a 'little p.p.' Their bodies are made quite differently.

"Are they? I didn't know that."

"Yes. I'll show you mine."

"And all the divineness rose in me," she later wrote, "and I felt as if rising out of my body as I slipped off my gown and my vest and stood there a moment—very simply—and all the wonder, how and whether was gone, while my child looked all at me just as ever, interested in what I had said but not any more—just loving simple interest, not a thought beside, and we had it together."

The pattern of life for each of the McCormicks was now well defined. Nettie was busy, fussing over her grown-up children, looking over Cyrus's shoulder as he managed the reaper business, aiding John R. Mott's International Student Movement or financing a missionary to China, to northern Minnesota, or to a mountain school in the South. Virginia reposed in the custody of a companion and nurses. Harold and Stanley were at Princeton, and Harold was soon to marry his childhood friend Edith, daughter of John D. Rockefeller, having succeeded in convincing his mother that Mr. Rockefeller's religion was "directed on lines exactly parallel to those of your belief."[3] Anita's financial affairs were handled by lawyers and accountants, and the distractions of daily life were filtered out by the household staff in the home she now occupied at 101 East Erie.

A widow for three years, she was free to concentrate on educating her son, an assignment she approached with strong convictions.

In her last year at the Misses Kirkland's Academy, she had written a theme which closed with an appeal to "overthrow the present system of education." As an adult she had come to believe that her school "received the pupil from the hands of its parents, but it did not take all of him. At the gate of the school, he, like the Gaul he was to learn so much about, was divided into three parts. His parents were told to retain two of them, keeping entire charge of his character formation and his physical well-being. The school assumed the task of developing his head machine." The result, she concluded, "was no thinking process on the part of the pupil—and no possession by him of such material as he had succeeded in uttering by rote. Discipline was a method invented for dealing with inevitably refractory human nature, for the easement of trouble for the population in general, and for individual teachers in particular." The child plodded through repetitious work, having "no free play to find one's own métier," and with nothing wanted but "strict adherence to a stamped pattern." Schools which should "flash the beacon light from high motives from hilltop to hilltop for humanity, fell into the device common to all authorities needing to hold their populace within their power"; they resorted to "fear of punishment and the hope of gain, the appeal to the selfish desire to escape censure, and to excel above others." She would not expose Em to that sort of miseducation.

Atmospheric changes signal their arrival, and in the nineties a stir in the air was beginning to be felt. Fresh breezes were forecast which would sweep through stuffy classrooms, clearing them of regimentation and learning by rote. To Anita, the prospect was exhilarating. Brother Cyrus had been the only McCormick child to attend public school, and while Chicago public education might have improved in the intervening twenty-five years, it was not good enough for Em. She wanted him taught so that his natural curiosity and goodness would be strengthened and his individuality encouraged.

In 1893, she had turned her drawing room into a kindergarten for ten children, carrying on through the winter and ending with a spring garden project—bulbs and seeds planted in window boxes which were faithfully watered by Anita and her three-year-old son. But she could not make a classroom for him beyond the kindergarten years, nor did she wish to. She had heard of the progressive accomplishments of the Chicago Normal School, financed by the Cook

County Board of Education, and of its inventive and combative director, Colonel Francis Wayland Parker,* a Civil War veteran who had inherited a dilapidated building without a library, laboratories, or gymnasium and a heating system so old that winter classes were often dismissed, and had transformed that archaic institution into a vital educational force in the city. For a decade, the freewheeling Parker had been inspiring young teachers in Chicago with novel ideas about child-centered schooling. As Anita began inquiring what education was available for Em, it was inevitable that she and Parker would meet and that each would find a natural ally in the other.

Although Parker had not been able to persuade the county school board to require more than a forty-week training course for would-be teachers, he had established a second year of "graduate elective work" and persuaded many students to take the course before beginning their work in the classrooms. Rejecting the traditional division of subjects and emphasizing "illustrative teaching with heavy use of pictures, models and field trips," he had abolished report cards and co-opted skeptical parents by enlisting them in parent associations and "mothers' meetings."

He and Anita had in common the conviction that each child has a spark of the divine and an instinct to use his powers creatively, and that all instruction should foster "the tendency of the soul toward freedom." Neither valued tools of learning (grammar, spelling, arithmetic) that were not put to practical use. A child who wanted to build a playhouse would gladly learn the mathematics necessary to complete this project; if he wished to write a play, he would happily practice grammar and spelling—that was the Parker theory. Away with the conventional emphasis on book knowledge and grades! "Correlation" was the Colonel's name for this system.

To many laymen and to business-minded Cyrus in particular, the most striking feature of Parker's philosophy was the extensive physical plant it required. Convinced that a strong mind and a weak body were incompatible, the Colonel was a stickler for gymnasiums and playgrounds. He also was an advocate of crafts—carpentry, pottery, cooking—not because he wanted to train youngsters to be carpenters, potters or cooks; workshops were a means of acquiring manual and mental skills.

Parker's bulk alone was enough to impress a child, and his hearty

* Born in 1837, Parker began teaching at the age of sixteen. After the Civil War, he went to Germany to study new educational practices. Before coming to Chicago, he was school superintendent in Quincy, Mass., and then supervisor of 42 primary schools in Boston.

laugh as inviting as an overstuffed armchair. Children climbed on his knee or sat by his side, chattering of their activities or listening to stories of his New Hampshire boyhood and his service as an officer in the late war. Katharine Taylor, who was to become head of the Shady Hill School in Cambridge, Massachusetts, recalled her early days at the Parker School, "when I went with one other student from my class to help in the kindergarten and opened the door and Colonel Parker was sitting on a low bench with at least half a dozen children all over him, telling them a story . . . and they listened spellbound and he doing it in language that they could understand directly. Warmth, ease, excitement, challenge." His confidence was overpowering. He once startled a faculty meeting by responding to some teacher's statement of "facts" and "principles" with the remark: "I think I shall formulate a prayer; it will be 'oh, Lord, preserve Thou me from the foregone conclusion.' "

Anita first met him when a friend brought her to the Normal School. Knowing little of his methods, she had inquired whether she might view one of his reading classes, to which he replied with considerable force, "we haven't any," which delighted her. She knew then that this was the place for Em, and by the spring of 1896, several months after he had been entered in the school, Anita was telling Nettie of the "wonderful way they teach down there, wonderful and most inspiring. It makes old bones get up and feel as if they might know and do something."

There was one drawback, however. Anita lived on the North Side and the school was on the very southern edge of the city, a long trip for a small child, even if chauffeured. Her solution was to propose that the mountain come to Mohammed; the Colonel must let her establish a branch school on the North Side. Having agreed, he was then asked to let her have two of his best teachers. He sent one, Miss Hattie Bradley, and she and a small group of children began regular neighborhood classes.

Meanwhile, Anita was educating herself, less by books than by seeing and listening. She visited John Dewey's Department of Pedagogy at the University of Chicago, and while not as enamored of Dewey as she was of Parker, she admired his courage. In 1899 she invited him to deliver a series of lectures in her living room, later published at Anita's expense as The School and Society and dedicated to her.[4] Earlier, she worked with the Colonel on a lecture course on primary education, also given in her home before an audience of wealthy Chicagoans.

Dr. Favill's advice had not been forgotten; consistency and regularity were important for Em. But there were occasions when they had to be put aside. In his third year with Parker, he was taken out of school in order that he and his mother could be near grandmother McCormick and Uncle Stanley, who had gone to California to supervise the construction of another house for Virginia. Anita assumed that suitable education could be found for Em in the Santa Barbara area, but found none. It was an omission easily remedied. We will create one, Nettie said. Hattie Bradley was thereupon summoned from Chicago and a small schoolhouse built for thirteen children and Em, so that he would not have to spend the months in California "in lonesomeness and idleness."

While Anita was introducing Parker's progressive ideas to Santa Barbara, the Colonel was fighting off the not-so-progressive politicians at home. Chicago's Democratic mayor, Carter Harrison, Jr., eager to extend his party's control over the public school system, had let it be known that he would welcome Parker's retirement. Parker's enemies on the Board of Education came in one cue, shook his list of recommendations for new faculty members in his face, and accused him of giving graduates of the University of Chicago hiring preference. Why that was objectionable was not explained.* On the question of the Colonel's reappointment, the board was fairly evenly divided, but the terms of many of the old board members, most of them pro-Parker, were coming to an end, and their replacements, hand-picked by the mayor, were expected to rubber-stamp anything Harrison wanted. If Parker was to be reappointed, he wrote to Anita in California, they would have to act before her return. And since it was thought that the vote of one board member, A. S. Trude, would be decisive, Parker urged Anita to do what she could to influence the outcome. "If that work at the Normal School is crushed out," she promptly telegraphed Trude, "the city will suffer greatly in fact and in reputation." But when the crucial mid-June meeting of the board was called to order, Trude was in Indianapolis, the vote deadlocked, and only one more meeting scheduled before the new, pro-Harrison board would assemble.

Then the mayor's troops bungled. A few days before the final meeting of the old board, it was disclosed that Harrison's corporation counsel, a long-time enemy of Parker, had tried to pressure at least one member to vote the mayor's way. Incensed, the member

* "How long must we stand this kind of thing?" Parker•was heard to mutter to President Harper of the University of Chicago, as an irate board member harangued him.

resigned and broke the story in the press. The mayor, who billed himself as a foe of vested interests, denied the charges of improper influence, but the damage was done. Harrison's henchmen did not now dare depose Parker. Anita, always ready to advance the Colonel's cause, was jubilant, and when she returned to Chicago, she and Nettie gave a sizable contribution to a vacation program conceived by the Colonel—field trips for poor children, giving them a glimpse of farm, woods, green grass, flowers, "the influence of a bit of God's beautiful world." It was the first of Anita's many donations to education.

In August 1898, after conferences with William Rainey Harper, president of the University of Chicago, it was announced that Mrs. Emmons Blaine would found a College for Teachers, to which she pledged $5,000 a year for five years, hoping the school would eventually serve the entire city and offer courses to people not working toward a degree.[5] Harper thought this might encourage dilettantism, but Anita pointed out that many who could not qualify for work on a degree had a serious desire to study. The following January, she raised her yearly donation by $1,200 so that the college could move into a larger building, and she continued her payments for seven more years. When a committee was named by the Civic Federation to "study the Chicago School System and learn its defects," Anita was appointed to it. She had once complained that her life was "vacant of work." It would never be that again.

She and Parker had discussed the waste of his energy in these annual battles with politicians, and Anita had asked why he need suffer them. Why not establish a private training school for teachers, so that he could work without restraints? She appreciated that her proposal "grieved him sorely . . . for his whole idea throughout his life work had been to do the thing as he saw it for *all* the children of the country. The Public Schools was the high road he saw for this public good." And yet Parker had barely escaped banishment by the friends of the mayor, and he was "almost sure," he said, "that the enemies of the School will win . . . and I must rejoice that the way is open for work." However, a private school could do lasting good only insofar as it influenced the public school system. Having entered that reservation, he picked up her suggestion and ran with it.

If we are to carry out your idea, he told Anita, there will have to be a teacher training school with a practice school attached to it on the North Side, as well as a slum school in the tenement district which would "show what education may do for poor children." It must have "an assembly hall for the people, parents, lectures, lessons that may unite home and school," and a place for social gatherings "like Hull House." Second, he said, there must be "manual training, the moving center of education, handwork and artwork, cooking, sewing, housekeeping—all correlated with the other teaching." Third, a kindergarten "to take the children early from the streets and make a little heaven for them." Fourth, a playground, green grass, a few flowers. Fifth, gymnasium and bathrooms. Sixth, classrooms. Seventh, a library for "sweet, good literature." Above all, "the very best teachers."

And that was not all. In his mind's eye, he saw a boarding school for children from out of town, a model rural school on a farm, a school printing press to publish leaflets for general circulation. The slum school especially touched Anita, who visualized "a roof garden, a hall for lectures, dances and theatricals, parlors, a room for the men of the neighborhood where meetings, games and billiards would combat the temptations of the saloon, as much air and sun as possible, all of this housed in a building of fine, simple architecture." She dreamed of their new school becoming "a common meeting ground for the different so-called 'classes' for communication of ideas."

Still Parker held back from a complete break with the public school system. It was his wife, ill with cancer, who convinced him that he could do more in a private institution, and after her death in 1899 he accepted without reservation Anita's offer of financial support. Anita prayed that "God may help me to do this work for the children."

Around two o'clock every afternoon, Mrs. Emmons Blaine, dressed in black, rode in her carriage down Michigan Avenue to an office she had rented on Monroe Street, where files, secretaries, and the problems of the proposed new school awaited her. Her heavy correspondence could no longer be handled by the secretarial staff at 101. The idea of the school was "pretty big," she remarked to her mother, "rather absorbing of one's means at first." Inexperienced in benefactions of this magnitude, she recruited other trustees to help administer her contributions and to advise Parker and the faculty he was about to appoint. Bringing outsiders into the project could endanger "vital principles," she acknowledged, but she did not want to be the sole monitor of expenditures. By sharing financial responsibility, she believed she would be freer to speak her mind. As co-trustees, she selected Stanley, who had become a director of the harvester company; Owen F. Aldis, an attorney and one of her late husband's friends; Cyrus Bentley, legal adviser to the McCormicks and husband of Anita's childhood playmate, Bessie King; and Dr. Favill.

Of the four, only Favill had a faith as indomitable as hers. Stanley shared his sister's idealism, but he proved an unstable committee colleague. Lawyer Bentley was a tireless worker, but his duty, as he saw it, was to protect Anita's fortune, and his formal acceptance was hedged with typical Bentley qualifications: "It is not easy to measure in advance the care and responsibility that will rest upon the trustees of the school which you are about to establish. I am, however, willing to assume my share of the burden and to carry it until I am compelled, in justice to prior claim upon my time, to relinquish the trusteeship, or until I find myself out of sympathy to Colonel Parker's ideas or methods (about which I really know very little), or with the views of my co-trustees." Owen Aldis was more blunt: he was "not born to be a reformer," and it seemed to him "highly improbable" that Colonel Parker had any very novel truths about education. Furthermore, he informed Anita, "I do believe in examinations, in competition, and in individual effort to beat others!" Within two months, Aldis had offered to resign. He stayed because Anita insisted that his criticism was valuable.

The cast of characters was set and each played a predictable part. Favill consented, Stanley quibbled, Bentley cautioned, Aldis carped, while Anita, who was paying the bills, summoned them "not to look for results or work for them, but to throw into the stream one's thoughts, one's deeds, one's self—and let it swell the tide as it can and will."

The call seemed to her so compelling; why then were these men so hard to arouse? The trouble, according to Missy, was that the others on the board were judging Colonel Parker "with the acumen of experts trained to financial and commercial enterprises," while Anita "took him on the other side of his nature and education," and that part of him could not be fathomed "except by the intuition of the spirit." Amiable Harold, who had no part in the enterprise, cheered from the bleachers; Anita was creating something "good beyond all computation." Mama thought so, too—"you are doing a great and estimable good to your race." It was "vastly interesting," Anita replied, but "just wait til a year from next fall!"

The work was "vastly interesting" partly because Anita was being forced to reconcile conflicting impulses within herself. She wanted the board to take full responsibility and yet could not quite free herself of the notion that the school was hers. The board discussed giving her veto power, dismissed the idea when she opposed it, then elected her treasurer, with Stanley as secretary and Aldis president. But that seemed wrong. Although disbursements were to be on order of the whole board, having the sole donor as treasurer might be misunderstood. So she and Stanley switched positions. In a note to herself, Anita had said that "the initial choosing of the Board of Trustees is mine, as the initial starting of the school is mine. But after the school is started, with its Board of Trustees, it at once becomes a matter in the hands of the whole Board."

It was not until January 1900, six months after the board had been set up, that Anita felt comfortable. Having renounced "all special responsibility," she was prepared to be only one of five trustees; if she was in the minority, she would give way, for "if something new shows, possibly correctly, that one's whole course in any matter has been wrong," she penned in her journal, "the new light should be simply taken as a guidepost, to swerve possibly in a new direction. Life is a series of such new lights. We should be quick to see and to take the new guiding."

Under the unalluring name of the Chicago Institute, Academic and Pedagogic, (neither Anita nor Parker would allow their names to be attached to it) the school began to take shape. Initially, Anita had planned to give $20,000 a year for seven years to the tuition-free school for slum children, but the board almost immediately decided to postpone the slum school in order to concentrate on a teacher's training school and an associated private practice school. Anita pledged $400,000 for the land, building, and equipment, guaranteeing in addition a gift of $95,000 for each of the next seven years, after which the school and its facilities would be hers to dispose of. She refused to endow it permanently. When cost estimates for the plant proved too low, she agreed to pay whatever the trustees thought necessary for facilities, provided that they did not, without her consent, spend more than $300,000 for the land and $400,000 for building and equipment. She personally selected the site—more than two city blocks on the North Shore, near the lake, Lincoln Park, the botanical garden, the zoo, and an academy of science.

The land cost her $425,000, not $300,000. The building threatened to cost over a half-million dollars, for Colonel Parker had invited each department head to submit an ideal plan, which the architect then amalgamated into one structure "of a simple and dignified appearance, expressing repose and scholarly bearing." It was to have four laboratories, three museums, two assembly halls, a large gymnasium, manual training shops, a swimming pool, an indoor playroom with a fully equipped stage, and a small observatory—all perfectly ventilated, lighted, and heated. There would be a model kitchen, a library big enough for fourteen thousand volumes, a picture collection of twenty thousand mounted photographs and engravings, outdoor playgrounds and gardens. This paragon of academies would house a training school for teachers as well as an academic school for children from five to eighteen, in which "a living and helpful relation of each child to the community is at once the goal of his development and the test of his progress." The institute was to open in June 1900 for a summer teachers' course and begin normal operation the following October.

According to the *Preliminary Announcement* in 1899, among the "educational doctrines" to be followed were that "the power of attention is an essential factor and must be stimulated and strengthened; that mental concentration may be enhanced by a correlated study of related subjects, as geography and history, science and mathematics; that knowledge and skill induced by the study of one subject are reinforced by the study of other subjects in relation; that self-expression in all its modes reacts upon the mind in developing thought-power; that training to habits of attention and self-expression tends to physical, intellectual and moral growth; and that the final aim of education is the highest development of individual ability and character."

That was the blueprint, and "Won't it be lovely," Anita said. Dr. Favill agreed, but they were a minority of two. Stanley and Cyrus Bentley were apprehensive; Aldis was appalled, for no matter how often estimates were juggled, they went up. And while the trustees were arguing over architectural designs, land prices, and their different ideas about educational theory, Colonel Parker's faculty, most of which had been with him at the Normal School, was given a year's sabbatical leave with full pay, so that the teachers could broaden their experience.

It was too much for Bentley and Aldis, already exasperated by Parker's nonchalance about finances, and they called him to account. Figures were not his province, he retaliated. When the trustees tried to economize, Parker resisted; when they refused one of his requests, he ignored them. Wilbur Jackman, hired by the board to administer the finances, told Bentley he had been under the impression that all of Parker's suggestions "were voted upon favorably, after some discussion, and finally adopted in the form in which he presented them." That had not been Bentley's impression, but it helped explain why more money was being spent than the trustees had authorized.

Spring came, it was time to lay the foundation, and the trustees were still wrestling with the constant upward revision of estimates. Then a strike was called in the building trades, not a brick could be laid. A settlement would raise prices further. Owen Aldis dug in his heels. "I wish to register my vote," he wrote Anita on 25 May 1900, "in favor of a new plan for a compact, plain, substantial, durable, well-ventilated, heated and lighted building, to cost not more than $300,000." He had no wish to hurt her feelings, but she was not a worldly-wise person, she did not "know how to be fair to herself at all times"; if she let architects, teachers, and contractors think that her funds were unlimited, she would demoralize the whole project.

As a stopgap, the trustees accepted the McCormick Theological Seminary's offer of space for the scheduled teachers' summer session of the institute. Plans to build were postponed. They would find temporary quarters for their school and wait until the following spring to begin construction.

Astonishingly, the Chicago Institute, Academic and Pedagogic, opened on time that September in a rented gymnasium in the Turngemeinde building on Wells Street. It had space for 600 students but an enrollment of only 195, of whom 68 were teachers. It was a start, however, and Anita was on hand the first day, registering children and helping them find their classrooms. By eleven, she told Nettie, "the rooms were as settled as if they had been at work for a week." Morning assembly, that daily convocation of students and faculty that was the keystone of Parker's method, was called. With the smallest children, including Em, gathered around him, Parker said he was "too full for utterance." Having collected himself, he told them that "they were part of a great experiment in education and must all work together to prove that boys and girls could learn in school without force."*

It was an incongruous setting, in a dreary business district. The school's temporary center, the gymnasium, had a high ceiling, with

* At these assemblies, Katharine Taylor told an interviewer in 1966, "Colonel Parker would say, 'What is the great word?' in a deep penetrating voice, and we would all say in unison, 'Responsibility.' Then he would say, 'What is our motto?' and we would say, 'Everything to help and nothing to hinder.'"

three stories of encircling small classrooms, the students walking from one class to another by way of a balcony overlooking the gym floor far below. The furnishings had been hastily assembled—blackboards, teachers' desks, and the old-fashioned kind of student desks which Parker hated because they were designed for passive students. Mixed in with Parker's Normal School faculty were teachers recently recruited from universities, all with excellent academic credentials but otherwise dissimilar. One professor, who lasted a short time, awed the children by holding his ruler threateningly over their knuckles. A pupil remembered studying French in a room that had been a tavern and reeked of malt. "And yet we believed in it enough," another recalled, "and we believed in the few gifted teachers, and then in our contact with Colonel Parker enough to want desperately to go on."

Above all, Em liked it. "Say," he told his mother, "that's a great school! It's fun to be up there." "I wish I could paint you a thing that came today," Anita wrote Missy. "Each child had written a play, it is to be acted, a Greek play, and the various ones were voted on to adopt, for playing, today. Em forgot his and when I heard they had decided, I burst out with regret, 'Oh I am so sorry that they didn't have a chance to hear yours!' Em with ardor, 'Oh, that would not have made any difference, they would have voted for Arnold's just the same, his was *undoubtedly* better, I could see it.' And then, 'but I think they would have liked a part of mine.' I can't at all convey the spirit of it, no sense of disappointment, the flowering of the spirit of the child—which it seems to me the competitive idea of most schools must at least tempt to be crushed. Here the idea was simply for all to join in doing this thing as well as possible, and he will enjoy playing Arnold's just as much."

The trustees agreed that the school spirit was splendid, but the administrative and financial problems were still "as bad as a Chinese puzzle." Ground for the new building had not been broken, the design was being whittled down, Bentley perceived a "lack of organization," and by November, the Colonel and he were barely speaking. Bentley now took the lead in urging a more modest building, one appropriate to an endeavor that was supposed to be primarily spiritual and intellectual, which was precisely what Aldis had recommended months before.

The modified plan was anathema to Parker.* For three years, he

* As it was to his dean, Wilbur Jackman, whose counterproposal was a $3 million permanent endowment for the school.

said, his friends had pushed him to accept Anita's offer and to abandon the public school system. He had acquiesced only because he had been assured that conditions would be ideal. Was he now expected to endure trustees who had no faith in him, one being downright hostile? He wanted "nothing to do with any ordinary school." Retrenchment would betray teachers who had taken a personal risk for the sake of better education. He appealed to Anita; surely she would not compromise their vision. But she temporized: "We must carry with us the imperfections of human arrangements—our own and other peoples, unwisdom of all sorts."

The trustees did not know it, but they were about to be rescued. President Harper of the University of Chicago had earlier proposed that the contemplated institute be a part of the university. The trustees had not then been receptive and even refused Harper a place on their board. A frustrating year having worn down the edge of their optimism, however, the chance to hand over their problems to an established institution had become more tempting. They reasoned that Anita's generosity was not boundless, that the Colonel's school would never be self-supporting, and that merger might ensure permanency for their venture. The university's financial resources and stability recommended cooperation, and as Harper pointed out, the university was as keenly interested as they in training teachers. It had John Dewey, chairman of the departments of Philosophy, Psychology, and Pedagogy for the past six years, who had a practice school committed to a child-centered education. Had not the Colonel himself said that Dewey was a better spokesman for his ideas than Parker?* If the two schools were joined, the Institute could draw on the academic wealth of the university; the university in turn could benefit from the practical pedagogical skills of Parker's faculty and Parker's reputation, as well as (though this was not said openly) from the considerable sums Anita had pledged to the institute.

Could any such partnership survive? The aim of the university, Bentley cautioned, was "scholarship"; Parker's was "character." Parker, suspecting that he and his school would be swallowed up by the larger entity, argued that the university system of distinct academic departments was contrary to his theory of "correlation," and that Dewey was dominated by this "departmental influence."[6]

For his own reasons, Dewey was almost as leery of the scheme as Parker. Built up over the preceding four years and only nominally

---

* So Anita told Max Eastman in 1942.

96

connected with the university, his Laboratory School was supported by private gifts, and Dewey and his ten teachers saw their existence threatened by the Blaine school with its more lavish funding. At a meeting of the institute trustees in January 1901, both Dewey and Parker stated categorically that neither would give up the headship of his school for the sake of merger.

From the standpoint of principle, it seemed an argument with little substance. Dewey, like Parker, advocated manual training and crafts, rejecting the traditional distinction between "culture" and useful work. Dewey respected the Colonel and had sent his own children to Parker's Normal School. It was not philosophies but personalities that clashed. A member of Dewey's faculty said he "had a feeling that in Colonel Parker's school, the mental processes of the child were being watched, much as one might dig up a bulb to see if it were growing"; Dewey "could see the whole landscape, where Parker saw only spots here and there."

Circumstances were on the side of compromise, and on 16 January 1901 Anita informed President Harper that, along with the institute itself, she was willing to turn over to the university her pledged future investment in it, estimated at $750,000. In return, the university would have to match that sum, devoting the total to Parker's work. It was a generous offer, but Harper did not see how he could raise the matching funds, and subsequent refusals by Parker and Dewey to give up a jot of authority seemed to push merger further off. Yet both sides went on talking, and at a meeting attended by Parker, Harper and Dewey, it was tentatively agreed that if the two schools did consolidate, a mutually acceptable plan of integration had to be worked out. The door was ajar.

Then Parker slammed it shut. He told Dewey a week later that life was "too short to begin again to build up under great restrictions, for the work that I wish to do. I would prefer to teach in a country school with all the conditions right than have charge of the largest institution with restrictions that could not easily be overcome. I may put too much value on my life, but I must consider these things long and well before I go into this new arrangement." While he did not wish "to be considered obstinate in any way," Parker wrote Dewey, he put "quality of work ahead of everything else." The clear implication was that quality would suffer from the merger. Since Anita and her co-trustees had previously agreed that merger would not be pushed through without Parker's consent, it looked as though it was dead.

Again the tide turned. Parker consulted with his faculty, for whom the question came down to whether their institute could "do more good by merging with the University of Chicago than by remaining on the North Side." When they voted thirteen to one in favor of consolidation, Parker felt obliged to go along with the majority, though to do so was "in decided opposition to my personal feelings." President Harper then tactfully asked certain professors to write the Colonel, expressing approval of his work, which he could continue at the university with perfect freedom. The inspired messages were reassuring. "We could hardly doubt the sincerity of such representation," Anita told Missy, "and hardly turn our backs on it on the ground of unsympathetic atmosphere—which had been our doubt."

On 4 March the institute trustees were informed that Harper had found the funds to match Anita's contribution and the debate was over. Papers were drawn up demarcating spheres of authority for Dewey and Parker. The institute, with Parker in command and consisting of a "pedagogic school," a kindergarten, and an elementary school, was to be established as a professional School of Education within the university. Dewey, working out of the Department of Pedagogy, was to be in charge of a secondary school, to be used primarily for teacher training. Should Parker leave his position first, his successor would be picked by the university trustees from among names put to them by the institute trustees. Should Dewey leave first, his secondary school was to be merged with Parker's.[7] No provision was made for Dewey's "lab school," and Harper thought that it would be "bad faith" to continue it while Parker was running his elementary school. But when the parents of Dewey's pupils offered to underwrite any financial deficits the lab school might incur, and when no one from the institute objected, Harper agreed that Dewey could keep it going.

The merger was signed and notarized. In June, the University of Chicago School of Education was officially established, and to it was attached the Chicago Institute of Colonel Parker. "You are always kind and always just," Parker wrote Anita on 13 June 1901. "I was very much worried, the discussion seemed interminable and the ideal fading." He wanted to be a good soldier, he would carry on. Jane Addams was sure that "with the personality of two such fine men built into it . . . it ought to be one of the finest contributions to education ever made."

Eight months later, Parker was dead, and all the old suspicions revived. The university authorities promptly called on the former institute trustees to discuss with them the appointment of a new director of the School of Education. Dewey was the obvious choice, but he would have to work closely with Parker's staff, which was loyal to the memory of the Colonel and jealous of its autonomy. Anti-Parker stories surfaced. Dewey had been heard to complain that Parker took advantage of the inevitable public confusion to denigrate Dewey's school and extol his own, and Cyrus Bentley learned from Jane Addams, an intimate of Dewey's, that the philosopher had a low opinion of the Parker faculty. Bentley himself told Anita that Dewey had been "subject to some influences very nearly hostile to our work in the past." Still, Dewey was clearly the best qualified candidate, and he was accordingly nominated and elected.

At once, his lack of sympathy became evident. He rarely participated in parents' meetings and attended institute faculty meetings only when he wanted to publicize his opinions. He discussed his plans for the institute with no one, preferring to announce his decision after the time for deliberation had passed. Quick to take offense if he thought his authority was being challenged, he threatened to give up the directorship on so many occasions that the phrase "my resignation" became a joke. Anita thought that "too much fuss" had been made over Dewey, that the press had "got him up so much too high," though she did like "the naturalness of his blurting out just what he thought."

Within weeks, relations had so deteriorated that older members of the Parker faculty came to Anita in desperation, begging her to intervene. They said that her recent talk at the school had been "the first real breath of Colonel Parker we have had since he left us."

The simplest way around the impasse was to erase all distinction between the two schools, but that took no account of Alice Chipman Dewey, who was principal of the Laboratory School and undoubtedly would be made head of any combined elementary school. Dewey's wife was admittedly brilliant, but although a certain "delicacy of feeling" prevented their saying so to Dewey, neither Anita nor the Parker faculty thought her suited to run their school. Without consultation, Dewey went ahead and recommended his wife as principal of a single elementary school, and the battle lines re-formed. Both sides courted Anita, who went to see Dewey, with no effect. He felt he could not reverse himself without losing "ordinary and decent self respect" and without calling into question "the honesty and good faith of my previous action." "My Dear Mrs. Blaine," he wrote, "you will see that it is a moral question of the most fundamental kind at stake." That put the matter beyond ajudication, since a moral question defies sensible bargaining. The incumbent principal of the Parker Grade School, Miss Zonia Baker, cried on Anita's shoulder: "I hope everything will be done to retain him [Dewey] except 'giving up the ship.' " Again Anita met with Dewey; again he claimed that surrender would weaken his authority, to which Anita replied that his authority was "quite unquestioned," and that "the only question about your authority is what you choose to do with it." When everyone had had his say, the two schools were merged, with Alice Dewey as principal.

The institute trustees had made one condition, which President Harper promised to honor; if Mrs. Dewey proved unacceptable, she would not be rehired after the first year. But was the pledge reliable? "Everything related to the welfare of the school," Wilbur Jackman wrote Anita, "hangs upon your firmness in insisting upon the fulfillment of the conditions. Almost every day brings new facts attesting to the utter hopelessness of the present situation. The faculty hope that your trustees will not under any circumstances yield a jot of your right or power to readjust matters. It would seem that the very purpose for which the school was founded hangs upon what you do in this crisis."*

Anita did stand firm, and at the end of the year Mrs. Dewey was not rehired. Both Deweys then resigned from the School of Education, and Dewey submitted resignations for all of his other positions in the university. President Harper, wanting to keep his word to Anita but under heavy pressure to retain Dewey and the prestige his name gave the university, was in torment.

It is not clear what happened at that point, but it is known that on the last day of Alice Dewey's tenure as principal of the combined schools, 5 May 1904, Dewey was writing President Nicholas Murray Butler accepting a position at Columbia University.

The University of Chicago School of Education did not collapse, and Anita later would help found another Parker-type school on the North Side. But the two great educational innovators had gone. Anita, who had wanted to liberate children from learning by rote and to give her son the best possible schooling, had been witness to and partly responsible for the clouding of Parker's dream in his last years and the angry departure of John Dewey from the Midwest.

* Paradoxically, Jackman, who held the position of dean of the College of Education, had earlier recommended that the Parker and Dewey schools be merged completely, and that Dewey be put in charge.

A number of North Side parents had been unhappy at the announcement in 1901 of merger between the Chicago Institute and the University of Chicago, for it meant the institute would move to the South Side, and, with both Parker and Dewey gone, they now approached Anita with the proposal that she carry forward the original plan for a school in their neighborhood.

She was amenable, but she was determined that this time the project would have a trimmer budget. There would be a kindergarten and eight elementary grades, with a high school to come later. Except for Stanley, whose growing eccentricities precluded participation, Anita invited the same trustees to help her. To erect and equip a Francis W. Parker School, she said she was willing to lend $45,000, and, at Cyrus Bentley's prompting, she asked for a promissory note payable in twenty years at 5 percent interest. A guarantee fund of $10,000 a year for the first five years would be set up, and she expected others to provide part of it. The school was to be "run on exact figures, so there is need to forecast every expense," she told Missy. And it would express the Colonel's philosophy: "Work to be really profitable need not be irksome."

From the University of Chicago, to whom she had given it, Anita got free use of the land on the North Side originally purchased for the institute. The same architect, James Gamble Rogers, was hired and told to design a two-story building, the focal point of which was to be an entrance hall dominated by a large fireplace, a Parker touch. There were to be spacious side halls, large enough for playrooms and museum displays, and the usual Parker paraphernalia—gymnasium, laboratories, printshop, clay modeling rooms, and an assembly hall. Pupils would "not be asked to spell and read by committing to memory combinations of letters and of words which have for him no vital meaning, but these subjects will be dealt with as they touch his actual daily experience." And order would not be maintained by the "old regime [of] whip and spur . . . fear . . . and factitious rewards." (The phrasing suggests Anita's hand in its composition.)

A contractor was employed, and a parents' committee took responsibility for finding $3,500 of the $10,000 annual guarantee, Anita agreeing to put up the remainder. But when enrollment blanks were mailed that summer, only eighty-four pupils tentatively registered, and the school needed at least a hundred to make ends meet. Nevertheless, ground was broken and construction begun. When the work fell behind schedule, a supervisor was hired to hound the contractor, who couldn't get along with the architect. It then turned

101

out that the parents would raise only $2,300 of the promised $3,500; this, coupled with reduced tuition receipts and an increase in the cost of everything, boosted the predicted annual deficit from $4,560 to $15,000. It was underwritten by Anita.

Heretofore, she had not given much thought to what she spent, but returning from a vacation that September of 1901 for a week of "shoulder to the wheel" work, she was seized by an inexplicable fit of economy. Her philanthropies were proving costly, exceeding $100,000 a year, their large home at 101 East Erie was expensive to maintain, and she decided that she and Em would move into an apartment in the Raymond on Lake Shore Drive.* The idea was ridiculous, Nettie said; unnecessary, was Dr. Favill's comment; unseemly, said Harold. "With an income of $50,000 a year, your present establishment is in no sense extravagant," Cyrus Bentley told her. "They were all very funny about it," Anita wrote Missy. She paid no attention to them. She and Em moved to the Raymond, where they played dollhouse for a month, by the end of which apartment living had lost its charm. The chauffeur then drove them back to 101, where the butler smilingly awaited them at the door. Bags were unpacked, clothing was returned to drawers and closets. Em ran about happily, inspecting his small gymnasium, the outdoor pool, and the tennis court in the backyard which had so agitated Anita's neighbors when it was being built—not because the neighbors objected to tennis, but because, when the carpenters, surveyors, and lumber haulers showed up, they assumed that Mrs. Blaine was constructing a kindergarten in her garden.

Anita had to admit that the Raymond lacked the amenities of 101, where even the tile drainage for the lawn had been laid out expressly for Em, so that he could run barefoot without getting his feet wet. In the rear garden, screened by a high brick wall from an increasingly noisy thoroughfare, the two of them had planted evergreens, an apple tree, a grape vine, and in a shady spot some violets given them by a favorite teacher. Inside those walls, Anita felt she owned quite an estate, and it was all for her son; "if I loved everyone in the whole world and loved them all very much," she told him, "I wouldn't love them all as much as I love you." She bought him a fox terrier puppy, the first of many adored pets—collies, mutts, cats, birds—and they discussed whether animals had souls. On the death

* Her expenditures for 1900 totaled $154,108.86, of which $105,261 was for the Chicago Institute.

of one of the dogs, Anita arranged a funeral complete with coffin, flowers, scriptural readings, and a grave in the woods.

Holidays were celebrated with a flourish and the Fourth of July, Anita's birthday, was always a special treat of feasting and fireworks. The Christmas Eve after their return to 101, the clan gathered—grandmother from across the street, other McCormicks walking the block or two from their homes—and after dinner hands were clasped at the hearth while Nettie read "The Night before Christmas." Stockings were hung, there was the grand opening of presents next morning, after which the front door was thrown open to admit carolers, and Uncle Harold dressed as Santa Claus sprang into the living room with a pack on his back. The day after Christmas, poor children were brought to the house and toys distributed. And after the greens and holly had been taken down, Anita went back to her desk, trying to put some order into her hours, knowing that "all one can do is to adjust and shift and apportion them, like little blocks."

There seemed never enough hours. Time had to be found for Em, for the Parker School, for fencing lessons,* for an executive committee meeting of the Board of Associated Charities, for conferences about a new art league, lunch with a Frenchman studying American schools, tenement work with the City Homes Association, meetings of the Audubon Society and the Consumer League. There were lawyers and doctors to be consulted, fund raisers to be interviewed, letters to Stanley and Virginia to be written, Bible study classes to be taught at the Home for Self-Supporting Women. With all this on her hands, she was relieved not to be pressed to take part in some intricate business negotiations which were going on at the turn of the century, and in which Nettie was taking the lead.

The rival Deering company had been giving the McCormicks brisk competition, and—with the assistance of George Perkins of Morgan and Company and of John D. Rockefeller (Harold's father-in-law)—Nettie, Cyrus, and Harold were negotiating a consolidation of the nation's two largest manufacturers of agriculture imple-

---

* "Among the well-known society women who find pleasure in the art of swordsmanship," according to an article in the Women's Supplement of the Sunday *Times-Herald* of Chicago, 13 March 1898, "are Mrs. Emmons Blaine and Mrs. Cyrus H. McCormick. Both of these ladies are exceptionally clever with the foils and have for some time past been taking instruction from Captain Yates, who is fencing master at the Chicago Athletic Association." The "Mrs. McCormick" mentioned was undoubtedly Anita's sister-in-law, not her mother.

ments. In conferences with her two sons, attorneys, and company officials, Nettie McCormick at sixty-seven was showing herself to be a shrewd bargainer. As principal stockholder in the reaper company, she had informed the Deerings that "the proposition or price must be very tempting to make me willing now. I do not prefer a combined organization at this time, per se, for its own sake." Privately, she told Harold that she was prepared to go ahead if Rockefeller was given a large enough share of stock so that when he voted with them, the McCormicks would control. A loan by Rockefeller of $4,500,000 in cash enabled them to gain over 50 percent of the stock. During the critical talks in New York in the summer of 1902, McCormick negotiators had met in one room, the Deerings in another, with lawyers shuttling back and forth arranging terms. "Oh! the toil in these rooms of these two weeks," Nettie wrote. "Oh! the night work of our dear boys!" But by 28 July, "for weal or woe," the die was cast "and a tremendous responsibility it was—perhaps never in the history of industry or trade or finance has such a mountain of responsibility rested upon individual members of one family."[8] The International Harvester Company had been born.* At the start it was producing 85 percent of America's grain-harvesting machinery, and the dividends of the consolidation were to make possible numerous philanthropies with which Anita was associated.

But life was more than philanthropy and high endeavor for Anita as she approached her mid-thirties. While she seldom went to other people's parties, she gave her own, always lightened by an informality and inventiveness she had not learned at the Misses Kirkland's Academy. At a party for co-workers on a child welfare exhibit, she provided male guests with Buster Brown coats and the ladies with pinafores and hair ribbons, and led them in a game of ring-around-

* Five companies were involved: the McCormick Harvesting Machine Company; the Deering Harvester Company; Warder, Bushnell and Glessner Company; the Plano Company; and the Milwaukee Harvester Company. For the first ten years, the affairs of the new International Harvester Company were managed by a voting trust consisting of a junior partner of J. P. Morgan (George W. Perkins), Charles Deering, and Cyrus H. McCormick. The Company was capitalized for $120 million. A fuller account of the negotiations is given by Virginia Roderick in her biography of Nettie Fowler McCormick.

the-rosie. She thought they ought to get the feel of what it is like to be a child. When Walter Damrosch came to Chicago to conduct one of his symphony concerts, she gave a dinner in his honor, to which she invited the cartoonist John McCutcheon and the sensational Isadora Duncan. After dinner, the party went to see "The Days of Old When Knights Were Bold" and ended up in Miss Duncan's hotel suite. It had been quite an evening, Anita wrote Em. "The waiters were finishing setting a large round table, Miss Duncan picked up some flowers to put on it, the whole thing went over on the floor, smashing dishes and glass and making one heap of debris. We all turned in to help pick it up, and set a new table. Meanwhile, Uncle Walter played and Miss Duncan danced."

On weekends, she and Em usually boarded the commuter train for Elmhurst, a prairie town sixteen miles west of Chicago, where she had rented an old country house set in the midst of an apple and cherry orchard, close by the Cyrus Bentleys and Bessie Bentley's parents. There she could play tennis on the Bentley court, and Em could run his dog and entertain his friends—"four boys out here for the day, a perfectly glorious day, and all day spent around and about with them. Football, tennis, games, jokes, a pianola which we bought recently. The attractions of the orchard house are growing, a chipmunk, two red squirrels, chickens. I take long walks and peg away at my desk."

While grandmother Blaine was alive, the two of them went to Bar Harbor for a month each summer, then, after her death in 1903, to their own camp on Upper St. Regis Lake in the Adirondacks, which became Anita's favorite retreat. Around them were forests of spruce, pine, and hemlock and scores of ponds and swamps which spread out from Paul Smith's hunting camp, a rambling hotel for wealthy guests. "I never saw anything like it," Smith told one reporter: "There is not a foot of land on that lake for sale this minute, and there is not a man in it but what's a millionaire, and some of them ten times over." Anita ended up buying three camps on Upper St. Regis, two of which she gave away, and hundreds of acres of wilderness—space enough to accommodate teen-age Em, his companions, her visitors, servants, dogs, numerous trunks, a grand piano, and a boat house.

"Camp" was a misnomer. Each was a small estate, accessible only by boat from Paul Smith's landing. Each had sizable, well-built cabins and dozens of outbuildings for cooking, laundry, and servants' quarters. When they went "rough camping," bearers carried their canoes, picnic lunches, blankets, and cold bottles of champagne;

105

money and nature were blissfully wed. The night skies were splattered with stars, the quiet broken only by the cry of a loon across the lake. Anita took long hikes with Em and his pal Elliott Dunlap Smith, and when her long skirts became irksome, she borrowed a knife and cut them off at the knee. During the official rough-housing period in the mornings, she often swooped into the boys' cabin and took on anyone in sight. There was boating, fishing, and swimming in the chilly lake, the butler standing on the dock and timing the races. In the evenings, an immense stone fireplace was ablaze with logs. Anita read, the boys talked or grinned sheepishly when she handed them Bibles. They were smiling, she told them, out of false shame: "Bibles are not something feminine but are books for boys, and boys should understand it, like it, and be helped by it."

The Adirondacks summer routine was broken one year by a train trip west to visit Stanley, where doctors, fearing incipient tuberculosis, had recommended mountain air and an active outdoor life. Stanley had bought a cattle ranch near Springer, New Mexico; that it had no fancy quarters for guests was an added attraction to Anita. She was fascinated by the Southwest, by its adobe huts and the contrast between the indigenous beauty and the junky trappings of a growing tourist trade. How might the "art qualities of the simpler peoples," she wondered, be preserved from the "great danger of being lost in their contact with our commercial standards?" "The things their little stores were filled with!" she wrote Missy. "Simply horrible compared with the real beauty shown in the adobe houses, and about them, further back, of the Mexican and Spanish." Anita and Em rode western style with the cowboys, chopped wood, and shared the chores; she had hopes "that a little more only will make me a 'long horn.' " The West was "real life . . . more educative than German opera." "This morning," she wrote Missy, "the foreman was skinning a cow that had died. I again was thinking of keeping E from it, but concluded instead that I would go along. It was very valuable as a marvel of nature, as contributing infinite contempt for my own ignorance, as an exhibition of the simple, natural, and thoroughly scientific way the child saw it. Many useful thoughts came to me."

There were other travels together: fishing in Colorado, threading their way through the currents with the aid of Indian guides; a visit to Grandfather Cyrus's birthplace in Virginia and a rediscovery of the old McCormick family camp near Iron River, Wisconsin. Later, when Em had entered Harvard, Anita took off for Cambridge on football weekends, and once to New Haven for a Yale-Princeton game to hear the band play "Reli on Eli," a song she had composed in 1905 with her cousin Chauncey McCormick.

Wherever she traveled, however, she was in reach of the long arm of Western Union and of urgent messages demanding a wired reply. A pad of telegraph blanks was an indispensable part of her baggage. Brother Cyrus, an apostle of a competitive economic system, was not put off by her addiction to telegrams but begged her to distribute her business and send at least some of her messages via a rival company. Along with the telegraph blanks, Anita customarily took with her at least two servants and a secretary. She stuck to trains long after air travel had become commonplace. On one occasion, Harold, a flight enthusiast who later had an "hydroaero" of his own which he brought to beach parties in Lake Forest for his guests' enjoyment, had tried to get her to go up with him. "If ever the thing looked harmless, it was then," Anita said, "for the conditions were perfect and seeing it go time after time gave one the feeling that it returned." But she declined Harold's offer. She would find it "thrilling, like the dawn of a new era," when biplanes made exhibition flights over Chicago in 1910 and an aviator flew his Wright biplane over the Loop, but "total dislike" kept her on the ground. Her McCormick forebears had been enamored of gadgets and mechanical progress, and Em took after them, but in that respect, as in others, Anita was a maverick.

An attractive, young, and rich widow was bound to have admirers, and as we shall see, Anita had her share. But there was only one who "understood what you are after, below the deeds and circumstances," who could appreciate one's longing to "open the oneness in us to others."

Henry Favill, the man who "always understood," her "beloved Aesop," had entered her "torn and shattered life" two years after Emmons's death, when she consulted him about her son's health.[9] Soon she was consulting him about her own "state of weakness." He had helped her "very much," she wrote him the day after one of their early talks; he had been "kinder than you knew probably, for when we yield to an impulse that springs from loneliness it is a great thing to have it kindly met." His words had rung "with the strength of mind over matter" and given her a feeling of confidence "which I seem to have lacked for so long."

Six years older than she, Favill had what Carl Sandburg called "the sad, stern power written on faces of some of the finest Indians —the deep quizzical thoughtfulness of a Lincoln face." Descendant of an Ottawa chief, "Returning Cloud," and proud of it, Favill had a massive head and a magnificent physique. He seemed, one colleague said, to be "of another age, an age more virile and heroic." There was a contemplative side to him as well, an ironic though not cynical tolerance, an unjudging curiosity about the world's oddities, and a calm indifference to conventional opinion. Morality or immorality seemed to him "chiefly a question of giving pain, and one ought not to give pain unnecessarily." He had been the only man with no business connections to be elected to the Commercial Club of Chicago and would become president of the City Club, the Municipal Voters League, and the National Committee for Mental Hygiene. Although gregarious and possessing "joyous vigor incarnate,"[10] he confessed to Anita his yearning for a "quiet withdrawing, so far as one's inner and personal life is concerned within the circle of one's individuality." Possessions seemed to him a burden, not a boon, and the sacrifice of self-respect to fashion ignoble. After all, one's needs were few—"to find repose and reward and work well done; and above all to recognize that, inasmuch as the only place of judgment of final value is one's inner consciousness, to cast one's life according to outside influence is to come into inevitable discord with one's deeper nature."[11]

Favill had that humility which accepts without regret or resentment the limits to ambition, and he saw, more clearly than Anita, the vanity of self-reproach when one fell short of the ideal. "How to be genuine in the midst of so much spurious, and not to be queer, or superior, or some other disagreeable thing is a problem," he wrote her. It was difficult "to draw lines for oneself to which others need not conform," to know "what to do with the mass of the things one does not approve but cannot on that basis condemn." It would be easier not to think, "but the habit never is overcome." When Anita was needlessly hard on herself, he reproved her, for while he believed in the "prime necessity of fully appreciating the gravity of failures," he was "equally sure that after that it is imperative that the chapter be closed and the next taken up with courage and determination." One must risk rebuff, he said, because there is "nothing so desirable to cultivate as a trust in every kind of life relationship."

Here was the strength of her father, the steadiness of Emmons, and an attitude toward life wholly compatible with her own. But even if she had wanted to be the "clinging vine" on this "sturdy oak" and to surrender the self-reliance fate had forced upon her, Favill would not have permitted it, for he was irrevocably, though unhappily, married. A nephew of Dr. Favill expressed puzzlement that "two such divergent personalities" as Henry and his wife Susan Cleveland Pratt should have married each other in the first place. "There was an aura of charisma about Uncle Harry that was obvious the moment you met him. Aunt Susie . . . was not beautiful nor was she homely; she was not loquacious nor was she excessively withdrawn." There appeared no "evidence of affection between them."

In his letters to Anita, he was punctilious. Writing her as a physician, he addressed her as Mrs. Emmons Blaine or "Dear Madam." Personal, handwritten notes began, "My Dear Anita" or "Dearly Beloved." By 1902, he had "only one word" to tell her—"as though I could tell you—how glad I am that you care, for me, about me, and what I do and am. Don't fail to realize that I know your spirit, even better than your word, and rate it as its value." Initially their correspondence concerned such medical matters as calomel and three grains of salicylate of soda for Em's sore throat, but before long they were discussing all of her tangled family problems. He went deeply into Virginia's case and, at Anita's prompting, advised Nettie in 1904 that in his opinion the existing medical supervision was ineffective; he would suggest "future arrangements to correct the weakness in the plan."

He paid Anita the respect of letting her see the darker side of his nature, his "loss of capacity to be enthusiastic," his inability to "see the compensations." But he was as certain as she of the unwholesomeness of becoming too absorbed in oneself and had a "rooted objection to the frame of mind that men get into when they begin to take care of themselves, and for my part I prefer to 'bust,' if it were not for the stupidity of it." That their freedom was circumscribed by other loyalties was an accepted fact. "What one might feel impelled to do as a matter of trueness to himself," he wrote her, "is not in the least a warrant for doing anything unless it proves up with the general situation"; the ignoring of that principle was "responsible for most of the blunders that we make."

They overthrew the sovereignty of the "general situation" at least once, however, and in a sealed letter to her son, to be opened after her death, Anita described that capitulation to passion: "Here in this sacred spot where I now breathe softly and peacefully in the thought of his beauty, I have had all the close communication, body and soul, that can come to two human beings—all of it that I could have from him and he could have from me. No words can make this plain to you, nor to me. I long for that illumination of spirit which can give this to you in its wholeness."[12]

Their intimacy was never suspected by Anita's family nor by the many courtiers who unavailingly pursued her, among them her attorney, Cyrus Bentley.

Married to Anita's girlhood companion, Bessie King, Bentley had known Anita since childhood, and as a young Yale graduate practicing law with his father had been a familiar figure in the McCormick social set. His prudent handling of real estate, wills, trusts, estate management, and corporation law made him a valued adviser. He had helped put through the merger of the McCormick and Deering companies and became International Harvester's first general counsel. His judgment, in Favill's opinion, was generally good, "though he might not see the indomitable quality in a quiet man who was not conspicuous." Bentley was fastidious, an epicurean (his camping equipment included a French chef), "very serious, very meticulous, rather severe," and with a "very astute legal mind," Anita said. His father had been president of the Young Men's Christian Association, and he, like other well-to-do professionals of his day, gave free legal advice to civic groups, especially the City Homes Association, in which Anita had a special interest. In addition to handling her financial affairs, he counseled her on her friends and her philanthropies, for she had given him the "privilege of talking about anything." In 1899, along with Favill, he had become a trustee of the Chicago Institute. Reliable, somewhat arrogant, at any imagined aspersion on his character or dignity he withdrew into his shell. He was, unhappily, miscast as a Don Juan.

She "never had a faster, truer friend than Anita," Bessie Bentley had once told Nettie, and Bessie's husband was aware of it. But Bessie was in the suburbs, busy with housekeeping and two young children, while Anita was in town, not far from Bentley's law office, and occupied with what he wistfully called "the deep things of life." A sweet word from her filled him with "unspeakable gratitude"; his existence at forty was "waiting and not much besides"; he was so thankful for "the perfect understanding" between them; she could regenerate his "lost soul."

Sufficiently staid to be shocked by his emotions, Bentley was nonetheless too enthralled to be put off by Anita's unresponsiveness. "The fact that there are others who are standing between us," he wrote her, "affects me as it would not affect you. There are many things which I am longing to take to you but which I cannot." Yet

110

he was comforted by knowing that "you do not want me to leave you," and if she was determined to reject him as a lover, he would be her guardian: she must not "take on new burdens," she must understand that courage was not "a perfect substitute for strengths," she must "learn to make the demands upon you conform to your ability to meet them," and she must forgive him for saying that "nothing seems to me so well worth doing as that which serves you. . . . I want to stand between you and care of every kind."

That she did not wish anyone stand between her and her cares was something his masculinity could not grasp. It threw him off balance, made him say the wrong things at the wrong time. He then was miserable, "just as I was more than once a few months back when I felt that my mistakes had made you wretched." He would do anything to prevent an estrangement. He could not endure that she should be unhappy—"least of all that unhappiness should come to you through me or on my account." After a telephone conversation one morning about a tennis date, he worriedly sent word that perhaps she did "not feel at liberty to cancel or postpone engagements which you may make with me. As things are now, though I have not changed, and cannot, I want you to have, so far as I am concerned, the freedom which seems to you (as you once told me) the first element of friendship." A week later, he was again apologizing, sorry that "suffering as you were last night, you should have had to go through that pitiful scene." But there was so much to be sorry for! What he would not give "to be able to say to you and do for you a tithe of what is in my heart. It is well toward morning but I cannot sleep. Oh, the vigils that I have kept."

A trivial difference led to a showdown. Anita, active in the City Homes Association, which had been set up to investigate and clean up rat-infested tenement houses where most of Chicago's immigrant population lived, was asked at the close of 1901 to take the presidency of the group. Bentley tried to prevent her accepting it; her primary duties were to her son and to the Parker School, he said sternly. "To aid you or even to work with you toward a common end, where everything we do together involves a denial of the paramount claims upon you, this I am no longer willing to do." He tried blackmail, threatening to give up his free legal work for the association if she took the job.* She took it anyway, and although he re-

* At least, Bentley said, she ought to confer with the other Francis W. Parker school before taking on other duties. There is no evidence that she did. In his book *Spearheads for Reform: The Social Settlements and the Progressive Movement* (1967), Allen F. Davis credits "Jane Addams

mained a steadfast friend and legal counselor, his romantic quest was over.

That same year, another suitor appeared. He was Raymond Robins, seven years Anita's junior, who had worked on a Southern plantation, mined coal in Tennessee, prospected for phosphate in the Southwest, managed a Florida company commissary, been a deputy postmaster, practiced law in Florida, migrated north to Washington, D.C., and then gone to San Francisco, where, as a crusading lawyer, he had been chairman of the Democratic city and county organizations and led the local William Jennings Bryan campaign for president. Following that, he mined coal, made money in the Alaskan Klondike, embraced the single-tax theories of Henry George, and finally joined the Christian Church and became a lay preacher—all before he was twenty-eight. He believed himself to be committed "to the voice of the social conscience as revealed in the common life of man." After a long bout with typhoid fever, he had moved to Chicago, where in 1901 he connected with Chicago Commons, a social work settlement founded by Graham Taylor.[13]

When Robins and Anita met, he was director of the City Homes Association's Municipal Lodging House, which took vagrants off the streets; gave them a hot bath, clean clothes, a place to sleep, and a job; and, if no job could be found, got them out of town as quickly as possible. The idea was, as Anita put it, "to rid the city of the tramps who infest it, by closing [police] station houses to them and furnishing a place where the minority of honest men who need a night's lodging can always get it, but with such restrictions that a tramp would never come there twice. In this way they would be forced to move elsewhere." As president of the association, Anita came to know and like Robins but was wholly unprepared for his avowal in the spring of 1904 that he could not sleep until he had told her that he wanted to marry her, "daring this great issue by the authority of an overwhelming love and the strength of a free and simple manhood." She refused him. Two days later, a second effusive message was delivered to 101. From the moment in Spaulding's store on a hot afternoon in July when she had lifted her veil and smiled, he had "felt a strange new thrill, a certain boundless undefinable joy, until that moment at Elmhurst on Good Friday night,

of Hull House and Mrs. Emmons Blaine" with "really launching the housing movement in that city [Chicago] with the establishment of the City Homes Association in 1900. They persuaded Robert Hunter, wandering settlement worker, charity expert, and radical, to conduct a thorough investigation of housing conditions."

when in speaking of the quickening life of your child you seemed the incarnation of glorious motherhood and the surging tide of my love swept all barriers away." She was his "seeress, singer of the sunrise. . . . I held thy hand once, and in the summer lightning, still of thy smile I see."

Getting nowhere, he did as Bentley had done. If she would not marry him, would she be his spiritual mother? Before she could answer that question, he had decided that this would not suffice, for "a mighty heart hunger from the memory of that divine hour of hope for the unspeakable blessing of your love sweeps over me." He saw her "glorious eyes in all their unfathomable beauty and tenderness"; "wave after wave of incommunicable agony" broke over his soul. The agony was unbearable: "If this present strain continues, I will either deliberately break up this terrible wheel-work of the brain or I shall go mad for lack of sleep." It had been many months since he had "gone to rest without your image the last conscious picture in my brain and now again the old sorrow is tugging at my heartstrings." He would worship her: "It is a master service you have done for me Anita Blaine. I know in my heart that I shall never pass wholly beyond the influence of your truth and nobleness in that supreme hour. For evermore, I shall thank Our Father for such communion and fellowship as may be freely given between thee and me. Never again shall I desire more, never again feel that I must take less."

Three months after that outpouring, Robins married and quit Chicago, to the relief of Bentley.

But the relief was short-lived. A new danger, as Bentley saw it, arose in the person of Carolyn McCormick, Anita's Baltimore cousin and protégée from the time of her graduation from Bryn Mawr in 1894. Bentley had got it in his head that Carrie was a "very strong and bad influence," and word of this got back to Baltimore. "My darling one," Carrie immediately wrote Anita, "it matters so little— the opinion, any opinion, even the best. I only wait after all to go to the bottom of it with you, certainly, with him if I can some day." Bentley had no intention, however, of getting to the bottom of anything with Carrie; his sole aim was to warn Anita against her young cousin's insinuating ways.

Anita seldom listened to gossip; anyway, she was fond of this lively modern relative with whom she could joke, versify, and have delicious late-night chats. Together, the two cousins had tramped through the Adirondacks woods and written songs. Carrie's letters vibrated with genuine affection: "My Dear Beautiful, could you guess how much I want you? And need you? And must have you? You are not here to sit down a minute by the fire or better still to creep into bed with! What wouldn't I give to have you?" And again: "Why can't I speak to you straight, and feel you close by and kiss your geranium eyes? I want to hold your hand because I love you." That was a privilege Bentley would have preferred to reserve for himself.

Affectionate Carrie had the added gift of sensing how to take as well as receive: "Gradually I have come to the place where I do not want even to thank you for anything," she wrote Anita. "It is enough that you are you, and that I can hold onto you. I suppose it is thankfulness that is in my heart, but it seems too great to be put into words." She did not treat her cousin as a philanthropist or martyred widow or paragon of civic virtue, but simply as "real and vivid and sure and beautiful," a clear river in which one could bathe one's "dusty travel-stained soul."

There can be no doubt that the cousins' friendship had in it no sexual impropriety. Why then did Bentley feel so strongly that Carrie's presence was "bad in its effects"? Was it jealousy? Prudishness? One can only surmise. Whatever his reasons, the anxiety was laid to rest by an announcement in 1907 of Carrie's engagement. "How shall I say it—how shall I not say it?" Carrie wrote Anita, "I am going to marry Louis Slade, and it is the best and the beautifulest and the brightest thing that ever happened in a million worlds if only you say to me 'it is well.' I somehow cannot go one step at all of the shining way until I feel your arms about me."

Anita was delighted; she immediately invited the couple to Chicago and gave a dinner for them. "We had thirty-five," she wrote Em; "it was very jolly. . . . Uncle Walter [Damrosch] came from Ravinia and he struck up the wedding march on the piano." It was "strange" to think of Caroline's being married, but grand "hearing all about their wonderful story of finding they loved each other too much to live apart—and so they have concluded to live together." Anita enthusiastically joined in the wedding preparations, but from then on the cousins saw much less of one another. Carrie had her husband and home in New York, and her women's suffrage movement. Anita would be spending more and more time on the care of Virginia, Stanley, and her aging mother, and on education in Chicago. Nevertheless, the affectionate messages continued. "With you in the world," Carrie was to write in 1917, it is "easy to visualize bigness and splendor and truth to the bottom—and vision—and so much beside."

The most pathetic, surely, of Anita's admirers was the Reverend William Lusk, an Irishman who lived at Paul Smith's the year round, and who showed up at her rented cottage on Em's eleventh birthday in 1901, when Anita was having tea and cake with her son. Lusk had dropped by to introduce himself and his mission, which was to bring the Presbyterian God to Adirondacks guides. Whatever a stranger's story, Anita was a courteous listener, and by the third cup of tea, Lusk appeared smitten. What an "air of grandeur!" Though "democratic and humble in spirit," Anita "walked the earth with the stateliness of a queen." That is how he recalled their first encounter.

Lusk was at loose ends that summer and, as became plainer on closer acquaintance, rather lackadaisical about his religious duties; wealthy tourists interested him more than the souls of Adirondacks Indians. Several days after their first meeting, he came upon Anita as she was walking along one of the trails with Em and two new arrivals, cousin Carrie and her father William. On a sudden impulse, Anita invited him to accompany them on a camping expedition. Guides had been hired, equipment collected and packed, and they set out across the lake for a distant high point surrounded by pines. The capricious Adirondacks weather was not cooperative; it rained for seventy-two hours, but "nothing could *damp* the deliciousness of it," Anita thought—beds on balsam boughs, good cooking, convivial company, and plenty of help.

On their return, a telegram awaited Lusk from an old friend, Arthur Brownlee, announcing his arrival at Paul Smith's. Why not bring him to lunch, Anita suggested.

If Lusk could have declined for his friend, he would have. He wanted no competition, and he knew Brownlee. The friend nevertheless came and at lunch said he had known Anita's brothers in college, which may have been true. He talked of his experiences as a miner and rancher, but confessed that his heart was still at Princeton, which he had left after completing ministerial studies. Without hesitation, Anita asked Brownlee to join their circle, and for the next two weeks they were together constantly. Stories were told around the campfire, sometimes until dawn. A phrase of Brownlee's —"Buffaloes always head into the storm"—caught Anita's fancy, for it expressed her belief that dangers should be met head on, and half jokingly she proposed they create an "Order of the Buffalo." Since a society ought to have an emblem, she ordered four tiny gold buffaloes from Tiffany's, and each member of the order was given a pin and name. Lusk became "The Rev," Carrie "Sammy," Brownlee "Willie Antelope," Anita "Lady Jane." They named their circle "Good Hope."

Underneath the highjinks, something serious was going on, at least for Lusk, who confided to Anita that too much of his life had been "spent among people whose view of life is wrong, whose atmosphere is vitiated and to whom life itself is sawdust." Thanks to her, he had been awakened from his "dogmatic slumber."

He went no further until the following year, when he, Anita, and Carrie tried to recreate Camp Good Hope. A newcomer to the Order of the Buffalo, Anita's sister-in-law Margaret Damrosch, remembered "the tossing sailboats, delightful and intoxicating climbs, woodsey smell, outdoor cooking," and their jolly evenings around the fire. But the spontaneity of the previous summer could not be recaptured. "The Rev" was gloomy. The winter had been long, and Lusk told Anita he was burning with a "hectic fever to find one who will come with me into the solitary places and transform this into gladness." She had aroused his ambition "to do something and to be somebody." He declared his love. Would she be his wife, or, as he put it, his "dear guardian angel"?

There were "a million reasons" why not. He was crushed, and, as Robins had before him, said that if he could not have her he must run away, which he did, to Ireland, where he married and became an Episcopalian.*

Not to be outdone and with Lusk out of the way, Brownlee also offered his hand. When it was not taken, he too escaped to Europe, leaving a note to say that Anita could "understand the hurry I had getting ready, otherwise I should have written a long letter (my first *love* letter)." She had word of him from time to time through Lusk, who reported that he had taken to drink and drugs, and she met him once when he called on her in Chicago and she tried to talk with him about his self-destruction. He ran out of the house, vowing never to see her again. In 1912 a report came that his sister had committed him to an alcoholics' rehabilitation center, hoping the treatment would cure the drinking and addiction to cocaine and morphine, and when he reappeared in Chicago, he was destitute and sick. Anita refused to see him, although she paid his hotel bills. Eventually, Brownlee went back to missionary work—the Epiphany Bible Truth Church in Chicago, where he tried to help losers like

* Not before writing her that as he "walked along the road the other day and watched them operate a stump-puller in a nearby field, I longed for some such instrument to come over my life and lift out stem and root friendships that have become too deep for me to eradicate."

himself. He wrote her begging letters from time to time, never referring to those luminous weeks at Camp Good Hope which to Lusk had stood "for what is truest and best and noblest in the world, the high water mark of human joy."

By now Anita had had her fill of missionaries. She had heard them in her parents' home, had had them in her own, had camped with them, had sent them checks, had been courted by them, and had concluded that each should hold his ideas "as a sacred sanctuary where those may worship who will, but where none should be dragged." She had lost interest in evangelism, and indeed in ecclesiastical organizations—"I believe that I disapprove of the Church entirely . . . that it does positive injury in the world." When her brothers asked her to join them in contributing to a religious magazine founded by her father and of which she was part owner, she replied she did not "sympathize with a project of a sectarian paper" and assigned her stock in the magazine to Cyrus, "thus ending any obligation on my part to the paper." Yet, she was still teaching a Sunday school class—"The dearest thing I have undertaken lately."

The basement was unfinished and the whole front entrance would have to be torn down so that a grand piano could be installed, but a brick, gabled, three-story Parker School had admitted its first pupils on the first of October 1901. The new principal, Flora Cooke, had been a friend of Anita's since 1896, when Bessie Bentley and she had spent three weeks with Anita exploring the geology of Mount Desert Island in Maine, collecting rocks for classroom study. "Prinny," as Miss Cooke was called, was a year younger than the school's benefactor, small, thin, brisk, a novice at administration, a devotee of the Parker philosophy, and, Anita informed Missy, "splendidly satisfactory to work with. . . . You would have loved to see our little school this morning, Miss Cooke so strong and brave and eager to make the work go on. . . . It must and will go on in its great mission of giving inspiration and high purpose to teachers. . . . How much of the world is in their hands!" (To Missy, Flora Cooke seemed like a wild flower, "drooping, delicately scented.")

There was so much to be done! Anita attended faculty meetings, morning assemblies, and school festivities; walked about the school with Miss Cooke, pausing to chat with a passing child and discussing him afterward; swept in and out of classes, listening and occasionally adding a comment. She volunteered as a substitute when a teacher was absent, sat beside the driver of the school bus and debated the best route for the children, chaperoned classes to the country to watch a sheep shearing; and wherever she traveled she picked up objects that might have instructional value. When Flora Cooke came to Maine to spend a three-week vacation with Anita in 1896, the two of them collected stones for the school—"examples of the most interesting formations," Anita wrote her mother. Cyrus Bentley had to carry a log for miles through snowy Michigan woods, so that Parker students could see where beavers had marked the wood with "their little industrious teeth, plied with such wonderful effect." Graduation week, a dinner for Parker seniors was given in the walled garden behind Anita's home, the trees sparkling with tiny artificial lights, a stringed orchestra playing in the background, and Anita gliding among the candle-lit tables. After dinner, she and Miss Cooke led the waltzes.

The Colonel would have been proud: the North Side school was a success. Everyone said so—except Cyrus Bentley, whose outspoken criticisms unnerved Miss Cooke. If she had not a "strong belief in Mr. Bentley's insight and judgment," she wrote Anita, she wouldn't mind, but if he thought that things were worse than they had been a year ago, "it cannot be considered lightly"; he would not be critical without "very good evidence." While not sharing Bentley's misgivings, Anita paid them the credit of commissioning her private secretary, Alan B. Eaton, who was also Em's part-time tutor, to analyze the work of the tenth grade.

His findings were disquieting: "a rather larger than usual amount of disorder of a minor kind, fooling around, horseplay, talking out loud, etc. . . . One had the feeling of a real something lacking somewhere. There may be a danger of failure to require certain things to be done or learned with absolute accuracy, even if they do not appeal to the imagination of the child, or are not on the face of them clearly of immediate usefulness."

The report prompted Anita to take greater personal responsibility. In the fall of 1906 she became assistant principal, something she had been "wanting to do for a long time, to get some of the technical side of the schoolwork," she explained to Miss Cooke, who thought it "too good to be true." For the next two years she worked alongside the principal from nine to four, and the experience convinced her of the justice of some of the comments that had been made by Bentley and Owen Aldis.

At soul-searching faculty meetings, Anita spoke out for "a fundamental element of essential educational value, the principal of completeness." She pointed to work tables strewn with paper and paint; coats left in a heap on the floor; ink stands scattered about, students carrying themselves sloppily, speaking carelessly and inexactly, coming out of classes "without having been possessed of the subject or even aroused by it." Perhaps in their haste to overthrow an objectionable marking system and with no method of checks and measures to replace it, they had "opened wide the door to all sorts of inexactness" and had "lost the balance between the child's choice and the child's necessity." Her fellow trustees heartedly concurred, Bentley having become "more and more fixed in the opinion that we have been departing too far from old principles and methods."

Faced with these shortcomings, the trustees asked, what would Colonel Parker have done? He would have searched for a "leader," they concluded, someone who could inspire the faculty, iron out administrative wrinkles, and spur the children to greater effort. Flora Cooke, who as principal had every right to resent that conclusion, acclaimed it; furthermore, four years earlier she had suggested just the right leader—Anita Blaine, or, she added coyly, "a Mr. Bentley who with keen eyes and understanding would make the weak places strong." Both nominees had sidestepped that trap.

The "leader" turned out to be a young man from the East, R. B. Nason, whom Miss Cooke hated on sight and thought bad for the children, uncongenial to the teachers, and a poor instructor who had "the ideals and methods of a cheap political boss." Anita, always hesitant to condemn, insisted that since the trustees had hired him, they must stand by him. You say so only because you haven't seen him in action, Prinny retorted bitterly. Forced finally to choose between Miss Cooke and the young new head, the trustees asked for his resignation, and Anita softened the blow by offering to put him through Harvard Law School.

Meantime, it was discovered that Emmons Blaine, Jr., lacked the necessary credits for graduation, having completed only three-quarters of the necessary work. The fault was not Em's. He had often been ill or away somewhere with his mother, but the deficiency was there, and nothing short of an earthquake could have been more unsettling to the Francis W. Parker School. Miss Cooke suggested giving him an unsigned certificate, with the understanding that he would make up the credits before it was signed, a suggestion which was repugnant to Anita: the graduation ceremony would then be a lie. Letters and phone calls flew back and forth. "These are not ordinary circumstances," Dr. Favill cautioned Miss Cooke (how well she knew it), for it could not be shown "that there was a school curriculum, including a perfectly definite understanding as to the amount of work required," an opinion Miss Cooke eagerly endorsed. The boy had "gone straight in all these years, doing his level best," Favill told Anita. That was not the point, she replied; her son "should not be made the occasion of forming policy for the school, and therefore he should take whatever comes of disappointment or surprise from a clear, straight, course with the thing as it is." She would leave it "entirely in the hands of the school authorities to decide" whether he graduated or not.

As Dr. Favill had said, the case was not ordinary. Em's school schedule had been modified to safeguard his health, with the consent of Anita. Three years before, Miss Cooke had suggested that he take a longer noon break, so that he could have lunch at home and be spared the overexertion of the post-lunch playtime, and she had recommended shortening his Wednesday hour of gymnastics. Somehow, Favill's diplomacy and the determination of an embarrassed Miss Cooke got them around the rule, and Em graduated with his class.

But the Parker School was still leaderless, or so the trustees thought, until they lit upon another young man highly recommended for his skill with boys. He was hired as principal in 1909 and survived until the winter of 1913, when one of the mothers told Dr. Favill that the leader kissed and embraced boys who went to his apartment on Sundays. The aghast trustees assigned Miss Cooke to communicate their anxiety, a task she did not relish. "Unfortunately," she wrote the young man, "there is a degrading practice, *not uncommon*. If you do not know this (which seems strange), Dr. Favill can enlighten you better than I. I only know that such a monstrous evil exists and that men, otherwise intelligent, have been victims of this form of revolting insanity. The *facts* of what you are doing, if they were known, would spell disgrace and scandal to our school, that is sure! Even though it meant that the school must stop because of your loss, I should let it stop and ask you to leave." He resigned, and for the next twenty-one years, until Miss Cooke retired as principal, no serious effort was made to find a successor. However, Anita kept looking—inviting such educational experts as the president of Harvard to visit and analyze the school, and traveling herself to other private schools to examine their methods and to search for new teachers.

Anita's attitude toward the school's dependence on her bounty was ambivalent. She appreciated that all the eggs were in one basket, and neither eggs nor basket would last forever. Yet, she shied away from every request to put the Parker School on a more secure financial footing. She may not have identified the reason for her reluctance, but behind it lay her feeling against freezing any existing arrangement. Who could know what changes time would bring—in the board of trustees, in education itself? She disliked tying things up. Meanwhile, she went on underwriting the yearly budget deficit, which would rise from $15,000 in 1902 to $60,000 by 1920, as well as unanticipated expenditures. That was all very well, Miss Cooke warned in 1910, but "the lack of permanency overshadows all the virtues which the school possesses." Salaries were too low, the building was overcrowded, no pensions were provided, and the facilities to train new teachers were inadequate.

Twelve years were to pass before Anita would authorize a "thorough study" of the school's future needs by a committee made up largely of first-generation Parker alumni, including Katherine Taylor, head of the Shady Hill School in Cambridge; Perry Dunlap Smith, a Winnetka educator; his brother Elliott, a college teacher, and Richard Bentley (Cyrus's son)—all of them childhood friends of Em. On behalf of the committee, Miss Taylor would renew the appeal to Anita to "decide what in your mind are the essentials in perpetuating this school; that you decide which of these you most wish to be connected with." She was by then the only original trustee still alive, none of the vacancies on the board having been filled, and Miss Cooke was on the verge of retirement. Long-range decisions could not be further delayed.

Anita did finally act, though only after lengthy meetings of the trustees at which she was maddeningly though politely insistent that every angle of every possibility be thoroughly examined before any vote was taken. At last, the school and its property were turned over to a new corporation whose trustees, besides Anita, included the two Smiths, Katharine Taylor, and Richard Bentley. Within two years, at Anita's suggestion, they had raised salaries to match the highest paid by comparable schools, raised the tuition, forced retirement on elderly teachers, instituted a pension plan, and begun planning a new building. Although Anita was laggard in providing the large sum she had promised the pension fund and had to be repeatedly reminded of her obligation, she came through. Tuitions were raised 50 percent. A parents' committee provided scholarship money, so that Parker would not be a rich child's school. In addition, on her own initiative, she gave a substantial sum to be used to cover any medical emergencies among the faculty. The school was on its own by the mid-twenties and its survival assured. Anita had given it more than $3 million, and another $1½ million had gone to its predecessor (the Chicago Institute) and other educational endeavors.

Her interest in the Parker School (it never ceased; at eighty, she offered to pay the salary of a new principal for five years) had been inspired by concern for the moral and intellectual welfare of her own child, but it had grown beyond that. She had developed a clearly thought-out educational philosophy, which she set forth in a talk to the Francis Parker Club in 1913. Reminding her audience that it was "still possible for cruelty, neglect and disintegration to be dealt out to children's minds and thoughts from those who are their caretakers," she observed that what children endure "is sunk in that wonderful silence of childhood concerning its own hardships—a silence that is proof first of its total trust in us and in life, and in the last analysis is composed of a sublime submission to the inevitable." Education's true purpose was the bringing of children to adulthood, "ready for their high destinies with energy conserved and strengthened, with vision clarified and intensified, with purpose deepened." This seemed to her "*the* spot at which to begin everything good for the world."

Nor was her interest in the right education of children confined to the Parker School or the University of Chicago Laboratory School. She was to recruit teachers for a new school in New Mexico; she started a Parker-type summer session in the Adirondacks, on the theory that the tourist economy of the region was corrupting the children of the native guides. She gave to the North Shore Country Day School in Winnetka, Illinois, and in the twenties helped found a school in Switzerland for the children of League of Nations delegates. In recognition of her work, she was invited to address a convention of the National Education Association, at which she said things many of the assembled teachers would rather not have heard. She dealt with teachers' salaries and with unionization, admitting that teachers were underpaid but asserting that campaigning for higher pay and better working conditions was not the teacher's job, it was parents'. The teachers' task was to teach. How like the rich, some of her listeners remarked, to underrate the importance of pay checks.

Until 1905, when Mayor Edward F. Dunne appointed her to the Chicago Board of Education, Anita had held no public office. She told the University of Chicago's President Harper that she had "finally and absolutely made up her mind to refuse the appointment" but had been persuaded to accept by "the urgings of those who thought they knew the situation." They had assured her that the mayor honestly meant to do something for the ten thousand children in elementary schools who were being taught in converted garages, warehouses, and store buildings rented by the city.

She knew that she would be in good company on the board. Dunne had also appointed Jane Addams, daughter of one of the wealthiest men in northern Illinois, already prominent through her settlement work at Hull House and perhaps the leading representative of the strenuous altruism of Chicago women; Dr. Cornelia DeBey, a champion of the working class;* and Emil Ritter, long associated with Dr. DeBey in a teachers' union. Although not on intimate terms with any of the three, Anita was classed with them as one of the four "reformers"—labeled "boodlers" by the *Chicago Tribune*, which was particularly hostile to Ritter.[14]

In theory, Anita and her fellow board members had control of almost every facet of public education in Chicago. Through a staff headed by the superintendent, they directed the hiring, firing, and promotion of teachers; the selection of textbooks; and the physical conditions of the classrooms. They could buy sites, authorize construction, control the instructional and clerical staff, and develop courses for the handicapped and the delinquent. It was a demanding job. As a member of the School Management Committee, Anita investigated the practice of prize giving, chaired a special liaison committee between the Home for Crippled Children and a new School for the Handicapped, and studied kindergartens. She devised plans for ethnic storytelling in public libraries, prefacing her recommendation with the remark that Chicago was so "particularly blessed with a variety of nationality . . . that there is no end to what might be done in arousing the interest of each nationality in its own heroes, and far beyond that, of arousing the interest of the various nationalities in each other's heroes." She wrote the controversial judge Ben Lindsay of Colorado to thank him for his contribution to "the final result which we achieved after much effort—the permission of the board to erect a school building adjacent to the new

* One newspaper (the *Record-Herald*) suggested that Dunne was recognizing the demand of Chicago's women teachers for greater representation on the powerful Board of Education.

juvenile court." She campaigned for a conference on truancy, believing that a study of the deficient child would lead inevitably to "a study of our deficient schools, of our deficient system."

Many of these efforts were distasteful to the politicians and businessmen accustomed to running Chicago, but so long as reformers on the Board of Education were in a minority, they were not taken too seriously.

The alarm bell rang when Mayor Dunne made additional, controversial appointments to the board in the summer of 1906—Anita's impetuous single-taxer friend Raymond Robins (who had recently married Margaret Drier, founder of the Women's Trade Union League); Louis F. Post, editor of a progressive news magazine; Wiley Mills, who had run unsuccessfully for the city council on a platform of municipal ownership of Chicago's streetcars; and John J. Sonsteby, president of a garment cutter's union and later to become chief of the Chicago Municipal Court. The newcomers were cordially welcomed by Cornelia DeBey, herself a gadfly and perennial foe of the educational and financial establishment.

The board then started to cut away at the superintendent's power to rate and promote teachers, after which it challenged his choice of textbooks, charging that he favored certain book publishers over others—an accusation that brought irate, interested parties to their feet. A series of fiery board meetings followed, during which a good deal of nonsense was spoken. One patriotic member hotly attacked certain textbooks because they had "not a single mention of George Washington, of Abraham Lincoln, of the Star Spangled Banner, kissing with its beautiful fold the blue empyrean." Another bristled at the insinuation that "dollars, sous, and pence" could sway the board in its search for the "best reader for the American child, bless his little heart."[15] Anita, thinking she could dampen the fire by pouring money on it, offered to pay for all elementary readers used in Chicago public schools herself, selling them at cost to the pupils. Her only condition was that the texts be written by local educators. The education and publishing merchants shuddered; the board's textbook committee refused even to discuss her proposal. She promptly dropped it.

The familiar pride in authorship which cannot countenance an opposing style or view was missing in Anita. Holding to the tentativeness of all truth, she put forth and withdrew her opinions, which were formed by her feelings, courteously and with no resentment. She could not be intimidated, but was not dogmatic. Thus, although not always seeing eye to eye with the school superintendent, she thought he ought to be supported wherever possible, since he was the designated administrative head of the system. To conspire against his express wishes seemed to her "subversive of all right principle in work—destroying any possible harmony and the unity of action which alone can produce efficiency in any organization." She had tried to take the textbook controversy out of politics, thereby avoiding the necessity of either accepting or rejecting the superintendent's recommendations, and she had failed. Now she wanted the board to move on to other matters and to renounce factionalism. Had there been calm weather ahead and a competent captain and complacent crew, her approach might have worked.

But Mayor Dunne, having been denied a second term in 1907, was succeeded by Fred A. Busse, a former postmaster and a Republican, who was elected on his opposition to municipal streetcar ownership. Some considered Busse a "barroom tough," uneducated and unprincipled.[16] Whatever he was, he wanted to be rid of Dunne's contentious board of education. In July, the terms of one-third of its members would automatically expire, and the new mayor planned to fill the vacancies with more compliant appointees. He should have bided his time, but he was impatient, and on the evening of 17 May notified twelve of twenty-one board members, not including Anita, that they were removed from office. Several days later, he ousted two other members for sympathizing with the dozen deposed "radicals." The "radicals," however, did not choose to be summarily deposed. After consulting a lawyer they announced that they would attend the next regular meeting of the board and challenge the mayor.

When Jane Addams and Raymond Robins came to her house to discuss strategy, assuming she was their unquestioning ally, Anita was in a quandary. Miss Addams,* whose mild manner could be quite misleading, was ready to fight.[17] So was Robins. Both were Anita's friends, on the side of right, and yet she felt that the question of the legality of Busse's maneuver was beyond her competence to judge. When Robins left, she told Miss Addams she wanted to be helpful but could think of no way. After further discussion on the telephone with Miss Addams and with Emil Ritter, the board

---

* Jane Addams and Anita, though not intimate, had been allies in a variety of common causes such as tenement housing and child welfare. Miss Addams wrote in 1898 to say "what pleasure my little visits with you have given me." She hoped Anita would take up "residence" in Hull House. She urged her to take the presidency of the Consumers' League: "We must have someone . . . impressive to the merchants."

president, on how that evening's meeting should be conducted, Anita conceived a possible way out. Customarily, when an old board was at the end of its term and a new one was to take its place, the first order of business was to call the roll of old members. Anita advised Ritter that between roll calls of old and new boards, she would formally request an opinion from the board's attorney on the legality of the mayor's removals. The suggested tactic was relayed to the "radicals," possibly through Ritter, and they agreed to go along.

Anita said subsequently that she had never spoken directly with any of the removed members about her intention, and that she had not promised to join any concerted protest. The exact truth is obscure. According to Louis Post, she had agreed not merely to ask for a legal opinion, but, if that opinion proved favorable to removed members, to then request the board's attorney to take legal steps to block the mayor.

As board members gathered that evening, Anita joined in an impromptu conference at President Ritter's desk, still puzzling over the question of a quorum. If the "radicals" had been legally removed by the mayor, she pointed out, there could be no quorum present. For her to make an official motion would be to assume a quorum, and thus prejudge the legality of the call. Walking back to her chair, she passed Robins and murmured, "It won't work."

The meeting opened; the secretary was ordered by Ritter to call the roll, but since the secretary was a paid employee and risked his job if he crossed Busse, he instead began to read a letter from the mayor's office, informing the board of several vacancies. He was interrupted by an angry member who protested that Ritter had directed him to call the roll. He went on reading; Ritter again instructed him to call the roll; he complied but called only the names of the unremoved members and said, "there are nine members present—no quorum present." "Call the remaining names," Ritter insisted. "Mr. President," the secretary replied, "in accordance with your instructions I will call the remaining names as individuals but not as members of the board. I do this under protest and upon the advice of my counsel." Whereupon he called the names of the removed members, each of whom carefully responded, "present as a member of the board of education."

Ritter declared a quorum present and gave the floor to Anita, as planned. Avoiding the word "motion," she requested a legal opinion from the board's counsel, and over the noisy attempts of some pro-Busse members to adjourn the meeting for lack of a quorum, the opinion was favorable to the removed members. Now was the moment for Anita to move that the attorney take the question to court. Instead, she asked the chairman "to test this matter and secure opinions from leading talent of the city, in order that we may have added to our attorney's opinion, the opinion of some of the most responsible minds of the city of Chicago." Ritter took her suggestion under advisement; someone jumped up and moved the meeting be adjourned. The motion passed, and it was all over. Ritter immediately dispatched his resignation to the mayor, certain that if he did not quit he would be removed.[18]

The "radicals" were furious. Louis F. Post, in the next issue of his magazine, *The Public*, accused Anita of changing course in midstream "without disclosing her change of purpose to members who had yielded their plan to hers." She answered that they should not have committed her to anything without letting her know: "It seems that you were all meaning to use my intentions for your own purposes, without making me aware of it." When the dispute reached the courts, the "radicals" won and Busse was forced to reinstate them and oust those he had appointed in their places, most of whom were business executives. But by then Anita was no longer a member of the board, her term having expired in June 1908. The mayor had asked her to serve another term, but she had declined.

She had not been comfortable with the wirepulling, the cliques, and the conspiracies. She had also come to believe that "the plan of selecting citizens of however great general intelligence or special fitness in other directions, but who had no special fitness for managing schools, and investing in them the final power and the management of schools on all questions, education as well as material, is a totally wrong one." Granted that public education had to be accountable to the public, it could not be well managed, day-to-day, by the people's elected representatives. They did not know enough, were too indifferent to the quality of teaching, and too reluctant to provide the necessary money. She had experienced what came to be called participatory democracy in education, and she didn't think it worked. She said all this in a farewell letter to the mayor, in which she recommended that emphasis be placed on "the teacher for the place rather than on the place for the teacher," and urged that the people of Chicago spend more money on education—the most important work of the city government.

In 1912, Anita ran on the Republican ticket for trustee of the University of Illinois and was defeated, after which, following her father's footsteps, she gave up any further thought of holding public office.

127

IV

PHILANTHROPY AND THE FAMILY

IV

During the Board of Education battle, Anita had tried to see her way "step-by-step, through an intricate and difficult situation," but her critics charged that she had dropped the banner of reform, and the accusation of betrayal hurt. Only because you have "abnormal standards of perfection and a conscience," Henry Favill told her, and both are "liabilities, not assets." Another way of putting it would be that she lacked the zest for maneuver and manipulation. In battle, survival may require the deceptive feint, action quickly taken without pause for full consideration of all the possible consequences. That was the tactic she wouldn't adopt, however, and henceforth her "politics," such as they were, would be played not in the backrooms but in the parlor, where candor, sincere intent, and the inspiring word must suffice. It was not that she failed to appreciate the necessity for compromise; of course, varieties of viewpoint and inclination have to be accepted; peace depends upon reconciling differences. Yet her heart was with the poet, not with the experts in the uses of power. She could contribute little to any discussion of the art of the possible; hers was the politics of frankness and full disclosure, however improbable the victory.

When Stanley later became the object of prolonged analysis, in the course of which his sister was interviewed, the doctors would comment on Anita's "wonderful versatility," her "fineness of ethical perception," her "utter self-abnegation." But because of these qualities, she "dallied inordinately with the relatively unimportant, and progressed slowly, painfully, and often with digressions from the practical goal."[1] Rightness for her had to be rooted in the intuition which gave rise to it, which could be annoying when there was urgent business to transact. But at least the hesitations were not based on any unwillingness to risk disapproval. "Don't be afraid of anything at all," she had advised a young cousin, "no matter how it hurts, or how the world whirls around; all the stormy things that rattle around you only hurt the person they come from." Missy's counsel had been, "Stand where you can reach out the helping hand," and she had done so, usually giving the benefit of the doubt to the person aided. Having hired two men to prepare her Adirondacks camp for the summer and do the chores, and then having to cancel her plans because of an outbreak of scarlet fever in the area, she paid the workmen four months' wages, not wanting them to "lose through my not being able to keep the engagement." When the Brooklyn Bureau of Charities helped her locate a former servant and sent no bill, she wrote that while she appreciated that the bureau's aim was to serve the community, she felt that "the time spent for a resident of another state would not fall within that," and that "I must pay for the time spent for me." If she was late in honoring a financial pledge, as was often the case, she added interest for the period of her delinquency. An overdue check to the University of Chicago would be followed by a second check covering interest, and a note saying that she was "not trying to make the University a paltry present" but would rather be "very exact about the accounting of the thing I undertook to do for it."

She was equally scrupulous about financial dealings with relatives. Along with an "enormous check" to Margaret Blaine Damrosch went an extra amount to pay for a safe deposit box; "a cunning touch," Margaret thought, "and so like you." The suggestion of Cyrus and Harold that Anita be reimbursed $8,049.97 which she had spent on Virginia's care was appreciated; she thanked them for "the thought of saving this expense from me" but she could not accept it, for the "amount is lacking receipts and accounting representation in the funds of her estate at a time when I was financially responsible for these expenditures." On another occasion, when an architect she had employed to landscape Virginia's property took time to draw Virginia into the project, Anita reminded him that "the most important work that you have ever done for my sister has never had any account rendered nor payment made. I know that this will be difficult for you to estimate, and I well remember your

132

word that you prefer not to make any charge for it at all. But you will remember my answering word that we cannot think of consenting to your spending your time for her without letting her have her rightful part of making a payment for it. This does not change our knowledge of your feelings in doing it for her in the least degree. No payment could stand over against that. But you can see that we could not have your taking of your office time without charging us for it."

Perspective depends on vantage point; falling leaves look different to the strolling beholder than to a street sweeper. Viewed from a cynic's angle, it could be said that Anita gave up nothing by her generosity, and that the satisfaction of helping others more than compensated for the incidental financial loss. But had the cynic been in her position, would he have done the same? She gave to panhandlers and charity organizers, paid off friends' debts, set the unemployed up in business, took care of hospital bills and funerals, financed committees, underwrote publications, buildings, summer camps, conferences. And she often gave without being asked. Reading a newspaper account of a family of orphan children who had been separated by being placed in state institutions, she wrote the judge offering to keep the children together until a relative could be found who would give them a home. She came near inviting one evicted poor family with numerous children to live at 101 East Erie and was dissuaded only by a reminder that she had only one guest room, and that it would be more practical to lodge them in a hotel. Hearing of a Kentucky coal miner trapped in a cave, she sent a doctor to the site and a check to the miner's wife. Families of the hundred men killed in a mine explosion in Centralia, Illinois, were each mailed $100.

If this is what Henry Favill meant by abnormal standards of perfection, she was a perfectionist, and it mattered little to her whether or not her generosity was expected or even needed. Cousin Chauncey McCormick, a major benefactor of the arts in Chicago, complained that he was never able to spend a dime if Anita was in the party. "It bothers me," he wrote her; "just why doesn't seem clear, but it does." He was unaccustomed to someone else paying. Anita, of course, paid by putting her name on the bill, for while she was rarely without a somewhat worn purse on her arm, it held only a lace-edged handkerchief, never cash or a checkbook.

By 1900, she had already evolved a code of philanthropy under which givers had "principles and preferences of their own, which may be more or less important to them, which they will want to have respected." These she called "the giver's rights." If the "wish is deep to give to the other person," the giver should not seek to "dominate the principles and preferences of the other person." Conversely, the receiver, "if he is to accept a gift from the bottom of his heart, must believe in the quality of the other's wish to give to him. Then he must, if he receives rightly, want to give due respect to the principles or wishes of the person who is making the gift. And he should make known his own principles and preferences freely, so that all is squarely understood. This, I should call the receiver's right." If an appeal to her came through a trusted friend, it was acted upon without investigation. A young painter whom Favill had recommended was invited to 101, and then and there Anita decided the artist would do "great work," helped get her "back where she best likes to be—in the woods," and provided "enough to live on while she works up things to exhibit, sell."

Loans, as distinct from gifts, might be conditional. A small-town Illinois attorney who wanted to borrow over $30,000 with which to repay debts incurred by illegal speculation and double dealings, was turned down initially because he was "not meeting the issues on my plane but that of your own convenience. . . . The only possible reason for doing such a service—if it were financially possible—would be that it should be a real service to humanity, even if only through one life." A barrage of letters from the would-be borrower followed, promising "not to engage in such devious methods again." Anita then asked Cyrus Bentley to look into the case. After investigation, he said that lending the man money would be "whitening a sepuchre." Nevertheless, she made the loan, but only on condition that the receiver sign a pledge to "pay back the money to the people I have wronged . . . run my business with honesty . . . try during all my life to find out what mistakes led me into the wrongs I have done and what other elements would have led me away from them . . . try during all my life to throw light on what is the best way for the community to deal justly with those who have broken such laws as I have and what is the best way to help them to do over their lives and begin again." Weeks of her time and of Bentley's law firm went into this one transaction, with a man Anita never met. He was back in three years, having not repaid his debts or his loan, requesting more. She cut him off.

On another occasion, asked to finance a small motion picture theater operated by an impoverished widow, Anita insisted on the right to select the films, so that she would not be investing in objectionable entertainment. Sometimes, she required an itemized accounting of how her money was spent—never from relatives, but

134

from William Lusk, who had turned to her when his ailing daughter faced a long and expensive convalescence. Lusk pretended shock at her demand; he was "putting everything between us on a higher than the business plane," while she asked for "an account of my stewardship." He said he "valued the check far more for the sympathy and understanding and affection that I thought it expressed than for the actual money it conveyed." The accounting was nonetheless forthcoming.

Most often, bread was cast on the waters and forgotten. Her sister-in-law Harriet Blaine Beale, whose brief marriage left her with an infant son and little capital and for whom Anita set up a $100,000 trust fund, said she'd never seen "such a spirit in giving as yours, and my one wish is to be a little like you, to make my receiving like your giving if I can." Where there was that bond of mutual respect, giver and receiver felt free; in its absence, both felt constrained.

Beneficiaries who needed endless evidence of her affection made her uneasy, and although the beneficence might be continued, it was done out of duty, not devotion. Cousin Lucy McCormick Jewett, whose husband's investments had reduced his family to poverty, was forever writing that Anita was her "one blessed privilege to go to. Oh! Dearie, don't you love me anymore? Please break this silence *any* way. If I have asked too much, tell Lucy, forgive her, and I will try to hard to make no more bills. Say to me, write to me *anything*, reprimand, but love me, *say* it too, or write it *please*."

Lucy's daughter Emita, whom Anita supported, was equally importuning. Forlorn Emita had "fallen into the hands of a villain" while in France with the YWCA in the First World War and had had an abortion. When she returned to America, Anita arranged for a medical examination, instructing the doctor to determine whether the abortion had harmed the girl physically, and "of course, the deeper thing to do is to help her to make life over." Emita later married a German-American musician, whom Anita gratuitously counseled not to be bitter because of what had happened to his wife in France. Taking umbrage at the implied reprimand, the husband avenged himself by reviling Walter Damrosch (a "pink tea conductor"), upon which Anita withdrew as an adviser but not as a financial sponsor. The checks kept coming, as did the abject communications from Emita: "Your severity is *terrible* for me to bear, loving you as I do. You *know* that your life is my religion." Anita did not reply. Nor did she reply to Margaret Damrosch, who wrote in anguish about an uncashed check for $875: "I am sending another. Do, oh do cash it, I owe it, I owe you so much more in every way that I can't wonder you won't take it seriously. But *please* inscribe your name across its back. It is a debt, you know. I just take everything, so as I hold out for this 'for conscience sake,' *do cash it!*" Letter and check were filed.

The filing was a way of forgetting. If Anita had been able to make more use of wastebaskets, she would have needed fewer files and secretaries. That which the secretaries did not file was passed along for other hired help to deal with. Accountants, lawyers, and investment counselors bought and sold her stocks, purchased mortgages and property, found tenants, prepared her tax returns, and saw to it that she had the income she needed. She could have delegated less vital chores but found it difficult. She had to make sure herself that the chauffeur could handle both her electric auto and a new gasoline automobile which she bought in 1908. Only she could renew her subscription to twenty-six magazines and to the opera, order gifts from Tiffany's or toys from F. A. O. Schwartz; and no one else could choose the guests for teas and dinners, decide who was to receive Christmas cards and flowers, keep her calendar, or schedule the fittings for new clothes.

When she and Em first moved into 101, she had tried to keep track of everything and soon discovered she could not even keep up to date on the meetings she was supposed to attend. And so in the late 1890s, she had hired her first secretary at $100 a month (more than the head butler's wage) and installed her in a makeshift office in the house. Before long, it was clear that a single secretary could not stay abreast of the rising tide of paper. In 1900, she was still "trying desperately hard myself to systematize and find where the limitations come in." "My things have been in a tangle," Anita confessed to Missy two years later, "nothing lost, but everything behind. The current things seem to have no space for the old and so the pile grows."

Eventually a system was worked out. Each day's mail was put in baskets for filing; the files multiplied (after Anita's death, dollar bills, sales announcements, and a long strand of pearls were found in them); and Margaret Damrosch, whose uncashed check was a casualty of that system, was convinced that her sister-in-law loved "files and alphabetical lists with a perfectly unholy joy." A second secretary had to be employed, a third, then a fourth. By the mid-twenties, eleven secretaries were on Anita's payroll, divided between three offices, one of which occupied the entire floor of a large downtown office building. Surrounded by a sea of paper, Anita when traveling was never without a small trunk of stationery, pens, pencils, holders, dividers, clips, and erasers. And if she planned to stay more than a day or two in a hotel, a filing cabinet was installed in her room.

Nevertheless, her affairs seemed to defy every stratagem to organize them efficiently. "I am enclosing Mrs. Blaine's gas and electric bills to you," a secretary would write Em's tutor, "for you to decide whether or not Mrs. Blaine would care to be troubled with them right now. Fritz [the butler] is very much afraid the light and gas will be turned off. Fritz tells me that two or three women have been here for their pay who seem to need it very much. One, the laundress, was crying because she simply did not know what to do without it. Another thing, which you will please tell Mrs. Blaine or not, at your discretion. Someone has been using her electric cab. It was taken out on the 18th of July and the driver was arrested for fast driving. Fritz does not think the machines are well taken care of."

Her unwillingness to delegate was a continual source of friction within the family, and her skill at evading suggestions for improvement was formidable. "Past experience," an irritated Cyrus wrote, "shows that your secretaries, when inquired of, know nothing about the business and they are not permitted by you to do anything but refer the inquiry to you, and you have been quite unable to give any attention to it. Besides this, you have failed in every instance to keep your promises as to reports." That was not how they managed things at the harvester company, of which Cyrus was president.

When she did get around to paying attention, Anita gave herself completely to the subject at hand, which meant that everything else was put aside, and the put-asides left to wonder why their letters and telegrams and bills went unanswered. After all, she had plenty of assistance. She never drove her own car; she never answered the telephone or the doorbell herself; she had secretaries whose devotion overrode overdue salaries, postponed vacations, and irregular hours. There were weeks when her correspondence got hopelessly out of control. Then, for a day or two, she would shoot off dozens of letters and telegrams, clean up her desk, promise to spend an hour every morning with her stenographer. But illness or travel or meetings or entertaining, or simply the desire for solitude, would take over, and the backlog would again build up. "The main thing necessary," Cyrus Bentley advised, "is bringing order and system to bear in the arrangement of days as fully occupied as yours must be." She thereupon set up a new system. After every telephone conversation, she dictated a memo of what had been said. The memos were revised, retyped and filed. Quite properly, each bill was recomputed

137

before it was paid, in case the store had made a mistake. Letters were returned to the secretaries for retyping if the margins were slightly crooked. When a dinner party was in the offing, up-to-the-minute lists of acceptances and regrets were required, not once, but two or three times a day. After each holiday, Anita expected detailed reports on what flowers had gone to each of two hundred or more friends and relatives. Other than carrying out such direct instructions, the secretaries were permitted only to make memos of "Things to Do" and neatly to stack unanswered mail. When asked any question by an outsider, they had orders to say: "I will refer your question to Mrs. Blaine."

If the system was not foolproof, it was at least intricate. The first condensed record of a telephone conversation was classified "C" and typed on the lefthand side of a single page. After the "C" notes had been assembled and placed near Anita's breakfast tray, she summoned one of the secretaries to take down corrections and amplifications, which were entered on the righthand side of the page and labeled "D." "D" notes were then read back to her while she rechecked her recollection of the phone conversation from penciled slips she had made, until she was satisfied that everything had been recorded accurately. When one harassed secretary had the temerity to suggest that the accumulated work needed more of Mrs. Blaine's time, she was told that "I am running the work, not the work running me." But when that same chastened secretary went to the hospital for surgery (paid for by Anita), the first thing she saw as she came out of the anesthetic was "Mrs. Blaine at the foot of the bed, holding a silver goblet filled with bright, red roses." She called her secretaries "Lambie" and "Darling" and they forgot they had been rebuked.*

Out-of-town visitors had similar experiences. Invited to come to Chicago for a conference with Mrs. Blaine, they were put up at the Drake Hotel, where they languished until she either was ready to see them or decided that she didn't have time. It frequently took heroic measures to get through to her. As Louis Slade put it, she "generally replied to the *second* telegram." "I wish life were not quite so exacting with you," Cyrus Bentley said sorrowfully, but he recognized that "radical changes are hardly possible any longer."

* A "vivid memory" of one secretary, Anne De Mooy, was of Anita, after hours of work in the study, walking out in the hall with her, "arm in arm (me with papers, briefcase, etc.)—and while I went down the stairway, she would remain at the balustrade upstairs—just as I reached the door, she softly called and wafted a kiss of goodnight."

An excess of scruple lay at the bottom of much of this procrastination. Anita felt on trial; she was both defendant and judge, cross-examining herself, questioning her motives, her sincerity. In her journal, she reproached herself for thinking too often of her "doubts and questionings and entire dissatisfaction about myself in every way," for letting prejudices [and] self will or pride" obscure the deeper knowledge that no truth is final and that "life is too big for us to understand." Hours that might have been spent on the business of the moment instead were given to lonely introspection.

She was constantly on guard against egoism. She would not authorize a picture of herself to be put in any newspaper, magazine, or yearbook. Asked to serve as honorary vice-president of an International Congress on Art Teaching in Schools and told she would be described as "Philanthropist and Patron of Art," she accepted the post but refused the description. She would not supply autobiographical information for a book on women in American history, because she did not see "that anything I have done warrants the assumption that I should be there." Having heard that a street near the Parker School would be named "Anita Terrace," she wrote the proposer that she did not "claim a monopoly of that name, and you probably do not know that I possess it at all. But if it were easy and possible, I think I could suggest to you many better names for the street." She declined to use her influence to get anyone a job in the harvester company.

In her treatment of servants, she was fickle—considerate one moment (she once sent all her help in cabs to hear Walter Damrosch conduct his own opera), severe the next. She threatened to dismiss a butler who had long been in her service because he had not left the dirty dinner dishes in the kitchen and come to the living room as requested, to hear a guest sing. When a $38 charge for his hospital care was mailed to her, she summoned the butler to the library and asked if he had instructed the hospital to charge her; when he replied meekly that he had not, she handed him the bill to be paid out of his $35 a month salary. The same dutiful butler, given a $5 tip by Nettie for having escorted her across the street, handed the money to Anita, who kept it. He knew she did not approve of her employees taking tips.

She might be dilatory, but she expected prompt results from her servants. Seemingly insuperable obstacles to achievement were no excuse for failure or delay. The day before she was to give a luncheon for ten, she rang for the butler, informed him that she had some yarn spun by Mahatma Gandhi, and instructed him to find ten silver boxes, each no larger than a thimble, in which the yarn could be placed so that her guests could be given a souvenir. He had twenty-four hours to produce the boxes. Off he went. Spaulding's jewelry store would take two weeks to make them, he reported, and Marshall Fields the same. "Try again in the morning," she said. After an early breakfast, the butler returned to Marshall Fields, found a floor walker who had not been at the store the preceding day, and explained the problem. "It's a hard one," the floor walker admitted. The two of them went to the silver shop on the ninth floor, consulted the manager, who in turn summoned the silversmiths. They all went to work, the butler waited, by eleven-thirty the work was done; he was handed the ten boxes, flew home, and gave them to Mrs. Blaine. "If at first you don't succeed try again," was all she said. "Mrs. Blaine did not like to take no for an answer," the butler later remarked.

It was different if the servants were not in her employ. Dining one evening at the Blackstone Hotel with a large party of guests, Anita was informed by an embarrassed waiter that she could not charge the bill because her account was overdue. The following day, she sent the waiter a personal note to say how distressed she was "to have been the occasion of such a trying thing as it must have been to you to tell me that a charge could not be allowed. Please accept my apologies for placing you in such a difficult circumstance."

She had too little vanity to mind apologizing and too much relish in the comic not to enjoy mishaps that were her own fault. One such mishap, involving her effort to reach Professor Irving Fisher of Yale, an economist she thought might be attending an American Medical Association meeting in Chicago, she described at length in a letter to Em. Mr. Fisher had been located at the Sherman Hotel by a secretary, and, hearing "a very nice firm voice over the telephone at the other end," Anita had asked,

"Is this Mr. Irving Fisher?"

"Yes."

"You don't know me, Mr. Fisher, nor anything about me, but I want to ask you about some work you no doubt would be interested to give advice about."

They discussed an appointment. That afternoon? No. Later? Sorry, but he had a long evening. The next morning? Yes, and please not until half-past ten or so. She sent her car for him.

"At the University of Chicago," Anita related, "they taboo the title of Professor and make a great point of being just Mister, so when they sent up his name, I thought, they like it at Yale, too.

When he came in, I had a violent shock. He was so young. My first thought was, 'it can't be he.' But he had said himself he was Irving Fisher, and after all, many people look young and are old, or he may have been an infant prodigy. So I forged ahead and tried to get the right end of preventive medicine to get him started on, when suddenly he broke in with, 'I don't think I am the man you want to see,' and I, 'well, will you kindly tell me who you are! Aren't you Mr. Irving Fisher of Yale?' 'No, I am Irving Fisher of the George M. Cohen musical company.' "

Em could imagine the sequel: "We both nearly collapsed with amusement. I told him about our plan [for a preventive medicine foundation] and got his advice in earnest and good advice it was, too, and I am going to his show, when he is to give me the best seat in the house." Two seats, one to sit in and one for her wraps.

Cyrus McCormick's decision in 1848 to locate in Chicago had been shrewd. There were fortunes to be made by speculators in real estate or in pork futures, and in the eighties and nineties the lowliest clerk or teamster with an extra dollar to invest could dream of riding with the rich. The city streets might be poorly lit, the slums a breeding ground for epidemics of cholera or typhoid, the city council run by crooks in the pay of streetcar and utility magnates, the state legislature dominated by other crooks who served the big packers and the railroads, but the people said "Let 'er rip." Civic virtue was a subject for satire. "Any man that wuud expect to thrain lobsthers to fly is called a lunatic," Mr. Dooley said of Chicago politics, "but a man that thinks we can be turned into angels by an iliction is called a rayformer and remains at large."[2]

During the depression of 1897, Anita had been absorbed by the education of her son and was slow to notice that hotels and restaurants were closing and department stores nearly empty, and that hundreds were sleeping on the floors of police stations or in empty cars standing on railway sidings. Had she moved in the circle of activist women of her class, such as Louise DeKoven Bowen and Mary Rozet Smith, she would have been more aware of what Henry George, in *Progress and Poverty*, and what the "rayformers" were saying. From countless platforms the socialist leader Eugene Debs was castigating capitalism for "slums, dives, bloated men, bedraggled women . . . babies cradled in rags and filth, aged children,

141

than which nothing could be more melancholy." Even Chicago's mayor, Carter Harrison, had started talking like a radical, berating the aldermen as "a motley crew . . . saloonkeepers, proprietors of gambling houses, undertakers . . . a low-browed, dull-witted, base-minded gang of plug-uglies, with no outstanding characteristics beyond an unquenchable lust for money, with a single virtue, and that not possessed by all, a certain physical courage that enabled each to dominate his individual barnyard."[3]

Young writers in the late nineties were exposing the underside of the city. An Irish immigrant, Francis Hackett, would describe how Chicago had rushed at him on his arrival "like a clanging brigade vomited from a fire house," how he was overpowered by the "dark huddle of the streets, the infamous congestion and the dirt."[4] Having seen Chicago, Rudyard Kipling told the press, "I urgently desire never to see it again; it is inhabited by savages."[5]

To the McCormicks, however, the city was a silvery slice of comfort, curving along the lake on the Near North Side and inhabited by the families of men who had fought free of the herd, quite unlike the brawling frontier town Anita's mother had visited thirty-five years before. Its energetic population had multiplied tenfold, the city limits had gradually surrounded and then incorporated adjacent villages, tall buildings now blocked out the sun, though wooden sidewalks still jumped crazily from level to level, thoroughfares were seas of mud in spring and fall and deserts of blowing dust in summer, the river stank of sewage and packing house waste, and dark streets echoed the ceaseless din of horse-drawn trolleys and delivery wagons which rattled past garish billboards announcing vaudeville shows and free lunches. But the conviction that prosperity was around the next corner hurried Chicagoans along, heedless of the noise and grime. It was an exhuberant town, to be rated by Lincoln Steffens as "first in violence, deepest in dirt; loud, lawless, unlovely, ill-smelling, irreverent, new; an overgrown gawk of a village, the 'tough' among cities, a spectacle for the nation."[6] But then, Steffens was a "muckracker," and an outsider to boot. Chicagoans, at least the more privileged and civic-minded among them, saw themselves in a more flattering light. "No sooner does one sniff the air of Chicago," one of them wrote, "than life becomes a turmoil of duty, every waking hour of which is burdened by some obligation."[7]

The "good government" element may have thought itself consequential; it belonged to the best clubs and dominated philanthropy and culture. But as historian Richard Hofstadter was to observe long after in his study of the period, it was "checked, hampered, and overridden by the agents of the new corporations, the corrupters of legislature, the buyers of franchises, the allies of the political bosses." In this uneven struggle, the "best people" were handicapped by "the regard for reputation, their social standing itself."[8] They could finance studies, prod the authorities, express moral outrage, but ward bosses like "Hinky Dink" and "Bathhouse John" had voices that carried further and their soup kitchens were bigger and better than the authorities'. Anita could write the mayor in 1903, having read in the *Tribune* of a heartless tenement ordinance passed by the council, that she must "storm your door to ask at headquarters if nothing can be done"; but nothing was done. Entreaties by the civic-minded made so little difference that even respectable folk wondered whether the populist governor of Illinois, John Peter Altgeld, was right after all in saying that "the very rich of our country are supported by dollars that are tainted by injustice." Yet if that was true, could the rich be taken seriously as reformers? And was reform itself enough, or might society require more fundamental reorganization?

In her journal, Anita recorded her dream of lying in a hammock on a "delicious summer afternoon with a magazine, browsing over many interesting thoughts from many minds on many subjects," and in the dream the question suddenly came to her: "Why should I be able to spend this afternoon this way, or as many as I please, in touch with any thought I please from all over the world? Not by an achievement of my own. Why should I therefore have the privilege of doing and having whatever I please, while so many who could do more than I, could make use of it?" She seemed to see "far ahead, coming just as surely as day follows night, a great time of organization of the human race. By that organization waste would be largely eliminated so that the production of the earth would be saved for all and by economy of human arrangement, greatly increased. By organization, all would have their place in the work of the world. All would give their work to the world, a certain proportion." And then anyone so inclined, not just Anita McCormick Blaine, could lie in a hammock on a lazy summer afternoon and read a book. On awakening, she would then pencil a note on a scrap of paper to say, "How I hate myself for talking of socialism and equality as against social distinction when I know so little about it . . . when I know so little what people have done, and when I know so little how to rate what they have done—and when I don't *first* do the first human thing before all else, sympathize with or at least see them sympathetically as they are."

143

On every side, Midwestern intellectuals and artists were rebelling against "the system," against selfish acquisition and mercantile dominance. Theodore Dreiser's *Sister Carrie*, published in 1899, was one of many realistic novels dramatizing the crushing power of that "giant magnet, Chicago." In his *Memoirs of an American Citizen* Robert Herrick was arguing that financial success came in direct proportion to a lack of ethical perception, and in *The Cliff Dwellers* and *With the Procession* novelist Henry B. Fuller was crusading for "a more sensitive and compassionate way of life." Frank Norris in *The Pit* ridiculed his central character for believing that "business principles are as good in religion as they are in LaSalle Street." The young, wealthy Chicagoan in Arthur J. Eddy's *Ganton and Company* loathed his family's meat business for its vulgarity.

In a journal entry, Anita commented that America seemed to be a "hobbling, blundering, heterogeneous, partly groping—and largely *not* groping, but blind and self-satisfied civilization." She perceived its baleful effect on her brother Stanley, who "suddenly stood arraigned before himself. He felt himself to be a partner in an enterprise that set forth assurance of certain fundamental rights to all, but which was in a dire situation not faced in its essence—a situation of chaos, whose methods were based on carelessness, whose intentions were deliberate discrimination. He saw with opened eyes, how, even in our best impulses of generosity, in their outcome of partial provision for some, we blind ourselves to the real needs of all, and comforting our hearts with stopgaps of charity, are lulled by their beauty, to forget the strong demands of justice and right and national honor."[9] Surely men would someday "revolt at the senseless inequality of the wealth-holding power of individuals, keeping only rightful and earned inequality of holding power—so that with proper safeguards of what affection should be allowed to do for its own, all individuals born will come into a common heritage of opportunity and of care."

She could imagine a "state of affairs where all paid of their own rightly earned product, in full and just proportion, into a treasury so filled to cover all of the common benefits needed by the community, to be disbursed by responsible agents for the public good." But for that ideal to be realized, each citizen would have to feel "by right that the business of the community was his own." She carried this vision no further and had no presentiment of the decline in personal responsibility which would accompany the rise of the welfare state, or of the impersonality of the bureaucracy (those "agents for the public good") which would mark the growth of governmental paternalism.

She did, however, to the consternation of Cyrus Bentley, begin raising awkward questions about her taxes. Was it right to have so much and share so little? Didn't she owe the government more than she was paying it? Behind her doubts lay a growing skepticism of private philanthropy, which diverted attention from the "processes that produced the surpluses" and made "the basic human needs of many people dependent solely on the will and whim of a small group of other people." Philanthropy, she concluded, was not a "good substitute for the adequate, complete, perfect filling of all community needs by the community as a whole, from the resources held by the community as a whole, which would belong to the community as a whole."[10] "When the race awakes to true individuality from class dreaming," she wrote in her journal, "I should like to be there."

She resolved the personal dilemma of her inherited wealth, not by divesting herself of it, but by accepting its benefits as a trust. "By circumstances over which you have no control," she wrote Em when he came into his inheritance, "there comes to you property accumulated by the efforts of those who belong to you and to whom you belong." Property was a privilege and an opportunity "no different from the opportunity you would have if you had accumulated the property yourself, but coming as it does, it frees you from the necessity of subordinating any good plans to the need for bread. It gives you the opportunity at once of letting free every incentive. The only rightful reason for holding property . . . is to do with that property for the greatest possible benefit to the race that created it, allotting to yourself and to your own in the process all satisfaction that seems to you rightful."

Such generalizations about social responsibility gave no offense; indeed many thought them admirable. But when Anita acted on her principles as a taxpayer, she sent tremors throughout the business community.

Cyrus Bentley first learned of what she had done when he picked up a newspaper one morning and read that Mrs. Emmons Blaine had scheduled her personal property at the office of the assessor in the amount of $1,005,063. It was the largest such individual listing ever filed in Chicago, and she had done it without consulting him. She told the assessor that "those able to pay the taxes should pay them"; that she had made "a very carefully prepared estimate" of her personal property holdings and had "endeavored to comply strictly with the spirit as well as the letter of the law."[11] Nettie thereupon followed her daughter's example, turning in a schedule of her own property worth of over a million dollars.

Backed by Anita's brother Cyrus, Bentley took up arms. By revealing the sources of her income, he told Anita, she had in effect forced every other major stockholder in the reaper company to do likewise, and since many of those stockholders believed that the tax law was *not* equitable—not to them—and that taxes on wealth should be fought rather than slavishly accepted, she had put them all in a highly uncomfortable position. That was regrettable, she replied; it had not been her intention to embarrass anyone. She was gratified* when Governor Theodore Roosevelt of New York, interviewed in Milwaukee, said that he wished "we had more people in this country like Mrs. Emmons Blaine; this country would need have no fear in this matter if all were like her."[12]

The controversy over her property taxes burned itself out, only to flare up again in 1906 in the press when the Square Deal Tax League brought forward evidence that International Harvester stockholders were annually bilking the county of taxes on $150 million worth of property. Paradoxically, in this instance Anita came to the company's defense, drafting a letter which on the surface appeared to repudiate her earlier act. The question of taxation in Chicago was confused, she wrote, and "the effect of the confusion is so universal that no one, by assuming that the taxation status is right and acting up to its present provision in literalness, would be doing more than jumping frantically into the situation and perhaps adding greater confusion, and a certain injustice, instead of contributing toward the real solution of a real injustice." While each taxpayer should pay his fair share, she said, it would do no good if only a few did as she had done. The statement was not all Bentley or Cyrus wanted, but it sufficed; family solidarity was restored.

Six years earlier Anita's name had appeared in the newspapers, this time on the front pages, and for weeks some radical ideas about household help which she reportedly espoused had been publicly praised and condemned, to the consternation of most of her family.

The background of the story was this. Anita at the time employed in her household two men and three women at salaries ranging from

* Gratified but not captivated. She never supported Theodore Roosevelt politically, and in a later letter to her son referred to his speeches as "bunco." She was happy with his defeat in 1908, after his "big stick and big talk."

$29 to $65 a month, one secretary at $100 a month, a part-time laundress at $1.50 a day, and several temporary odd-job servants. Each was paid neither more nor less than the average wage, though there were fringe benefits. If they were too old to work, they were pensioned; former retainers were lent money to start out on their own; all her employees and their families were provided with medical care, one tubercular secretary being supported for years in a sanatorium. None of this called for special comment. What had been found newsworthy was Anita's decision to reorganize her staff on labor union principles. "Her servants work but eight hours a day," the *Chicago Post* reported, "a system having been adopted which divides their duties into 'watches,' or 'shifts.' The innovation applied to cooks, maids, butlers, laundresses, coachmen and all the others belonging to Mrs. Blaine's establishment. Those whose duties begin at six o'clock in the morning are relieved at two o'clock in the afternoon by a force that stays on watch until ten o'clock at night. The system was introduced about ten days ago and is said to have proved highly successful."[13]

Anita could not imagine why the papers found this so interesting, but if they were going to publicize it, why didn't they get it straight? True, she had told inquiring reporters that "the relation of capital to labor in the case of domestic help, being one of power to exact conditions, it behooves capital to give consideration to the subject of conditions." But the "unauthorized and inaccurate" stories they wrote were so twisted, it would be "a hopeless task to attempt their unravelling."[14] Nevertheless, she tried to explain what she had done, and her explanation simply set off a new round of press comment. The *Baltimore American* addressed an unflattering open letter to her; the *Baltimore Sun* called her a socialist (a year earlier the same charge had been made because of her sympathy for striking tailors in Chicago); the *Chicago Times-Herald* reported that other wealthy women feared that "such a concession would bring servants to the belief that they could get everything they wanted." The kinder critics dismissed her as an "idealist." It was all well and good for a McCormick, one editorialist remarked, but what about the middle class? She was bombarded with letters and cuttings. "So many people ask me about it," Harriet Blaine Beale wrote, "and I am weary with assuring them that your home is run very much like any other, and *not* with relays of sleeping car porters replacing each other." Still, there were relays. For a woman of her means, Anita could be said to live simply, at least not ostentatiously, but she did want round-the-clock service, and if an eleven o'clock supper was to be provided for her evening guests, someone must be there to prepare and serve it.

If the principle of a more balanced relationship between employer and employee was right, it was right for the harvester company as well as for households, and she was a principal stockholder in the company. Thus, when Stanley began a campaign in 1902 for a profit-sharing plan to include all Harvester workers, she was the only member of the family strongly to support him. Cyrus was not against it *if* the plan strengthened the loyalty of the executives and would help to avert unionization. What he could not accept was participation by all the workers. Over his objection and after months of family discussion and the threat of a strike, Anita and Stanley won their point. Profit-sharing was introduced, and all employees with at least five years' service—except for one trouble-making union activist—were to share in the benefits.

A decade later, when a commission of the New York state legislature, headed by Democratic state senator Robert F. Wagner, revealed that women were working all night in unsanitary conditions at a Harvester twine mill in Auburn, pulling loads weighing up to a hundred and fifty pounds, Anita again intervened in a dispute over company policy. With the report of the legislative commission fresh in the public mind, she accompanied Nettie, Jane Addams, and Miss Addams's good friend Louise DeKoven Bowen, who was also a prominent Harvester stockholder, to Cyrus's office. It was not a surprise visit, he was prepared for them, and the ladies left satisfied that he would do all he could to improve the conditions of women's work. Before long, men had replaced women on night shifts in both the Auburn and the Chicago twine mills, and $50,000 had been appropriated by the company for dust-removal equipment.

Within the year, however, the company was embroiled in another controversy, when it was faced by a strike at the same Auburn mill, and Cyrus, rather than raise wages, recommended that the plant be dismantled and moved to Germany. This time, it was Nettie who stepped in, telling her son that "wisdom bids us walk more circumspectly." The decision to dismantle was reversed, to Anita's considerable relief. The memory of the Haymarket murders in 1886 was still vivid. Concession and cooperation were preferable to confrontation, and the prospect of violence was repugnant. When two men were arrested on the charge of dynamiting the *Los Angeles Times* building in 1910, Anita had at first been sympathetic to the defendants, doubting their guilt, and was gratified that Chicago's Clarence Darrow had been retained to defend them. But when they admitted planting the dynamite and said that the act had been one step in a three-year program of terrorism, she lost all interest in them. Murder was unjustified, whatever the provocation.* And so, she thought, was the *Times*'s refusal to recognize the right of labor to organize.

Greed for profit and greed for power "must be damned alike." As she had said to Cyrus when he balked at meeting with union leaders, sensible men learn to accommodate, however deep or just the grievances on either side. She liked what she heard at the City Club in 1912, when labor leaders spoke "straight from the shoulder" to Chicago's elite on what their union stood for and of the kinds of employers they were up against—"the man who came with superabundance of culture gotten out of books to patronize them, having none; the man who wanted their help to plant shrubs and sidewalks but opposed them in legislatures when they were fighting for life conditions; the man who would buy their leaders, thinking to settle them and their struggles with a check." If only such frank interchange were more widespread and "lead to getting together on lines that are common," she wrote Em.

Why was it, one wonders, that so advanced and public-spirited a woman was not in the front ranks of the suffragettes, or at least on the sidelines waving a check? By Anita's early forties, ladies from good families, including cousin Carrie, were marching in the streets demanding their right to vote. Like Carrie, Anita frowned on female passivity, but she blamed it on women themselves, not on laws or men. The cramping restrictions of her own upbringing—the assumption, for example, that higher education was the prerogative of men—were not connected in her mind with any built-in, institutional deprivations imposed solely because of one's sex. As an adult, moreover, *she* had not been patronized and had encountered few "keep out" signs. Then there was the matter of style. The Pankhurst sisters in England seemed to her ludicrous and the feminist disruption of the 1913 Inaugural parade in Washington vainglorious. Imagine, she wrote Em, "their prancing in just ahead of the Inauguration to get the wind of our greatest, most dignified national ceremony for their sails." Women were certainly entitled to make their

* This applied equally to execution by the state. She signed a petition in 1912 against capital punishment—"Sorry I did, for I knew too little about it. But . . . it may though start a real effort against capital punishment . . . and that would be good."

149

opinions felt, but not by "breaking furniture." Yet she allowed Jane Addams to persuade her to host a suffrage meeting at 101 East Erie, because "one morning must be given, plus hospitality, to the cause." Unexpectedly, she was impressed by what she heard and saw that morning. The ladies present were rather like herself, not a bit "faddy," and "one nice thing about it was that there were no men. Dragging a lot of men along as escorts to the would-be voting ladies never did appeal to me." Nor did female chauvinism.*

It was the experience of registering to vote in 1914, the Illinois legislature having the previous year passed a bill giving women the right to cast ballots for state offices, which carried her the rest of the way. "Well," she wrote her son, "though I went in as casual-like as you please, I can tell you it was a sensation—a sensation of the real thing. The simple thing of walking in and registering myself as prepared to vote on things gave me more feeling of how unreal it is not to, than yards of argument. Opening the door, I saw some several gentlemen stretched out in barber's chairs. I thought at first I must be mistaken. But not at all. I found a table with political looking men sitting around it quite ready to ask me questions. The first was my residence, whereupon they informed me I was in the wrong place. I took me off to East Ontario Street, where I found a large white sign pointing me to the basement of a house. I went down, encouraged by seeing another woman ahead of me. Here I found quite a clean room, a stove, a table and three men writing and one bossing the job. I again politely—I had all my manners with me— waited for the lady who came ahead of me. She was being interrogated as to residence, birthplace, years in the city, county, and then her age. She said 72. I felt myself give a jump of surprise and wondered if my reckoning was correct, for if she was 72 I was at least ninety. The officials were very polite and wrote it down with increased respect, and one of them murmured, 72, whereupon she— 'oh, I meant I was born in 1872!' When she got straightened out and dismissed, I raised my right hand and swore and had my set of questions fired at me and in a minute found myself out on the street again a voter, which is more of a sensation than you will ever have out of it. For when you have just naturally known that you will do it in the course of time, it must be one thing. But quite another to have looked on at it all your life from outside, as it were, and never to have expected to do it, and then to find it very suddenly thrust into your

* "There isn't anything versus marriage," Anita wrote her young cousin, Kyle Adams, "when you know the man whom you want to give your life to. And that's all there is to it."

hand—it has quite a feeling." From now on, men and women must work together as equals, for "the longer the separation is maintained, the more emphasized it becomes."

There were so many separations! If she could just "*see* right" and perhaps "light the way for others to see by living, talking, or writing," perhaps they could be bridged, "though we be not here when it comes." She no longer expected much leadership from the church in the many tasks of reconciliation. Preachers talked of sin and urged their flocks to shun worldly lusts and to live soberly in this evil world; Anita's father had founded a seminary to propagate that gospel, and her mother was financing missions to spread it. But the religious doctrines and institutions of her childhood had come to seem cold and oppressive; after Nettie's death, Anita would refuse to join the other members of her family in endowing the McCormick Seminary. "I wish that I could spare you this," she would write the head of the seminary, "and I can only pray that down below the facts of the moment, there may be for you too, as there is for me, a deep peace." When a member of the seminary faculty remonstrated with her, telling her she owed something to the memory of her parents whether or not she accepted Presbyterianism, she replied that her duty was to God and that she did not feel "that my obligation to Him could conflict with my obligations to my Father and Mother, because they, being now nearer to Him, would know and see and be helping me to fulfill my obligations to Him as I can find them." The distressing part of having to refuse, she telegraphed Cyrus "is that I love you and I want to be with you. But then comes the wonderful part —to be with each other, as we do, each as he sees and is led. I come to feel that there is no togetherness so great as that." Anita had felt obliged to explain at length her reasons for not participating: the seminary "would still be training ministers to do those things or meet those questions" which were not central to the religious experience. Seminarians were burdened by "a leaden insight that a soul setting out to teach of God should not be bound by or carry. . . . I had long felt a difficulty about the Presbyterian Church." Grace, Anita thought, had to be earned through "this thing we call struggle, effort, fight," and that strength was "not through swaddling clothes."

She could sympathize with her mother over "all the sorrow we bear, all our sadness over the things going wrong in the world," but she had outgrown the theology of her youth. Aware of it or not, Anita in 1901 represented what William James hailed that year as the "victory of healthy-mindedness within the church over the morbidness with which the old hell-fire theology was more harmoniously related";[15] the conflict of good and evil was "swallowed up in a higher denomination, an omnipotent excitement which engulfs the evil, and which the human being welcomes as the crowning experience of his life."* Jesus had said "the truth will make you free," and she believed that. But one ought not expect to convert another person to one's own truth, she wrote in her journal, "not to try to, not to want to, not to go through life with that as the goal to which others must be brought, for therein you may make a great mistake, and as your idea changes you may discover it. If that is even your *inward* desire, differences in life will be uncomfortable. If it is not, they may be helpful." Each person had "a divine right to every shade of his own," and each was destined to change: "The sun sets and the day seems ended, but it rises again and another day begins. And so we may go from one step to another."

To meet Anita Blaine was to be carried away by a compelling grace and goodness. Barriers fell, communication was instantaneous. She listened eagerly, interrupting to say, "Oh, *hold* that thought!" This was more than courtesy; the attentiveness and sympathy sprang from a deeper source. The stranger, having heard only of the public personage, was unprepared for the woman. Perhaps he had been told that she was a benefactor of the Consumers League, active in the Chicago Playground Association, head of a kindergarten committee set up by Jane Addams, trustee of a new school of civics and philanthropy, member of a committee to prevent tuberculosis, partisan of a federal bill to prevent food and drink adulteration, even a lobbyist, for Anita had gone with Miss Addams to Springfield for her "first dip into that begrafted atmosphere." The stranger might have known that her name appeared on letters to legislators urging a law requiring professional training of workers in state charitable and correctional institutions, a law to create a national children's bureau and another to conserve the sand dunes at the lower end of Lake Michigan. He might have heard of her gifts—to the Municipal Voters League, United Charities, Hull House, the Women's Trade

* James's further comment is pertinent to Anita's attitude: "The idea of a universal evolution lends itself to a doctrine of general meliorism and progress which fits the religious needs of the healthy-minded so well that it seems as if it might have been created for their use."

Union League, and summer relief for workers in the city. (To Miss Addams, she had expressed "the earnest hope that your group of department store heads will see fit to incorporate in their arrangements, as a regular provision, the half holiday on Saturday through the months of July and August.") What the stranger probably would not have known was the intensity of Anita's inner life, the night hours of meditation, the exacting self-scrutiny recorded in diaries and journals. Nor could he be aware that her most time-consuming commitment was not to the public but to her family.

Em's health had stabilized in his teens, as Dr. Favill had predicted; it was Nettie, now seventy and totally deaf, who had become the problem, who still thought that her children, the youngest of whom was over thirty, had to be instructed on the application of a poultice when they sneezed. It was she who had to be watched over and steered away from tasks that were too taxing. A determined woman who is used to the driver's seat is not easily steered, however. When Nettie in 1905 took it upon herself to supervise the renovation of one of Virginia's houses, Anita had to write the architect, in confidence, that he was not to consider "any word in this work, of any sort, as authoritative direction except mine." "What a blessing honest open candid difference is," Anita had written Missy in 1898, and how she would have given "all the worlds I could possess" for a true meeting of minds with her mother.

The care of Virginia had been in dispute since the 1890s, Nettie veering from one treatment to another. Against Anita's advice, she had ordered the doctors to send the sick girl to Chicago. Back home, Virginia wandered aimlessly from one relative to another, arriving distraught one night at Anita's at eleven o'clock. It took four hours to calm her down, and Anita, unnerved, went to Cyrus to ask whether he and she should not now take full responsibility for their sister, and do it firmly. The situation had become "ominous." She toyed with the idea of making a secret pact with Virginia's head nurse to send Nettie only pleasant reports, but gave it up. Missy had counseled against it: "The care of Virginia is a consolation to your mother. . . . Better not abridge it. . . . Just stand under to help bear, and decide without seeming to do so."

Then a scandal threatened to erupt which made it all the more urgent to circumvent her mother. One of the nurses alleged that Virginia's doctor was an alcoholic and an opium addict, and Anita and Cyrus quietly dispatched the always available Missy to California to investigate. Innocent of drugs and addicts, Missy reported that everything seemed normal, but when Cyrus and Anita themselves confronted the doctor, she tearfully admitted taking a small daily dose of opium. Although they tried to keep this from their mother, Nettie somehow got wind of the story and was "in that state of mind," Anita said after one fruitless conference, "where she grasped anything you said of the doubtful, and what you said of the household's being quieter, Sissy happier, etc. went almost unnoticed." During a brief stay with Harold and his wife at their summer home that year, Nettie had carried on day and night. "This constant unrest," she would sob, "Oh! If only I could be at peace!" She would suddenly leave a room, exclaiming that her heart was skipping; she prayed aloud until she cried herself to sleep in the early hours of the morning. It was too much for Harold. Virginia's doctor was "a constant menace to Mama's welfare, mental and physical," he told Anita; she would have to go. And so the doctor who had made the patient reasonably content during fifteen years of illness was dismissed, and Anita could reassure her "dearest and preciousest of all Mothers" that all cause for worry had been removed.

Nettie was not that easily consoled. She complained that no one minded what she thought, no one asked her opinion, no one wanted her. And then Anita would embrace her and ask how she could say she felt "like a ship on a wave, when you have a haven and a nook in so many corners of the world, where you belong and where you are longed for. My Honey, I should think that the feeling would rather be that you are torn in pieces, rent in twain, by being wanted!" Meanwhile, Anita and Cyrus were taking steps to assure that their mother did nothing to further upset Virginia's precarious equilibrium.

With the hiring of Grace Walker, a former teacher and dietician, as Virginia's keeper and companion, their problem was solved. At last, someone qualified was in charge, and someone who understood that although there were four trustees legally responsible for Virginia's welfare—Nettie, Cyrus, Harold, and Anita—Anita was the first among equals. When an escorted visit to Chicago by Virginia was contemplated, it was Anita who informed Miss Walker of exactly what to expect. No schedule devised by a protocol officer for a visiting head of state could have been more precise, more painstakingly mapped out than Anita's schedules for her sister's reception. Each detail was checked and double-checked and telegraphed to Miss Walker in advance: dinner at ten minutes to seven with immediate family present, Virginia's portrait by Cabanel in its usual place on the wall, the elevator in use with someone to run it, doors to the basement fastened, the front door unlocked but ready to be locked during the meal, a car available at all hours, three nurses in attendance.

The sheltering of Virginia was total. With Anita's backing, Miss Walker was to serve for forty years as buffer and screen, absorbing the shock of ill-advised meddling and filtering out the unpleasantness in reports sent to Rush Street.

Stanley's deterioration presented more agonizing problems. Although Anita and Cyrus had agreed that no questions "of any sort whatever" were to be brought to Nettie by anyone without their permission, the deepening psychosis was too obvious by 1906 to be concealed. The knowledge of it brought Nettie to the verge of a nervous breakdown.

Withdrawn as a child, Stanley may have resented Harold's athletic prowess and social poise, but when the two brothers entered Princeton in 1891, Stanley seemed to have come into his own. A popular member of the Mandolin and Guitar Club, it was he, indifferent to the shadings of social status, who got the first invitations to the best clubs. Tall, slender, clean-cut, grave, he graduated cum laude and was carried off on his classmates' shoulders after a rowsing commencement speech. An upstanding, fine-looking fellow, his friends thought, though perhaps a bit reserved.

That was the outward appearance. The inner reality, as Anita was to recall, was that Stanley always seemed to be "holding himself, too much, under all provocations, to the finest point of gentleness and patience and forebearance"; he "never laid down the law for himself." Having been taught not to reveal his body to anyone, he associated sex with a wracking conviction of his depravity, and in college he had begun to masturbate. Feeling unutterably evil, he was far too reticent to confide even in Anita, the one person with whom he could speak openly. No one knew of the harness he had invented for his ankles and wrists, so that he could not touch himself in his sleep.

With Harold's marriage a few months following their graduation from Princeton, Stanley was the only child at home with mother, and Anita later regretted she had not "taken a strong part in getting him to do some act of breaking away"; it would have been better if he had "felt worse and been more drastic." But these were afterthoughts, the product of Anita's own hard-won independence. At the time, she had responded to Stanley's unhappiness by saying she "knew very well what he meant and felt" and had "gone through the same."*

Nettie's decision in 1895 to take her youngest son to Europe and the Middle East, where she could have him to herself, had met with no resistance within the family, ill advised as it was. In Paris, she hid his books. In Alexandria, she hounded him to elevate his taste by more religious reading. Wherever they went, she cultivated the acquaintance of Presbyterian ministers, whom she brought back to the hotel for improving talks with twenty-one-year-old Stanley. She criticized his spending more money than was necessary for dinner or for the writing of a telegram. She was barely civil to friends he met. If he planned to spend an evening with them, she tearfully begged him to be home by nine-thirty or ten. If he was late, she was awake and waiting. To win his sympathy, she lied to him that she had heart disease. He was allowed to take singing lessons because they would "widen his chest and develop his lungs," but when he pleaded to remain in France to study art and music, she hauled him off to Switzerland—just long enough to build up his health—and then insisted that he return with her to Chicago to take his place in the reaper works. He wanted to remain; she was determined to leave: Paris was unthinkable as a residence for him, the winters were too severe. When he asked "how much better is Chicago," she replied that in Chicago he would be "among his dear ones, and that is a good deal." She then consulted Cyrus and Anita long-distance on Stanley's desire to stay in Europe. "Thoroughly impracticable," Cyrus replied. Anita wrote that "it might do him good to be left on his own responsibility."

There was a brief truce in Egypt, where Stanley fell ill with what looked like typhoid. Since local doctors were not to be trusted, they returned to Paris and nights of nursing by Nettie, and when he was better, the argument was resumed. Stanley repeated that he would prefer that she return alone, and that there was "nothing which I should rather do than to pursue art here this winter." She pretended shock "that he could possibly feel *that* sentiment."[16] Finally, she

* There had been an eerie incident in the summer of 1885, which Anita reported to Stanley's psychiatrist, Dr. Kempf, in a letter of 11 July 1929. The family was vacationing on Buzzard's Bay in Massachusetts and set out in a launch for New Bedford. "At some point there was a sudden explosion. I think a steam-pipe burst. . . . Stanley had been in the direct line of the steam and hot water and . . . received the whole force of it. I remember the anguish and terrified feeling about him and in his face. . . . I only learned afterward the extent of the burns—which was very great."

gave in, but only after Stanley had agreed to take rooms at a Mrs. van Pele's, where they sang hymns on Sunday evenings.

Within a week of Mama's departure, he had been seduced (he confessed his sin to Harold, who was passing through Paris on his honeymoon), and six months later he was back in Chicago in the reaper company, where he was a fifth wheel. Cyrus was president and Harold vice-president; compared to them, Stanley knew nothing about business. He must learn, they said, so that he could become the family financial expert.

He seems to have made a sincere effort to be what they wanted. He studied contract law at Northwestern, took a part-time job in the McCormick Estates Office helping manage McCormick real estate holdings and nonreaper investments, and superintended the reaper plant from 1889 to 1901. Then he was made comptroller of the company. He continued to live on Rush Street, where he was allowed no privacy, even in consultations with his doctor, who was quizzed by Nettie as to whether Stanley's habit of dressing and undressing in a particular room had in any way enslaved him: "You cannot wonder that I feel that no one can arrange his little affairs of dressing in comfort as well as his mother." The door to his room had to be left open at all times. When he was out late, Nettie instructed a maid to telephone and order him home. When he returned, he was expected to kiss his mother goodnight, so that she could smell his breath. At dinners for friends, he could not serve wine. Only when Anita offered him her house for his entertainments did things go more smoothly, and he could think that "there's really nothing to this dinner business, it's just a matter of digging up an equal number of males and females."

Wealth weighed on his conscience. He dealt with his guilt by proclaiming that the McCormick money belonged by rights to the workers who had created it.* He contributed to the Socialist party and read the novels of Jack London, but that was the extent of his socialism until he bought the ranch in New Mexico where his egalitarian sentiments had full play. He found a manager who was in accord with his scheme to run the ranch cooperatively, and although the cowhands didn't understand socialism, they liked Stanley. He broke horses, rode mountain trails, and joined in cattle drives. He seemed for the first time to be at peace with himself.

When Anita visited him in New Mexico in March 1902, she asked

---

* He had made a will which left nearly all his wealth to Chicago charities and McCormick employees.

whether he ever thought of returning to Paris; he ought, she said, to "do the thing that seemed to call him." There was no reply, and she did not press the question. Neither then knew that Stanley's ranching days were about over. He began quarreling with the manager and the cowhands, accusing them of ingratitude and of not appreciating values he considered important. In 1903 he returned to the East, where, at thirty-one, he met the woman who was fated to be with him when he slipped into insanity.

Katherine Dexter of Boston was the twenty-nine-year-old only daughter of a prominent Chicago lawyer who had died when she was fourteen, leaving a considerable fortune. Spirited, well-educated, one of the first women to be admitted to the Massachusetts Institute of Technology, where she had studied biology, Katherine was as imperious as she was attractive. Too rich to need Stanley's money and too shrewd to be impressed by his politics, she perhaps saw him as a complicated knot to be untied. Or she may have been intrigued by his odd ways of courting. Instead of flirting, he tried to engage her in discussions of socialism, after which he lapsed into gloomy introspection. When they were apart, he wrote her self-deprecating letters, which she saved for days and then read all at once.

It was sufficient for Anita that Stanley seemed to have found someone he cared for. But how much did he care for her? He was up one day and down the next, uncertain of his own emotions, uncertain whether Katherine really did prefer him over other men. "Now Stanley," Anita told him, "the only advice I could give you would be to be patient, and not want this girl, or any girl, if she belongs to someone else and not marry this girl, or any girl unless she is really the girl that you utterly love." Cyrus's opinion was sought; he was skeptical, doubting whether Katherine had "affection enough for it to dominate her feelings for you." "I don't know that my nature calls for that," Stanley answered, "I think my nature is like Katherine's and perhaps I do not need that."

In the spring of 1904 they were engaged. Nettie, who judged Katherine to be hard, proud, and irreligious, wrote a curt letter of congratulations. Anita said nothing of her premonition that Miss Dexter would not be "the big love" her brother hoped for. Stanley brooded, warned his fiancée that she was tying herself to someone who had "never done anything worthwhile," and confessed his masturbation, which did not shock the scientifically trained Katherine.

Then she had second thoughts. She announced that she was leaving for Europe and that Stanley was not to follow her; she needed time to think. There was to have been a farewell meeting before her departure, but Stanley canceled it. Katherine then broke the engagement and departed.

Two weeks later he caught up with her, and on 15 September they were married in Geneva with Nettie present, whispering to the groom that his bride was "so selfish, even her mother's maid says so. She's so unkind to her mother."

For ten months, none of the McCormicks saw the newlyweds. When the couple returned to Chicago after a prolonged tour of Western Europe, it was not known that the marriage was unconsummated and that Stanley had avoided Katherine by locking himself up in his room. Within a year, he had thrown over his job with the Harvester company and moved with his wife to Washington, D.C., where she enjoyed the diplomatic round of the winter season. From there, they made their way to Brookline, Massachusetts, so that Katherine could do graduate research in biology and be near her mother. That was when Stanley fell apart.

It took Anita many years to understand what had happened to him and why. When he was growing up it had been Anita's delight that he could bring her "any annoyances or troubles, big or little." Now it was evident that her sympathy had been unavailing—that while she had managed to "really cut the connections" with her mother and Cyrus, Stanley had not. His illness seemed to her more tragic than Virginia's, "because we knew years ago that she could not fully recover," whereas Stanley's life "was so full of rich promise in every way." That he had struggled with a strong sexual attraction toward Anita herself, and that this had added to his anxiety, came as a blow. She blamed herself for having overestimated his capacity to withstand strain. When he had complained of fatigue, she, from her strength, had told him that it would "pass into unimportance whenever you see the situation as it is." She had had no inkling of how close he was to collapse until one afternoon when she had urged him to stop trying to keep up with Katherine's social pace, and he had brutally turned on her, accusing her of leading a hermit's life, of wasting her time with dreary teachers, and of smothering her son as Nettie had smothered him. They were the first unkind words between them and she was in tears. She begged him to see a doctor. He said he preferred to study fencing and German. But as she was about to leave the room, he looked at her with his old friendly expression and said, "You know it's alright between us." They were the last coherent or affectionate words she was to have from him.

159

At a party in the summer of 1906, he froze on the dance floor, perspiration pouring off his face, and had to be led home. He could not speak for days. When he stared into a mirror, a dog looked back at him. Then he saw nothing. By fall, his eccentricities were accompanied by periodic attacks of indigestion. He became obsessed by weather and bought eight different weights of underwear, to be worn according to the temperature. Katherine wanted a child. He tried, again failed, and on 16 October abandoned her on the street in Boston and disappeared. When he showed up several hours later, he explained that he had tried to get a shave but that all the barbers were against him. The following day, he attacked his dentist and returned home with a protesting German teacher in tow. He became violent, and held imaginary conversations. An alarmed Katherine telegraphed the McCormicks.

Fortunately, Nettie was not at home. Harold came to Boston immediately; Anita followed, suggesting that Dr. Favill be summoned, to which Katherine agreed. They would "do this thing together," keeping Nettie out of it. Stanley was taken to McLean hospital.

Those early hospital visits were a horror to Anita. Gazing into space, her brother would cry out, "Jack London! I'm glad to see you." He sang, shouted, fought with his attendants, and, when restrained, yelled, "To Windsor! To Windsor!" He ate like a dog, lapping the food from his plate. He stared at objects in his room, shrank back in terror, pleaded to be killed, tried to hang himself with the drawstring of his pajamas, provocatively cuddled up to his male nurse. In his delirium, he wept at his inability to have sexual intercourse, struck his nurses, asked them to show him their private parts. When Katherine came, he remained in the bathroom or hid his face behind a newspaper until she had gone. Curiously, a sketching pad and pencils relaxed him; when he drew, the doctors told Anita, "there was no indecision in his manner, and most striking of all, while he was thus employed he could talk without slowness, without hesitation, and without the exhibition of nervous laughter."

A month later, December 1906, he seemed to have improved. Anita rushed up to him "with such utter gladness" and threw her arms around him. At the time, he seemed to her "well and in his right mind, almost." She stayed three hours; they lunched, played cards. But after she had left, he had a relapse, and Katherine abruptly informed Anita that she no longer would consult the McCormicks about his care: "This may be hard for you and for Stanley's family —if so I am very sorry, but it is the only solution for me of what will otherwise be an impossible situation."

It was the first of Katherine's many ultimatums, and it was re-jected. Cyrus Bentley, to whom Anita turned for advice, confirmed her opinion that Katherine, having said she would share responsi-bility for Stanley, had no right to cancel the agreement unilaterally. Katherine replied that Anita's affection overwhelmed and harmed Stanley; that Nettie's influence was a "profound moral blight"; and that the extravagant McCormick way of doing things, calling in three doctors where one would do, had become intolerable. Further-more, she would not accept Cyrus Bentley as an intermediary, for he was Anita's accomplice. The distrust was reciprocated, for while he respected Katherine's force and intelligence, Bentley thought that she was not always truthful, had an "uncertain temper" and was "far too sure about that which is essentially uncertain."

Katherine played a skillful game, "the end being," Dr. G. V. Ham-ilton wrote Anita, "to outwit everybody." Everything was "secon-day" to that, he said, including "her husband's good." Against her were Anita, Bentley, Favill, and Nettie, and to a lesser extent Cyrus and Harold, who would have rather have let Katherine take over if she was going to be unpleasant about it. Contrary to Katherine's wishes, Dr. Favill continued to see the patient, reporting back to Anita from Boston on Christmas 1906 that "it would be enough to have the legitimate distress over Stanley, but quite outside of that is a great weight, partly of doubt, partly of foreboding, over the perfectly unnecessary situation created by Katherine's attitude. I have such a struggle within myself not to tell her what she is doing and counsel with her." As for Nettie, he wrote, no one could know "how much she must be grieving over the restrictions upon her." Only Anita's repeated entreaties kept Nettie from bringing Stanley to Chicago. "*Do nothing* and say nothing that could possibly come to the other side," she begged her mother. "The situation which we feared might develop is imminent," Anita wrote Bentley at one point. "I'm afraid that mother might at any time urge upon you and the physicians her ideas respecting treatment and care and may even seek to take independent steps. I have so far been able to control her disposition to act independently, but for some time I have thought that she might get quite beyond my control."

They tried to persuade Katherine to have the marriage annulled, take a generous settlement, and go away. She couldn't be bribed Katherine shot back, and she wouldn't take orders from the McCor-micks. She was agreeable, however, to Stanley's being removed to a private home in Massachusetts and, eight months later, to an es-tate near Santa Barbara, California, which he had originally helped plan for Virginia. No quick cure was now looked for. Permanent arrangements had to be made, and the California court was asked to appoint legal guardians.

In August 1908 there were further family maneuvers. A noted German psychiatrist was called in, and Anita went to California to be on hand. She thought Stanley recognized her, but he did not say so. When she entered his room, he began to tremble all over. She got a rug and put it over him and wheeled him into the sun, saying it was a bit cool. His trembling wore off; he murmured several words she caught, and some she didn't. Once he said, "It is a long pull," and she said, "Yes, but not too long for us."

The psychiatrist's verdict was grim—dementia praecox, a disease which was supposed to be organic and to worsen progressively. "It seemed at first as if hope was taken away," Anita wrote, "and it had gone toward darker, not lighter, still—hope!" Favill gave her what encouragement he could, adding, "I wish I could see you a bit, to be sure you were not too lonesome."

A deadlock had been reached with Katherine, whose curtness or icy silences blocked all dialogue. Nevertheless, each side recognized that some compromise had to be devised. Finally, Katherine consented to settle for less than sole legal responsibility for Stanley; she would accept as co-guardians Favill and Bentley. The uneasy truce held for seven years.

The loving conspiracy among Anita, Cyrus, and Harold to shield Stanley and Virginia from their mother and to protect Nettie from herself also held firm. They winked at Mama's petty economies—having her shoes patched or her cheap broken china mended—and if she complained because her dressmaker bills were too high, Anita had her billed for less than the correct amount and made up the difference. "It never occurs to her," Anita confided to the dressmaker, "to question the rising prices of houses built for missionaries, but her devoted maid seems to feel she will not get clothes she should have because she does not wish to spend so much on herself." A live-in nurse hired by Anita had to be disguised as a poor young social worker who wanted to attend school in Chicago and had no place to live. When Nettie became agitated over the cost to her of furnishing a sitting room for Virginia's nurse, Anita won her over by assuring her that her "exception taken at the expense of it is well grounded. I had not seen it in that light before. I could have done the room much less expensively, and if what I was trying to give was right, and good to give, I should have given it. And to make myself feel at all right about it I have paid the bill so that it may really be my gift, wisely or unwisely. I am not doing this because of your feeling about it. That was right, and beautiful and between us. I am only doing it to satisfy my own idea."

Anita cast about for treats and surprises with which to reassure Nettie of her children's love. Since her mother could buy whatever she wished, however, only the most unusual, unexpected gift could serve the purpose.

The inspired idea came in 1914. Why not build Mama a summer home in exclusive Lake Forest, where both Cyrus and Harold had houses. It would have to be more modest and cheerier than Harold and Edith's forty-four-room Villa Turicum with its thirteen identically furnished bedrooms. Nettie had never been comfortable there; it was like an ice palace. Moreover, Edith, for all her intelligence, was far too worldly for her mother-in-law, who disapproved of elegant dinners served on gold plates, menus printed in French, and protocol which required that no servant be addressed except through the chief steward or Edith's personal secretary. It was said that Edith's three children— Mathilde, Fowler, and Muriel—saw their mother by appointment only.[17] No, Nettie ought to have her own, simpler house in the country, and the gift must be kept secret until the details had been worked out.

Harold offered a parcel of his lakeshore land, near Cyrus's but not too near, and the three of them agreed to hire an architect to draw up three alternate plans, from which Nettie could choose. "Only make sure that she is happy with the idea," Harold cautioned.

Anita picked a lovely fall Sunday to break the news. She drove her mother to Lake Forest for a walk through the woods to the spot where an unsuspecting Nettie had been led once before. "This is the place where I had planned to have a house," she had said then, "but that's all past." It seemed a good omen. A mysterious portfolio was produced and the architect's drawings laid out. Nettie, pleased and flustered, asked whether Anita was quite sure Harold was willing to give her the land. Satisfied on that point, she began to compare the plans and with great relish took apart the proposed designs, the architect having been forewarned to let her have all the fun she wanted, never mentioning expense. She fiddled with the stakes, decided which trees to cut, and, as they were leaving, asked to have a last glimpse before the digging started.

A cable from Harold in Paris was awaiting Anita when she returned to 101 that afternoon, withdrawing his offer of land. She was dumbfounded. She wired him to reconsider, reminding him that their mother's heart was in the project, and that "what she needs now is a cable from you putting your heart into it for her." Before he had a chance to reply, Nettie telephoned to ask, "Won't Jack Frost get us if we don't dig soon?" At last, word came from Harold: the house could be built, but Nettie must agree in writing to certain conditions, which Anita interpreted to mean that Edith had made a fuss and Harold had given way. Of course there could be no question of conditions. She conferred with Cyrus, a site on his land was selected—really better, Anita told herself—and then, armed with the portfolio of designs, she walked across the street to her mother's and was greeted with a happy, "Let's go out and look at the place." The change in plans had to be explained. Nettie turned away, the inspired idea was ashes, and Anita left, doubtful whether anything could be salvaged.

Twenty-four hours later, one of Nettie's nephews died and she was busily occupied with the arrangements for his funeral. Taking advantage of the distraction and saying nothing to her mother, Anita met with the architect, commissioned work to start at the new location, trusting that Nettie would recover her enthusiasm when confronted by the reality of house and garden. By the spring of 1915, "earlier disappointments had been forgotten."* The House in the Woods had become "a tale of joy"; there it was, ready to furnish and move into. "If there is pleasure in it for you, then its full purpose is accomplished," Anita said. "And at every step, in every corner, it is filled with love."

The gift of the House in the Woods was followed by an eightieth birthday party that year, planned by Anita to the smallest detail of Nettie's dress. Cyrus and Harriet brought eighty pink roses, Anita's present was a heart-shaped pearl locket. A photographer was hired to memorialize the event. Eight small cakes, each with a lighted candle, were brought in, and scenes of Nettie's life were shown on a stereoptican. Five-thousand dollars had been spent on telegrams around the world, asking for birthday messages to be sent, pre-paid, to "McCormick, Chicago." For that one evening, the controversies

* "If she [Nettie] could but know," Anita wrote Em, "what it has been to me to see her go through such a distress and disappointment, with the agonizing feeling that Edith's flat refusal put into it, in such fine sprit, she would almost be consoled for going through it."

which had divided the family even before the death of Cyrus Hall McCormick in 1884 were unmentioned.

The cause of the old family quarrel was not acknowledged to be the fact that some McCormicks were richer than others and that Cyrus's family was the richest. To survive, family feuds must acquire more elevated rationalizations, having to do with rights and justice.

Less than a year after Cyrus's death, his brother Leander had had published a *Memorial of Robert McCormick*, which asserted that their father had invented the reaper and given it to his eldest son to refine and market with the understanding that the profits would be distributed equally among Robert's children. Cyrus's family had said nothing publicly about Leander's allegation, though privately they pointed out that, during the early battles over patents, Leander, his brother William, and their mother had sworn repeatedly that Cyrus was the sole inventor of the machine. Such claims and counterclaims were part of Anita's inheritance, and she would forgive no one who, as she wrote her Uncle Leander in 1895, "sought to show my father's life to be a lie."

With Leander's death in 1900, the argument seemed to have been buried. "All that is over now," Anita wrote Missy, "with all the army of half-seen things, left to be woven into truth." But in 1910 the charges were revived in an article by Katherine Medill McCormick, the wife of one of Anita's cousins and mother of Robert Rutherford McCormick (cousin "Bertie"), who was to become publisher of the *Chicago Tribune*. A pamphlet along the same lines followed, signed by two other cousins, Hall McCormick and James Shields, and the smoldering controversy again caught fire. When Anita learned that a committee in charge of sending invitations to a lecture at her home had included Hall McCormick among the invitees, she wrote him that "as the occasion is given in my name as well as at my house, you will understand that I not willingly include yourself. Of course, I refer to my understanding that you have been occupied with Katherine McCormick in trying to demonstrate that my father was an imposter."

If their McCormick cousins were going to defame the inventor of the reaper, Anita and her brothers felt duty-bound to counterattack by setting up a Historical Association to sift the evidence and prepare a legal brief defending their father's honor, which meant additional secretaries and office space. Anita gave herself so wholeheartedly to the project that Cyrus Bentley, nominally in charge, reminded her that one could overdo research: "It is possible that somewhere in Persia is a letter from your grandfather expressing his pride in your father's achievement and otherwise disposing effectively of the claim advanced by Leander and Hall. This is possible, but it is so extremely unlikely that we should be guilty of extreme foolishness if we ransacked Persia on the possibility." Undeterred and not satisfied with what had been done, she hired another researcher, who was told by Bentley that if he did not hear from Mrs. Blaine, he should "write to her directly, but do not be surprised if she fails to answer promptly. You will have many exasperating experiences of this sort."

Paternal loyalty did not wholly account for the time, money, and energy expended in defending Cyrus McCormick's good name.* There were financial considerations as well, understandable only in the light of what had happened following the reaper's invention in 1831.

After Cyrus had shifted his operation from the family farm in Virginia to Chicago, his brothers and sisters had followed him, some to work for him, others to be helped to start their own businesses. But it was Cyrus who had drawn them to the Midwest and he who was primarily responsible for their fortunes once they were there. Resentment was inevitable, particularly by his two sisters, Amanda Adams and Mary Caroline Shields, whose husbands were not moneymakers. The resentment was magnified when Cyrus willed his entire fortune to his immediate family, leaving nothing to his widowed sisters or the orphaned children of his brother William. Nettie and her children grew richer, while the Adams family, which had a high incidence of alcoholism, get-rich-quick husbands, and improvident wives, grew poorer. Naturally, they turned to their wealthier relatives for assistance, and it was forthcoming. Anita and her brothers put promising Adams children through school, saw their small enterprises through hard times, and paid medical bills. Anita, unhappy that her father had ignored his two sisters in his will, discussed with Harold and Cyrus the possibility of establishing a trust fund for the benefit of needy cousins. The trust might have been set up had not the argument over the reaper's parentage been revived in 1910, when it was realized that the cousins were in effect saying

* "Dealing with Hall McC's performances would be exceedingly hard," Anita said to her son, "except that it makes me so mad that the fury helps."

that because Cyrus had stolen the invention, Anita and her brothers were living in luxury that was not theirs by right. That view, expressed quite openly the following year by one of Amanda Adams's children, Anita interpreted as attempted coercion. At a meeting in 1911 with an Adams cousin, Anita spoke the final word on behalf of herself, her brothers and her mother: "We could not give one cent to any relative on the strength of the proposition that Cyrus McCormick owed them anything, for it would make him out to be a robber and a thief." She would not be stingy, but generosity would be on her terms, not theirs, and as her father's first obligation had been to his own family, her first obligation was not to her cousins but to her son, who was nearing his twenty-first birthday and would soon come into possession of that part of his father's estate which she had carefully conserved since 1892.

The sickly boy who had been prone to attacks of nausea and fever and was never away from home on his own until his sixteenth year, was now a sophomore at Harvard, studying engineering, cheering the football team, and falling in love with a Vassar girl, who, alas, told him she was "positively sure as it is possible to be that I never shall feel that way toward you." Anita gloried in his growing up. If she was anxious about him, it was only that "in the scramble for things," he might be drawn away from his "real spirit—which as yet, is not tinged with sordid or selfish ambition—and be hurt." She acknowledged "the dangers of the usual trend today for boys who are unfortunately not born to the necessity of work," but she did not think her son "would quickly follow a trend not innately his own." He was, however, "already deeply in love with the automobile [which] leads away from nature." Harvard was his "opportunity to be in touch with a great seething, growing, doing world," and she had no plans for him except to see him "walk his own way." If he was indifferent to poetry and overfond of automobiles, she would overlook it and stand by, "ready to enjoy and sympathize and advise if that is wanted." He bought a motorcycle while at Harvard and wrote Anita that he "was not going to tell you for fear you would worry, but I decided you would rather have me tell you, and I dislike exceedingly having secrets from you on any subject."

Em had the heavy-lidded Blaine eyes, large ears and beaklike nose, a shy pleasant manner, and a practical turn of mind—the only one in a camping group likely to have a needle, thread, and stopwatch. When he went to summer camp, a letter to his mother had expressed his matter-of-fact attitude toward those around him: "We got to the other side of the second lake, and then had lunch. There was just so much lunch to each person. Some of the boys wanted more corn-bread and some wanted more donuts. So they traded. In a little while, nearly everybody was trying to trade something for something else. I did not trade anything and was entirely satisfied." He had, at twenty-one, his grandfather McCormick's respect for mechanics and efficiency, tinged by his mother's moral outlook. "We are but cogs in the great machine," he wrote her, "and the important thing for us is not to break and go to pieces under the load, but so stand the stress and help drive the works along."

After completing graduate work in engineering at the Massachusetts Institute of Technology in 1916, Em was ready to "help drive the works along" but uncertain whether to do it in engineering or experimental farming. Nettie had always assumed that the grandson of the inventor would "naturally gravitate to the business of the family," but he had no more interest in manufacturing than Anita had. Henry Favill, who owned a model stock farm in Wisconsin, favored a farming career and proposed that Em study at an agricultural school for a year, buy some land, and work it, which "sounded mighty nice," Em told his mother; "it looks as if the only way to decide which I shall do will be your time-abhorred method of throwing a penny."

Whatever Henry Favill thought commended itself to Anita, but at fifty the habit of shopping around for reputable opinion was as strong as ever, and she sought the advice of the secretary of agriculture. Her son, she wrote, was "thinking very definitely" about farming: "Associated as he is with the International Harvester Company, I ought to say that his thought is not going along that line at present at all. It is the opposite end that he is thinking of. Agriculture from the agriculturalist's point of view, with possible research, experimentative and demonstration of improvement in that field is what is on his mind." There is no record of the secretary's response, but Anita soon had Em's own preference: "Anyone of the three, harvester, engineering, or farming—would no doubt offer sufficient field for good work, and I have come to feel that . . . it must be decided on the basis of taste. One can surely do the best work in the field which one most enjoys. On this score, the harvester would be eliminated for reasons which you know. You see, I am now on the farming side of the swing."

A week later, the strongest advocate of farming was dead. Henry Favill had gone to Massachusetts to talk to the New England Dairy Association. Word came that he had pneumonia. He lingered a week, long enough for his wife and son and several friends to reach Springfield and stand by helplessly, and died a few hours before Anita arrived. It was "as if the storm which sweeps a forest had uprooted the greatest tree and left the scrubs unscathed," Em wrote the young lady at Vassar.

Anita was plunged into the "blackness of silence." Two years earlier, Favill had agreed to let her have some part in the material arrangement of his life, and so let her "into another chamber of it," she had told Em, "beautiful in the satisfaction of sharing with him what I have to handle, beautiful in that he gives me that satisfaction." Gone was the companionship which had "seemed the one thing that lifted care off you," Harriet Beale wrote Anita, all the hard things would now be "so much harder without him to lean on." *The New Republic* of 4 March 1916 editorialized that Favill "had that character common to all big personalities, the inspiring suggestion of a free and unqualified natural force."

When Em telephoned his mother in Springfield just before the funeral, his voice seemed to her "like an angel speaking into Hell." He at least understood what it would mean to have no "Dear Aesop" stopping by for lunch, "dropping out only to drop in again," filling her rooms with his "beautiful presence." In the weeks that followed, she tried "to pick it up in its darker shade and get good out of it and into it, and the stored sunshine that has been given us should come back to it in time." But her house was "a terrible blank," every corner of it crying out with the "shouts of the beauty and joy he brought in." He had wondered "how well or wisely one orders life." Now there was no life to order.

She sent $68,000 to the Favill Memorial Laboratory at St. Luke's hospital, and $25,000 to the Henry Baird Favill Foundation. Em, "the only one who really knew him," was all she had left, and "oh my blessed one, how I love you! Do you know?"

While Favill's estate was in probate, the opportunity arose to buy his Milford Meadows Farm in Wisconsin. Two appraisers submitted a detailed inventory of the value of the land, building, and stock; Anita and Emmons sold some securities; and in October 1916 the name of Emmons Blaine, Jr., appeared on the farm records as "Proprietor." The land had made his grandfather's fortune, and the land would be his future. Remodeling was started on a small house for Anita's use.

Neither guessed that the future would also include a freckle-faced girl Em had recently met in Lake Forest—Eleanor Gooding, educated at Miss Porter's school in Farmington, Connecticut, and the daughter of a New Hampshire Unitarian minister. Anita had heard her name mentioned but was unaware of her son's tender feelings until she went East in October 1917 for a wedding at which Em ushered. He then told her that he had put the question to Eleanor and had the answer he sought. "In the twinkling of an eye," the face of the world changed. "How I waited that day to get to her I don't know," Anita wrote Nettie. "It seemed an eternity until I could take my daughter in my arms. Oh the blessedness and wonder of it! I am afraid you can't know, for you didn't wait twenty-seven years for a daughter." She was off to New Hampshire the next day, wondering if Eleanor Gooding's parents would look upon her as "an interloper, the accomplice of a robber, and throw me out after a sufficient hospitality." She hadn't been in the Gooding house five minutes before they were weeping and laughing together and she felt she "just belonged." She promptly dubbed Eleanor "Pete" —Pet plus E for Emmons.

It was a postcard New England December setting, the streets snowy, the colonial church "exquisite in shape and taste and lit by innumerable candles." The Reverend Alfred Gooding read the service, Walter Damrosch played the organ, Anita wore her long ermine coat: "You know how she can wear those things that are so beautiful themselves," Margaret Damrosch remarked, "and somehow dominate them so that they seem really beautiful but of no consequence." Eleanor was poised, Em pale; his aunt swore she heard his knees knocking. After the ceremonies, the couple drove in an open motor car to White Sulphur Springs, West Virginia, having been saved the embarrassment of streamers and tin cans on their car by Anita's butler, who during the reception had moved their suitcases from one automobile to another so rapidly that no one knew which the newlyweds meant to take. In their rooms at the Greenbriar Hotel, they found soft quilts and blankets. "You certainly are a sly one," Em wrote his mother, but being an honest young man he added that because the nights were very cold, Anita's linen sheets had been replaced by the warmer, if less elegant, cotton ones of the hotel.

The young Blaines had planned to make their home on his Wisconsin farm. A month before their marriage, however, the United States had entered the war in Europe, and Em, rejected by the army because of his doubtful medical history, was bent on serving in some fashion. Thinking that his engineering skills might be worth something to the American Shipbuilding Company in Philadelphia, he applied for a job and was hired; the couple then set up house in a nearby town. He bought a Ford, "so that henceforth I shall travel in style," he wrote Anita, and in addition could "make it easy traveling for four or five other men." In case she thought the purchase was an extravagance when he already had a larger car, she would appreciate why he "didn't want to go to work in a Cadillac." There being no opening in the engineering department, he was installed first as a clerk, then as foreman of a railroad crew.

Hog Island, where the shipyards were located, had been swampland and was still dismal and damp—possibly the worst area in the country for colds, Em's doctor had told him. Plant discipline was sloppy, and orders might be countermanded twice a day. Em accepted the disorder with his habitual stoicism; the choice of service had been his after scrupulous consideration of alternatives. He had informed the military authorities that he was too inexperienced to "get the most out of the farm in the way of production and general efficiency," and that since he had "considerable training in mechanical engineering" he had secured work with a firm that was building merchant ships under government contract. If the authorities knew of any other work for which he was better qualified, he would "gladly and willingly do whatever the board directs in this matter." He had been told to stay where he was.

The house they rented was in Lansdowne, a suburb of Philadelphia, where a Cadillac and a high income were not curiosities. Eleanor was already pregnant, "almost too much to believe" for Anita, who was "awed and trembling with happiness by turns." Em had been Nettie's first grandchild, his child would be Nettie's first great-grandchild. A new lease on life! And "so wonderful" to share her son with Eleanor, "such a marvelous feeling that he is ours—that *we* have him."

In October, Eleanor wired that Em had a cold and possibly a light attack of grippe; there was no reason to worry. Anita took the next train to Philadelphia, and when she reached the house on Friday, 4 October, she began struggling for her son's life before she took her hat off.

An influenza epidemic had transformed Philadelphia into a plague city. Forty percent of the doctors were stricken, all services were cut, nothing was to be had for the mere asking. Anita telegraphed for a specialist from Chicago; hired three cars to take anyone anywhere, day or night; rented rooms in the Ritz Hotel in Philadelphia; assigned someone to take telephone calls and deliver messages, and managed to secure four nurses. Eleanor had been trying to take care of her husband without going into his room but had been so desperate that she had nursed him through the previous night. Anita at once had her driven to the hospital. "General Foch didn't put more into his campaign," Margaret Damrosch said later.

On Sunday, Cyrus Bentley, Harold, and a fifth nurse arrived. On Tuesday, Eleanor's father and mother came from Portsmouth, New Hampshire, and were joined the next day by cousin Carrie Slade. Em developed pneumonia, became delirious, and died at four o'clock Wednesday morning. Anita, Harold, and Cyrus Bentley immediately went to the hospital to inform Eleanor.

Entering the somber house that morning, Margaret Damrosch felt as if she "couldn't bear to cross the threshold." The first things she saw in the downstairs hall were bottles of Poland Water and Carrie with a pencil and pad in her hand. "I said 'how is Emmons?' and she said, 'you know he has gone.' I spoke to Harold. He was walking around in an overcoat. Then I went upstairs and sat at the top of the stairs on the second floor just miserably crying. There was an air of wretched quiet about the house." For four nights, Anita had not taken off her clothes or rested. She came out of her room, spoke to Margaret, and passed on down the hall. No undertaker could be found that day. When they finally located one, he collapsed and sent a substitute. No coffin was immediately available, no hearse. Carrie and Margaret wrote the death notice, got off telegrams and cablegrams, and tied white roses on the door of the dead man's room.

The morning of the funeral, Eleanor was brought back to the house, and as she and Anita came through the gate, the coffin was being carried out and laid on a carpet of flowers. The drive to the crematory seemed endless. Eleanor's father read from *Thanatopsis*, brother Cyrus spoke a few words, Anita read the twenty-fourth psalm. "Then the door opened," Margaret Damrosch wrote her family, "and the coffin covered with flowers was slid in, and it was an extraordinarily beautiful moment when you saw the little tongues of flame begin to lick the trailing roses with which it was covered. I can't describe it, but something elemental and beautiful. In a few moments, we all left, except Eleanor and Anita."

The doctor who had been in attendance was instructed by Anita to say nothing about Em's illness. "I always regard what is told me in a professional way as a matter of confidence," he replied huffily, "and you may be assured that anything connected with Emmons' last hours will be looked upon not only as a matter of confidence, but as something sacred." She had only wanted to be sure. Wires and letters of condolence piled up. "To have had such a son," Jane Addams telegraphed, "to have seen him develop under an ideal system of education into manhood . . . I can't bear to think of you torn and wracked afresh."

But there was a lifeline to hold to. Two weeks later, Anita carried Eleanor off to Chicago and installed her in a bedroom at 101 to wait out the remaining weeks of pregnancy. This battle would not be lost if Anita could help it. Eleanor was not told that she had a toxemic pregnancy, or that the doctors had said that unless her condition improved, they would have to take the baby to save the mother's life. Anita asked Eleanor's parents not to come to Chicago, since their daughter might then guess how precarious her condition was. She summoned a specialist from Baltimore, hired round-the-clock nurses and had the hospital kept in readiness in case of emergency. An entire floor was requisitioned and redecorated.

Barely a month after Em's funeral, Eleanor gave birth prematurely to twins, a stillborn boy and "a vigorous girl weighing about four pounds," who was placed in an incubator, a rarity in those days. The ambulance in which mother and child returned to 101 was equipped with devices to purify the air and maintain a uniform temperature during the journey. A canvas canopy covered their exit from the hospital, and no one was permitted to enter or leave during the baby's removal.

It was as it had been a quarter of a century before—a life taken, a life given. And now as then the uppermost question was what the father would have wanted Anita to do.

V

THE WORLD AS A WHOLE

V

The United States was at war, and Anita never doubted that Em was
a war casualty, as surely as if he had fought and died in the trenches.
If there could be any comfort taken from his sacrifice, it was that
the war against Kaiser Bill was just, and that America's commander-
in-chief was a man of integrity and valor.

Woodrow Wilson had been a college classmate of Anita's elder
brother, and Cyrus was instrumental as a Princeton trustee in getting Professor Wilson, then teaching at Wesleyan, appointed to a
new chair of public law established by the McCormicks, endowed,
Cyrus wrote him, "as much on account of our personal regard for
your ability as because of our deep interest in the subject of the
department."

Anita shook hands with the future president at her mother's
house when he came to publicize his Quad Plan for Princeton,* and
from that day on he commanded her full confidence—so unlike Theodore Roosevelt (a "bellower") and William Howard Taft ("weak
as water"). She solicited his opinion when Em was searching for an
alternative to military service and his reply was "upholding to us
both." "I believe that what he is doing," the president wrote, "since

* Woodrow Wilson was at luncheon today at Grandma's," she wrote Em
(4 February 1909). "He is very interesting. I was especially interested in
his plans for Princeton, if they can be carried out. He wants to abolish
all clubs and put the whole university on a homogeneous basis."

177

he is doing it enthusiastically, will be as much service to the Government, if not a greater service, than what he could do as a single soldier. . . . In any case, I shall honor the motives by which he is prompted." Anita would have few heroes in politics; Wilson was one of them. She was thrilled by his high-minded speeches and offered to give the money to print one of them. When her offer was refused by the government, she did it privately, arranging for its distribution at military induction centers.

Although the achievement of a lasting peace in the world came to occupy more and more of Anita's thought, she was always behind the government when it was fighting a war. She and Margaret Damrosch nearly got into an argument when Margaret said of the Spanish-American war in 1898 that she didn't consider it "a pure philanthropic war." "We held back as long as we could," Anita replied, "with any manly blood flowing in our veins. . . . When you consider the atrocities . . ."

During the first months of the fighting in Europe, she shared Wilson's hope that the United States could stand aloof, although Germany's ultimatum to Russia shook her. " 'Stop mobilizing within twenty-four hours'—an almost impossible thing to acceed to," she wrote Em. "Now, I don't trust the German Emperor in any of it." With the sinking of the Lusitania by German submarines in May 1915 (one of Anita's cousins was among the twelve hundred casualties), she came "face to face with the fact that civilization has not yet worked out any other method of settling differences of power between nations." But if her country had to become involved, she wrote Wilson, it must not become "just another bloodstained warrior, blindly lusting after power"; it must "stand for the right as we see it" without bringing "barbarism and brutality to its defense." He replied that hers was "the voice of a friend whose good will and whose opinions I peculiarly value, for I know how sincerely you think and how candidly you speak. A beginning can be made in the direction you point out, and I shall try with all my might to make it."

The president of the United States was not the only high official on whom Anita was showering her opinions in 1917. She dispatched a personal letter to "My Enemy, The Kaiser," notifying him that while America had "taken freedom and equality for all human beings and justice and fair dealing for all alike as the foundation rock of the law of love," Germany had set out to "wipe them out for purposes of your own." And yet, "our spirit must be great enough to bridge the gap between what we oppose in you and your own better nature—hidden somewhere, because you are a human being. And we must be ready, while we oppose you with a hand of iron, to lend you the hand of help toward a better destiny." Using German inadvertently in conversation, Anita apologized, for she was "so hating their ways." She likewise refused to hire a gardener, in August 1915, in part because he was of German origin. Nonetheless, she at first defended German-Americans: "Let us respect their silence and their sorrow while they stay in an enforced quiescence; we are not playing at making a stand in the West for Democracy."

It was an inauspicious moment for tolerance. Hate-the-Hun propaganda was inundating the country by late 1917. More than fifteen hundred persons would be jailed for disloyalty, German books removed from libraries, and the teaching of German forbidden in schools. The spreading hysteria did not leave Anita untouched. She felt it her "stern duty" on one occasion to notify the president that two friends of the McCormicks might be spies, and in the spring of 1918 her hardening anti-German sentiments threw Flora Cooke and the whole Parker School into an uproar.

A Parker boy of strict religious upbringing had written in the school magazine that he did not "believe in murdering my fellow men and therefore would not join our country's forces if I could."[1] Through Miss Cooke, Anita summoned the bewildered lad to 101 East Erie, where he waited nervously for an interview with a woman he had never met but had somehow offended. Anita sailed into the living room, tall and erect, questioned him closely on his opinions and their religious origin, got an admission that the word "murdering" was poorly chosen and that he had no objection to serving as a noncombatant. When he agreed to publish a statement withdrawing the word "murdering," Anita was ready to forget the indiscretion.

Cyrus Bentley was not. He had been making inquiries, he said, and had uncovered a "profound pacifist tendency" in the Parker graduating class. The more he thought of it, the more his patriotism was affronted, and he put it to Anita that the flow of opinion and expression could no longer "be regulated with exclusive reference to the rights of free conscience, free thought and free speech." They must act to rid the school of disloyalty, for which they needed Flora Cooke's cooperation.

Miss Cooke was not about to cooperate, having, as Bentley surmised, "cherished peace-loving views." When he proposed that the young pacifists be expelled, she threatened to resign, asserting that "one could not spend one's life teaching children to follow their consciences and then allow them to be punished when they did so." "You are fortunate," Bentley answered, "if you have always been able to serve your *highest* ideals. I think in a time like this, when there is so much to be done, and so many conflicting views, we ought to be willing to serve *high* ideals, even if we do not consider them for us the highest."

As she had done so often in the past, Miss Cooke turned to Anita as arbiter. But Anita was of two minds and suggested that they appeal to a superior authority—President Wilson. Why Wilson, Bentley asked irritably, considering his "peculiar twist of pacifist bias?" The remark was brushed aside and Anita wrote the White House in April 1918, outlining their quandary. The president replied that he valued her courtesy in consulting him and was "very deeply concerned about the treatment accorded those people who do not show an active sympathy with the war but take no active measures to oppose it, and whose offense is merely one of opinion." In his judgment, "we should in our treatment of such people vindicate in every way our claim that we stand for justice and fairness and highminded generosity."

The commander-in-chief had spoken; Anita swung toward leniency. After considerable telephoning, a compromise statement was drawn up and approved by the school trustees; they would "labor in all possible ways" to persuade the lukewarm "to become loyal to America." The statement then had to be presented to the faculty and students for approval. Again Anita hesitated, and again she turned to the president. Once more he cautioned against raising "questions of disloyalty unnecessarily." He was afraid, he wrote, that "we are getting in a suspicious attitude toward people who are not really disloyal but merely unreasonable. We never know until a crisis like this how many of them there are in the country, and yet upon reflection it is evident that most of them do very little harm." That settled it. "I want to help carry out the government's program faithfully and entirely," Anita answered. And having seen "the right course," she wondered "that I could have seen it differently." It was the school's duty to educate, which included guiding "thought that is in a pro-German direction into appreciation of freedom of thought."

Summer vacation was at hand, and when school reconvened, the war was over. No student or teacher had been dismissed, and Anita's attention meanwhile had been captured by the Wilsonian crusade for a League of Nations.

"Peace arrangements would of necessity be world considerations," she had written Wilson in 1916, "and in particular could not be decided upon without the cooperation of the United States"; America could contribute "something at the end of the present conflict toward world protection . . . offering our quota toward the enforcement." Shortly before the president left for Paris to present his League of Nations plan to the victorious allies, Anita telegraphed her hope of "world cooperation to maintain freedom" and her belief that Americans were "ready for the thing you represent. . . . Our real war is not over but only entering another difficult phase."

At a meeting in Chicago of the League to Enforce Peace in February 1919, she delivered one of the main addresses, extolling the constitution of the League as "the Magna Charta of human freedom and human cooperation." She gave the organization $5,000, signed a pro-League appeal, and contributed funds for the defeat of Senator Henry Cabot Lodge, who was pressing for reservations to the peace treaty. Nothing seemed more urgent to her than routing Wilson's isolationist enemies in the forthcoming 1920 presidential election. Despite her misgivings about the lackluster Democratic candidate, James M. Cox, he was Wilson's heir and more for the League than against it. Accordingly, when a railway car of Republican internationalists crossed the country to campaign for Cox, Anita, identified in the public mind with her Republican father-in-law, joined them. "The Democratic Party," she declared, "gives us a straight road to the fulfillment of our national duty and we should take it."[2]

She wrote a five-page plea for a Democratic victory and paid to have it printed in the *Chicago Tribune* the day before the election.* It contained no reference to the Democratic candidate but concluded with a characteristic rhetorical flourish: "We have caught the spirit of our sons. When civilization needed our help, they turned the tide. It was done then. The League of Nations is built upon the labor and sacrifices of our youth. Let it carry their spirit to the uttermost parts of the earth." Her secretaries telephoned Anita's friends and acquaintances in Chicago, asking for their signatures on an appeal by Republicans and Independents for Cox and the League, but only Flora Cooke, Graham Taylor, Mr. and Mrs. Harold Ickes, and a few others were willing to give their names.† Even cousin Chauncey

* Along with Ida Tarbell, Carrie Chapman Catt, and M. Carey Thomas, she also signed an appeal on behalf of the Cox ticket to the "Women of America."
† Anita had no hesitation about trying to enlist her family, friends, and neighbors in her causes. Fellow property owners on Upper St. Regis Lake

McCormick, a warm supporter of the League, would not sign, convinced, he wrote Anita, "that if Mr. Harding is elected, the Hoover Element et al. in the Republican Party can get us a League of Nations that may be a step in the right direction, provided always we can avoid the pitfalls of having it said and believed that a Republican victory is a repudiation by the people of the League idea."

The nationwide Democratic defeat that November was deeply discouraging to Anita. "Since the events of last fall," she wrote an ailing Wilson a few days before he left the White House, "the feelings within me have left me dumb. I do not understand it at all. I know that I want to have patience while the dust is blown away or while the heart is changed." But the nation had voted for "normalcy" and she could not reverse that. She could only look for other, narrower openings "toward the truth." A Congregational church in Chicago received her financial support because she admired the minister's "desire to use his key position as a kind of sounding board, where fresh and fearless notes may be struck." She gave $20,000 to an Englishman interested in "inter-allied" education for orphan boys in France. And for each cause to which she contributed, a dozen others were added to the pile of requests that the secretaries sorted and filed.

In the quest for a "clean vision" of her duty, Anita sought guidance from the dead as well as the living, from her husband and son who were not there—and yet were. Her interest in psychic phenomena had been freshened in 1917 by reading *Raymond*, an account by the English physicist Sir Oliver Lodge, of communication with his only son who had been killed in the war.[3] So great was the book's popularity that the superintendent of Scotland's largest insane asylum had issued a public warning against flirtations with the occult: "I have known a person who had lost her son following the procedure in vogue at present, under advice first hearing of him through mediums, then getting into touch with him herself and receiving messages from him, some as impressions and others as audible words,

---

were petitioned on one occasion. On another, she had "a good deal of fun with Uncle Harold," she wrote Em. "The Chicago Playground Association suddenly found itself without a president . . . and I thought, why not Harold. . . . So they made him a director, and at the first directors' meeting he was nominated and elected President."

then increasing her circle of spiritual acquaintances and living more for her spiritual world than for this, to the neglect of her husband and household til finally God conversed with her in a low musical voice at all times, and confided His plans for the future to her. I would ask spiritualists where in this case does spiritualism end and mental disorder begin?"[4]

Lodge had answered that question for Anita in his preface to *Raymond*: "The amount of premature and unnatural bereavement at the present time is so appalling that the pain caused by exposing one's own sorrow and its alleviation, to possible scoffers, becomes almost negligible." It was essential, however, "to keep the region of communication true and clear of all illusion."

Learning that Lodge was coming to America in 1920 for a series of lectures on spiritualism, Anita wrote to inquire whether he might lead her toward that "perfect light from whence I get the glimpses." Would he allow her to come and see him, but without his knowing who she was, and would he put her in touch "with the clearest method of possible communication?" She enclosed an envelope addressed to a friend through whom he could reply. She signed herself "Z Young."

It was a cautious overture, contrary to her customary straightforwardness, and the subterfuge was soon dropped. Before Lodge arrived in Chicago that February, she had revealed her identity and invited him to stay at 101 and to address the Parker School assembly. Given her initial wariness, Lodge was overwhelmed by her swift and unqualified acceptance of him as "one of the family, rather than one who a short time ago was a stranger." Her talk with Lodge "strengthened her hope and eagerness for communication with people who had died whom she had loved," according to Katharine Taylor. "She felt at times that their presence was with her . . . and that they did exchange thoughts." Lodge understood her desire for anonymity: "Strange mediums or fictitious ones about whom I know nothing are to be avoided; when I tell my secretary to make an appointment for you, I shall not tell even her who it is but will tell her to reserve a few dates in July or August." The appointment to which he referred was for a séance with a medium in Detroit, from whom Anita subsequently had a "wonderful confirmation." She came away "with no question whatsoever."

The correspondence with Lodge continued after his return to England. He thanked her for sending him some of her automatic writing, not having known previously "how much you were in touch with the other aspect of things. The messages are stimulating and helpful to many people I am sure, and the receiving of them must have been a good experience."

Early on, Harriet Blaine Beale and Anita exchanged messages each was getting from "the other world," but by February 1921 Harriet's faith had waned, while Anita's had grown so intense there was concern for her sanity. For instance, she wrote Virginia's custodian, Grace Walker, accusing a mutual acquaintance of rifling her files at 101 and removing confidential material. Then, in November, she announced that voices had ordered her to attend the disarmament conference in Washington and personally deliver a message to the delegates. "Dearly Beloved Brethren," she was to say, "I am bidden to come here to bid you greeting from those who have given their lives in the service of their countries. The only work the conference has to do is to find God. God is everywhere."

Cyrus Bentley tried to head her off, warning that further neglect of her affairs would mean her legal exclusion from Virginia's trusteeship. "Isn't it possible," he asked, "for you to seek Sir Oliver Lodge's advice—I recall his public warning against the thing that you are doing. And if you go to Washington, will you not stop in Baltimore and talk with Dr. Meyer; you seem to us ill." Nothing Bentley or her family said could dissuade her from setting out for the capital. From a hotel there she wrote Cyrus and Harold of trying to set up appointments so that the word of "the Most High" could be heard at the conference and of her round of visits to the offices of Secretary of State Hughes and of Basil Miles, secretary of the American delegation. She reported having gone on Sunday afternoon to Hughes's home. She was turned away and "told to write to Secretary Hughes what the thing was that I wanted to tell him of, which I did, sending him a note and asking to see him at once." The voices told her to go to his house on Monday morning, and that he would take her to the conference: "I went at nine o'clock, and learned that Secretary Hughes could not see me, and that he referred me to his secretary at the State Department for an answer to my note. . . . I returned to the hotel, and was instructed to go back to the State Department in the afternoon and to ask for the answer. I did so, and a letter ready to mail was handed to me, signed by his private secretary. I read it there. It said that it would not be possible to address the conference, as no one is permitted to address the conference except the Plenipotentiary Delegates. I asked that I might have an answer which would indicate that my full letter had reached Secretary Hughes, and that I was receiving his reply to it. I was informed that he had left the office, and was told that he had been in great haste.

I sent the letter to his house to await him. I had no answer to this letter. I returned to the hotel and received instructions to see Mr. Miles and tell him the whole. I went to his office that afternoon, and after waiting for some time I saw Mr. Miles between appointments and told him as concisely as I could the whole—and left with him a pencilled note of the message which I had written as I waited. He said Secretary Hughes had taken up the question in the Committee, including Mr. Root and Mr. Lodge, and he hoped they agreed with him that no one should address the conference, that if one was allowed to, others would not understand."

For seven days she traveled from office to office, leaving notes, being informed by underlings that she should telephone at a later hour. "I was not well for a day or two," she wrote Harold, "I had some slight infection. I am better now and well again." She was mistaken, and the illness finally drove her home to her worried family.

Shortly after her return, Harold came to the house, and they talked for hours. Afterward he told Nettie that he believed "we will win out and bring Anita back to us to *stay*, by gentle presence." She came down with pneumonia, and after a slow recovery seemed subdued. At least that was Bentley's impression. He attributed the Washington folly to her having been overtired and having dwelled too much on Em's death.

Anita drew a different conclusion from her experience: she had not been hearing the voices properly and henceforth would find and follow "the real leadings." She would set herself "a new mark within —to make the bodily machinery carry its part—to let the mind be the proper director, and to bring the spirit in harmony with the divine." She was determined to keep at it. Two years later, on fifty pages of penciled scrawl, she recorded a communication from her father; another séance produced a forty-one-page account of other messages from the unseen world. She said nothing to Bentley or her family of these ventures into the beyond, and she expected absolute discretion from her secretaries.

Henry Favill's role of adviser-at-large was now to be filled by another physician, Roger I. Lee of Boston, whose admonitions reminded her of his predecessor's. She must "let up," not undertake "anything serious or solemn the whole week," and on "Sundays and occasionally on a weekday, you are going out to a House in the Woods, but the work will not pursue you there." The work did pursue her, because that is how she wanted it. Even on vacations, one doctor said disapprovingly, she took her resting "too strenuously." Anyway, on Sundays she did not wish to spend her time in the

House in the Woods at Lake Forest. She preferred to have lunch with Eleanor in Winnetka, where she could romp with granddaughter Nancy, play the piano, and entertain the six-year-old by singing "Of Speckled Eggs the Birdies Sing."

In the closing months of 1922, her internationalist fervor was rekindled by the formation of a new League of Nations Non-Partisan Association, to which she pledged $10,000. The makeup of its executive board, Republicans and Democrats, seemed to insure partisan neutrality. Cousin Carrie's husband, Louis Slade, who served in New York as national membership chairman, invited Anita and Chauncey McCormick to organize the work in Chicago and help plan mass meetings throughout the country.*

Chauncey was willing. "I suppose to start we must name chairman, vice chairman, sec., etc. more or less arbitrarily," he began. No, said Anita, not yet; we must first think it out carefully. He waited while she thought and while she bombarded the New York office with queries. What should be the exact relationship between the national office and the proposed Chicago group? Should each local group report its plans to the national office? Should the national office pass around such reports to every other local group? Shouldn't each local group be autonomous in its fund raising? Louis Slade suggested a Chicago mass meeting in April; Anita replied that April was too soon. No plans were made, and by late spring Slade was becoming impatient. His New York office had instigated meetings in forty-five large cities and was sending speakers and organizers on nationwide tours. Why was nothing done in Chicago? Something had been done, Anita answered. She had invited two prominent Chicagoans to head their local group—Carter Harrison, whose five terms as mayor had made him a Chicago institution, and Frank Lowden, former Republican governor of Illinois. After both had turned her down,† she had tried to persuade Alexander Legge of the International Harvester Company to take on the job. He also had declined, on the grounds that the company owned foreign prop-

---

* The Treaty of Versailles had been rejected by the U.S. Senate on 19 November 1919—with and without reservations—and by now it was clear that President Harding had no intention of leading the country into any association with the League of Nations.

† Harrison wrote her that Americans were "infants at the diplomatic game. We enter a conference with all our cards spread on the table—before the game is ended we learn to our mental chagrin and material cost the deck has been shifted on us and that we are playing with marked cards, a few of which are held up the opponents' sleeves!"

erty and there might be a suspicion of a conflict of interest. She was searching for someone else.

Chauncey himself was becoming restless at her resistance to taking one step until the right leader appeared, but no appeal from him or the New York office could budge her. Cousin Carrie was sent to Chicago to nudge Anita, after which Slade wrote Chauncey that he thought she now did understand the situation "thoroughly," and if Chauncey would lean on her a bit, they might go forward. All the leaning produced was a firm restatement of her intention to do it her way, in her own time, and a reminder that if the national office didn't like her methods, they were free to take the job out of her hands. She wanted nothing less than "a foundation which is not built on impulse, which is not originated in ways of momentary feeling nor which contains uncertainties."

Nothing happened in Chicago until the following year, and by then the forthcoming 1924 elections were making it difficult for the association to retain its nonpartisan image. Spurred by the Senate debate on United States membership on the World Court and by the recent death of its patron saint, Woodrow Wilson, the association dispatched a professional organizer to Illinois (Chauncey was out of town) with orders to inform Mrs. Emmons Blaine that she could cooperate or not, but Chicago was going to be organized. She managed to persuade the emissary to set up a temporary group— the Illinois Committee for International Cooperation—after which she and Chauncey took the train to New York to explain to Slade why prominent Chicagoans such as Jane Addams, Julius Rosenwald, Walter Fisher, and Charles Merriam thought that the association was on the wrong track, and that the League issue should not be introduced into the political campaign. At a national executive committee meeting, she pointed out that her cousin Medill McCormick, United States senator from Illinois, then owner of the *Chicago Tribune,* and an "irreconcilable" on the League, was up for reelection. He would not on his own bring up the League, but if he were forced to do so by the association's interference in the campaign, he would "no doubt use all the meretricious arguments" and his "publicity organ will spread these and only these widely." The executive committee listened and disagreed. Political neutrality would "completely wreck our organization. . . . Leading Democrats would resign immediately under the impression that we were surrendering because of political pressure from without." Whereupon Anita and Chauncey themselves resigned from the association, and with Anita went the financial support she had furnished since its birth.

After the elections and the inauguration of President Coolidge, however, she was invited back on the board and accepted, willing to be "allied as far as I could with any organization that was carrying the League of Nations as a cause." The board welcomed her with smiles. "I have known no one," the chairman said, "who, after being voted down on a matter upon which they felt deeply, behaved as splendidly as you have. Your whole attitude is a splendid lesson for us all, and we appreciate it." She subsequently joined an informal finance committee of a newly organized Illinois branch of the association, served on its executive committee, and gave it almost $100,000 over the next two decades, as well as $170,000 to the national office.

It is not flattering to be called eccentric, but to be regarded as "a character," as Anita was by her mid-fifties, is to be complimented. How charmingly old-fashioned, they said of dear Mrs. Blaine—those long, loose, wrap-around dresses, the lace collars and rolled up stockings, the bloomers which reached below the knees, the small straw or velvet hat perched on top of her head, the closet full of shoes handmade to fit her narrow feet, the drawers of cashmere sweaters and scarfs and the three-button French gloves ordered by the dozen from Altman's in New York. How original to defy the short-skirted, bobbed mode of the twenties. And her house, so untouched by fashion—its heavy chairs with their arms of carved eagles' heads, the massive dining room table from the late nineties, the enormous tufted sofas and large fringed lampshades and the brass fittings in the bathrooms.

Accustomed to her surroundings and her daily routine, she saw no reason to change them. In fair weather, the Cadillac was brought to the front door of 101, its presence announced by the butler. A mink lap robe would be thrown over her lap. She would be driven to the lakeshore, step out, stride briskly for a half-hour or so before being picked up by the chauffeur and taken home. Nearing sixty, she still loved to waltz, and playtime with granddaughter Nancy was as lively as the rough-and-tumble she had enjoyed with her small son.

She and Harold had the same playful streak in them, but, unlike Anita, Harold was a fashion plate—stiff collars, detachable cuffs with sapphire links, colorfully striped shirts, fancy waistcoats, gray spats, and an emerald or pearl stickpin adorning a gorgeous silk tie. The gossip columnists referred to Harold as "a rich playboy," which was misleading, for he was not frivolous and certainly not dissolute. He was simply fun-loving.* "There's something about Harold that bubbles," a friend said. True, he had had constant reminding by Anita that "as head of a family, as a man and a citizen, responsible for many people," he really *must* decide what he was going to do with his life. And she did think that his upbringing had been "quite mismanaged." But when she admonished him, he would take her hand and say, "But Anita, haven't I done what was expected of me?" Hadn't he graduated from Princeton, married the daughter of John D. Rockefeller, fathered five children, and worked for the harvester company? Admittedly, he was fond of flying, whistling (he once gave a whistling recital over the radio), fine clothes, and women; and he enjoyed playing patron to the fledgling Chicago Civic Opera Company. But didn't he deserve some sympathy for putting up with a wife who, having discovered Karl Jung, spent most of her time in Switzerland, and whose life, Anita readily admitted, was full of such "arbitrary artificialities" as a million dollar emerald necklace.

It wasn't Edith's extravagance that he minded, Harold would explain, it was her lack of understanding. Why wouldn't she make an effort to see his point of view? Why, for instance, couldn't she accept his friendship with a lady he had only tried to help deal with a nasty marriage? "You see," he said to Anita, "I have never had many *real* friends and here is one. I made real sacrifices. Why cannot Edith now? And let me have this happiness? I would harm no one." How was he to find companionship with a wife who took their three children (two others had died in infancy) and stayed abroad eight years?

Anita could not bring herself to censure her pet, but the truth was that more than one lady had seemed to be Harold's true love. For several years during Edith's self-exile in Switzerland, Harold's name had been coupled with Ganna Walska, a Polish singer, about thirty, once widowed and twice divorced, whom he had met when she sought his help in his capacity as benefactor of the Chicago Civic Opera. In 1920 he had asked her to marry him if he could free himself of Edith and had been turned down; her heart was in her second husband's grave, she had replied. But her seductive re-

---

* And childlike. Writing to Anita from the Adirondacks in 1925, he said he had learned "so much about *simple living*. . . . If you could have seen me washing the dishes after the meal . . . going to the market and ordering only what was needed . . . you would have said, 'Can this be Harold?' —but it *was* him."

fusals became fainter with each proposal, then inaudible, and when Harold went to Switzerland in 1921 to ask Edith for a divorce,[5] Ganna Walska was deposited in Paris to await the outcome of his interview.*

When Edith said yes, an exuberant Harold raced back to his Zurich hotel room to wire Ganna the good news, only to be handed a telegram informing him that she had just married Alexander Smith Cochran, an American millionnaire of recent acquaintance; she hoped that she and Harold would "always be good friends." He left for Paris, took a room in the hotel where the Cochrans were honeymooning, and excitedly telephoned Ganna at seven in the morning. She invited him to come up for coffee.

Mr. Cochran was still asleep in an adjoining room, while Mrs. Cochran coolly poured coffee, asking if Harold wanted sugar or cream. He wanted neither. He wanted her, and he demanded that she leave her new-found husband and marry him as soon as his divorce from Edith was final. She said she would let him know. He waited a year for her answer.

Meanwhile, his youngest child, sixteen-year-old Mathilde, announced she was marrying her Swiss riding master, Max Oser, then in his forties. Hearing of the engagement, Anita wrote Max that "it would be good to meet together. There are deep places that we should go into all together—I mean you and M and Harold and I. I only say 'I' because M has no mother near her and although I cannot be all of that, I can be some of it—and I love her dearly." Edith put Max down as a fortune hunter, all the McCormicks except Anita and Harold opposed the match, and Mathilde was persuaded to postpone the wedding until her eighteenth birthday. By then, Ganna had rid herself of Alexander Cochran, taking with her a sizable settlement, a car, a house, and the jewels and furs he had lavished on her.

The publicity generated by Harold's courtship of Madame Walska sent shock waves through the executive offices of the International Harvester Company, of which Harold was president, having reluctantly taken over from his tired older brother. Notoriety of this sort, Cyrus sternly pointed out, was unbecoming; it shook the confidence of stockholders. Harold offered no defense, other than the fact that he had not asked to be president of the company and would be happy to get out from under. His resignation was accepted and the

* Edith returned to America to negotiate the final terms of the divorce, and there announced that their Lake Forest mansion, the Villa Turicum, would be transformed into "a Mecca for devotees of psychoanalysis."

presidency taken over by Alexander Legge, a former cowboy who had worked his way up through Harvester ranks.

The press, however, was not finished with Harold. On 12 June 1922 he entered a Chicago hospital for an operation that provoked even more publicity than his courtship of Ganna Walska. Reporters identified the doctor as V. P. Lespinasse, a prominent Chicago surgeon whose specialty was urology and who had been awarded a diploma by the American Medical Association for his experimental work on spermatogenesis and sterility. He was described by the *New York Times* as the dean of gland transplantation and "author of the saying that 'a man is as old as his glands.' "[6] Harold threatened to sue newspapers which asserted that he had had a transplantation of monkey glands to revive his sexual powers, but the stories did not stop.

Two months after the operation, Harold rejoined Ganna in Europe, married her, then remarried her under Illinois law at Nettie's House in the Woods in February 1923, with Anita smiling and sixty detectives guarding the grounds. Anita wrote part of the service. After the ceremony, the ebullient bridegroom greeted reporters with "Hello boys, this seems like old times. You know, I've been in the newspaper so much, I feel like a newspaperman myself." He was good copy.

Nothing in Anita's past had prepared her for this new, tempestuous sister-in-law. The child of Polish farm workers, Ganna Walska had a dusky beauty, a monumental ego, a driving ambition to be hailed as a prima donna, and, according to one musical director, "an impossible voice." She pictured herself as buffeted by malevolent winds of destiny, dragged down by the rude rabble and by critics who were stupid or jealous. "People made about me quite wrong impression," she wrote Anita in her idiosyncratic English, "and they imagine that I am foolish, vane, consited personne who imagines that she can sing because she is pretty and through her husband's money tries to push herself. As a matter of fact I am entirely, not consited, but wrongly or rightly, (to be seen some day!) quite sure that something is in me and that I should deliver a message and leave something behind me as an example. I want other people to know that Harold did not marry a foolish woman, but a person who wants to give at cost of terrible suffering and undiscrable misery."

Foolish or not, she was Harold's wife, and that made her dear to his sister. "What you have gone through you only know," she had written Ganna before the marriage, "but there is nothing that can be gone through within or without that has not its sacred lesson to teach. Only pray to learn it." She longed to have "beloved Ganna" in her arms; "it is that that I wait for." To them both she said: "You had to find it. It was there to find. It was yours. It is all one road —the seeing, the findings, the attaining, the giving, the sharing." When publicity-shy Harold had hesitated about returning to Chicago from Europe Anita said that she had "no respect for the ear to the ground and fear of publicity which may not happen, and if it did happen would not be worth so much consideration. I think you two should settle that wholly on your private wishes. I hardly think anyone could advise."

Two years later, when the marriage was in ruins, it was Anita who comforted him; he must give himself "the quiet untroubled chance to know what the experience teaches and where it leads." Bolstering her "pet" was one of Anita's lifelong assignments. She told him he should "welcome the experience, not deplore it—come up, not down —be glad, not sorry."

The American concerts Ganna had planned for herself, postponed once because Harold had to be operated on for appendicitis, were a tragicomedy, and Cyrus was outraged. It was shameful enough to appear on stage, he burst out, but this tour, coming on top of the monkey gland scandal, was more than an offense against good taste; it was, he repeated, an offense against good business. Harold hung his head. What could he do? He could not prevent the critics from panning his wife's performance. And it was not as if he had been deceived. Ganna had told him before their marriage that everything was secondary to her career.

He was to find out what she meant. She now said openly that she tolerated him only because of his money. She spurned his affection in private and humiliated him in public, writing in her well-edited autobiography that he had been led to "idolize the physical expression of love" and had become "insatiable in his search for the realization of the physical demands—insatiable because they were unattainable for him anymore." She, on the other hand, was "an idealist who was able to put so much value on the richness of his soul that she could not even imagine the possibility of his preferring to seek further for a gross and limited pleasure, rather than being satisfied with the divine companionship of the spiritual love she was willing to share with him."[7]

If Harold felt cheated, so did Madame Walska. She had banked on family connections to advance her career, and what benefit had they brought? She was unaware that Anita had whispered a word on her behalf in Walter Damrosch's ear, and that he had had to explain apologetically why he could not let her "very pretty sister-in-law" sing in his performance of Beethoven's Ninth Symphony: nature had given Madame Walska great beauty, but from the "absolutely unanimous accounts of my musician friends who have heard her, her voice is absolutely devoid of charm." "What a tragedy," he wrote Anita, "if only she would leave art alone, she would be much happier."

No precautions were taken to keep these scandalous goings-on from Nettie, for at eighty-eight she was content to know little. On Christmas Day 1922, she entertained three young men she had been helping to educate; then, after the holidays, she went to California to see Virginia and Stanley. The following June, she came down with a cold which did not respond to treatment, and on the Fourth of July, Anita's fifty-seventh birthday, the end was near. The dying woman murmured snatches from the Bible and two verses of "Home Sweet Home." Twenty-four hours later, as the nurse was counting her pulse, she looked up and said, "How lovely! How lovely! How lovely!" and was gone.

In the last thirty-four years of her life, she had given away nearly $8 million; yet she left an estate valued at $12 million, out of which $2,536,641 was paid in taxes. She also left considerable personal property, which was to be the cause of further friction between Anita and Cyrus because of Anita's procrastination.

Nettie's Rush Street goods were put in storage and the jewelry in a bank vault,* where they stayed for thirty-one years, despite Cyrus' frequent requests that they be distributed. He wanted a decision, Anita would not decide until the true inwardness of the situation had been revealed to her.

It was the same old conflict that had arisen again and again in their differing approaches to the supervision of Virginia. As co-trustees, Anita, Cyrus, and Harold were authorized to invest and spend Virginia's money, and to determine where and in what manner she was to live, who staffed her household, and what doctors saw her. A rough division of labor had been agreed to. Anita let Cyrus handle the investments; he let her have charge of Virginia's wardrobe, music lessons, household comforts, and the selection of physicians and nurses. But there were disputes over such details as the maintenance of Virginia's extensive gardens or the costly decoration of her rooms, and Cyrus repeatedly ran up against Anita's

* Except for Nettie's wedding ring, which was put on a gold chain and passed around among her children, who wore it in turn for several months.

193

disinclination to share the decision making, even with her co-trust-ees. They differed over the proper salaries for Virginia's employees, over whether and when to sell three houses Virginia did not use—in Alabama, Massachusetts, and Canada—which were costing $60,000 a year to keep empty. Anita would promise to look into it and to prepare a report, months would go by, and finally Cyrus would wire that although neither Harold nor he had "any desire to take arbitrary action, we feel strongly we should not wait on your reports." Bills piled up. The architect of one of Virginia's houses waited for $5,543 with which to pay the contractors. Grace Walker relayed his request to Anita, Anita was not available, and Cyrus then stepped in and asked Miss Walker to "please wire me your recommendation so that this item may be paid promptly, if correct."

Conflict was unavoidable, since Anita took it for granted that she must have "the directing part" in the management of Virginia's life. "As the executive member of the family council on her affairs," a consulting psychiatrist, Dr. Adolf Meyer, was told, "and also the natural one as her sister, it is right that I should do so." She was happy to consult her two brothers so long as it was understood that nothing would be done without her permission. "I simply put before you the two ways of our meeting requests of the other," an exasperated Cyrus wrote. "Any word from you generally takes precedence over other things, but I have a feeling that it is almost hopeless to expect an answer promptly from you to a telegram. It gives me a feeling of being far away and not in touch with you. It is hopeless for one side of the interrogation to be usually prompt and other side of the interrogation dilatory." Tired of "standing on the sidelines looking on," he once dared to express his impatience to one of Anita's secretaries and was rebuked by Anita: it was "not correct and not just to those who are not finally responsible to send such messages through them."

Harmony would be restored briefly. Anita would become absorbed in some new organization or a summons to offer her thoughts to some notable on a public controversy. Weeks later Cyrus would complain about yet another unpaid bill: "Is it not possible to place a vexed question like this (upon which so many good people are awaiting reply) into the hands of some secretary who will not forget it?" Whether over the division of their mother's property, the planning of a centennial celebration of the invention of the reaper, or the care of Stanley or Virginia, they were at odds. "All our actions seem to be based on the premise that *time counts* for *nothing*," he told her. You are being "exceedingly anxious," she replied; she would not be hurried. But what was he to do when one of her secretaries telephoned him to ask him to approve payment of a year-old, $5,000 doctor's bill for Virginia, and Anita could not be reached? He must wait until they could discuss it, she answered. Eventually the bills were paid, but the bickering went on until their sister's death in 1941.

For almost sixty years, Virginia had been isolated from the everyday world, her whims gratified by the luxuries $21 million could provide.* She became a plump, harmless old lady who had to be humored to keep her from crying. Every day was like the day before. She was led downstairs at eleven each morning; played croquet until lunch, rested; was taken for a drive; had tea, dinner, a motion picture; and was put back to bed at eight o'clock. The mysticism of her teens no longer burst forth in hysterical prayer, and at the end, her pleasures and her faith were those of a child. "I love to think what I will tell Jesus when I see him," she said shortly before she died.

Harold had kept as clear as he could of the line of fire between Anita and Cyrus. Technically, he shared responsibility with them as a co-trustee, but he was eleven years younger than Virginia, still a boy when she had been taken away, and was never close to her. And in the last ten years of Virginia's life he had had his own troubles. In 1931 he had been granted a divorce from Ganna, on grounds of desertion, which cost him a reputed $6 million. "I have my life, he has his," she told the press, "every artist must have her rights." Then each of Harold and Edith's three children was married to someone at least twenty years older. Pretty Mathilde Oser and her middle-aged Max stayed together in Switzerland until their two children were grown; then she left him and returned to America. In 1921, son Fowler, who was to become president of the International Harvester Company, married Anne Stillman, the mother of his Princeton roommate, thereby giving newspapers an opportunity to recall that the lady had been involved in a well-publicized divorce amid mutual accusations of adultery. No sooner had Fowler married "Fifi" Stillman than his restless, plain sister Muriel followed his example by picking a mate from her parent's generation.

Of the three, Muriel's history was the most calamitous. Having played at acting, singing, and owning a stylish dress shop, she belatedly attached herself to, or rather annexed, Elisha Dyer Hubbard,

* She left no will. The money remained within the family. Anita, along with attorney Judson Stone and the Continental Bank of Chicago, was named administrator of her estate.

a near-invalid and veteran of the first world war. He survived five years of marriage, from which Muriel emerged a brutal alcoholic, who insisted that Major Hubbard's dog accompany the funeral procession, whereupon her brother Fowler walked out of the house, saying his sister was "mentally unbalanced." She was self-centered and cruel, treating her social inferiors with the same contempt she showed for her social equals. In that sense, she was democratic.

Edith Rockefeller, Ganna Walska, and the example of his children might have convinced anyone but romantic Harold of the blessings of bachelorhood, and he did stay legally unattached, though not uninvolved, for seven years after his second divorce. Then, in 1938, convalescing in southern California from a series of heart attacks, he married his nurse, Adah Wilson, thirty years his junior. Anita was the marriage's sole supporter within the family. "One usually congratulates the bridegroom to be," Fowler's wife wired Anita, "but as no word can reach the fortress of the Good Samaritan Hospital have decided to congratulate you and the doctors for a rare and beautiful mess." Muriel placed drunken phone calls to her father, who was hiding out in Virginia's Pasadena house, but the calls never got through because Anita saw to it that all incoming communications were monitored. On the wedding day, Anita was in Chicago, but she followed the ceremony in her mind's eye: "My Dearest," she wrote Harold and Adah, "I can't go until I give you word of my evening. It was all so wonderful. Your marvelous flowers with your wonderful double letter began it. Eleanor came to dinner with me. I played the wedding music just before we went in. We drank a toast to you. . . . We go together into the promised land. Thankfulness and joy and love."

It turned out to be Harold's only tranquil marriage, marred only by a breach-of-promise suit in 1938 for $2 million filed by a Mrs. Olive Colby. (It was settled out of court for $12,500.) Adah looked after him until his death three years later, after which she remarried, had a son, and lost her life by falling from the rim of the Grand Canyon.

We have gone far ahead of our story, leaving Stanley behind. His days were uneventful, and over the years he grew calmer but no saner. It was the interminable fight for possession, swirling around him, that filled the stage.

In 1923, shortly after he was settled in Santa Barbara, Stanley had been visited by Cyrus Bentley, whose account of their meeting did nothing to ease Anita's anxiety. Bentley had concealed himself behind a screen in the music room, awaiting the hour to strike for Stanley's automobile ride. "The bated breath in which the nurses made their few remarks," he wrote, "and the long intervals of silence between these suggest nothing so much as the customary conditions of a funeral. I should myself expect to go insane if I were to spend many moments daily behind bars with my keepers just outside, acting as if they were in the presence of death."

The seven-year truce with Katherine had worn thin. Anita had taken Henry Favill's place as a co-trustee, and she and Bentley stood guard against any encroachment by Stanley's wife. In 1927, Dr. Adolf Meyer of the Johns Hopkins medical school (one of Virginia's physicians) had been selected to oversee Stanley's treatment as well, but had been dismissed on Katherine's allegation that he accomplished nothing. In retaliation, Dr. Meyer accused her of promoting unproved theories on endocrine disorders, to his patient's detriment. Another prominent psychiatrist, Dr. Thomas Salmon, had then been hired, and he also was driven to quit by Katherine's veiled threats to have him fired if he ignored her recommendations. To Anita, the Salmon incident "was like the firing on Fort Sumter in the Civil War. It was frightful."

Having failed to agree on one doctor, the trustees decided to employ a team headed by Dr. William White, a Freudian psychiatrist who, in Anita's judgment, had a "very keen mind, a great deal of sense and judgment, but above all a wide experience and wide amount of knowledge from handling tangled affairs." Dr. Edward J. Kempf, a younger man who had worked with White at St. Elizabeth's hospital in Washington (and who later was to treat Harold's daughter Muriel), was taken on as the resident psychiatrist. While not "inclined particularly toward psychoanalysis," Anita liked Kempf.

The supervisory team might have survived if Katherine could have overcome her deep hostility to Bentley. As he and Anita awaited her arrival for a trustees' conference one morning in a hotel room in Santa Barbara, she telephoned that she was "not coming to the meeting, and I am not coming to any more such meetings. I am through with it." She asked Anita "to say to Cyrus Bentley for me that I think he is not playing square, he is not expressing his ideas. He is stalling."

Bentley, who had his pride, resigned on the spot, and Katherine proposed replacing him with Cyrus and Harold.

It was a shrewd move from Katherine's standpoint, since Cyrus, in Bentley's words, was "wont to follow the indirect and devious paths of least resistance which may take him in one direction today and in the opposite direction tomorrow," and Harold was an even weaker reed ("essentially an opportunist," Bentley thought, though "with backing he can stand firm") and cheerfully admitted it: "When Anita and Brother are together, I almost universally, gladly, fall in line without further consideration or discussion, whereas, when they differ, it presents a problem to me." The only trustee with a will to match Katherine's was Anita, who felt she had no choice but to "co-operate handsomely." Her two brothers were appointed.

But the compromise could only camouflage the animosity. The tug of war went on, the McCormick trustees conferring among themselves in a secret telegraphic code devised by Anita. She was "Alpha," Harold "George," Cyrus "John," Katherine "Mary," and Stanley "Crane."

On Dr. Kempf's orders, the bars had been taken off Stanley's windows, the nurses let go of his arms when he walked, and he was allowed to go to the bathroom alone. Sketching parties on the lawn of the estate and hikes in the nearby foothills had been organized. A beach cottage was rented so that Stanley could take a dip in the Pacific Ocean under the watchful eye of a life-saving crew in a boat anchored just beyond the surf line. Kempf now thought it safe for Katherine to spend three weeks at Christmas in Santa Barbara.

When she arrived, Stanley embraced her casually, bolted for the front door, was seized and brought back to his rooms. Katherine stayed five months.

According to Kempf's diagnosis, Stanley was "timid, introverted, masochistic," Katherine "dominating, aggressive, impulsive and sadistic." "If she will be fair and patient," he wrote Anita, "he will either accept her as she is, with full knowledge of her interest in other men or reject her completely. Either evolution will be progressive, and I don't care which way it goes provided that she will be fair and truthful. Of the latter attribute, I am not so sure that she will come out fully to Stanley's satisfaction. We must wait. I will certainly not let her fool him no matter how much it hurts him or her."

Neither the diagnosis* nor Kempf's treatment was tolerable to

* "If we consider the entire picture of his life," Kempf wrote toward the end of 1927, "all its stresses from childhood until his illness, such as the strict Puritanism of his home making his sexual traumas abnormally severe, the seductions by his nurse Marie when he was a little child, sup-

Katherine. She charged him with alienating Stanley's affections, refused to guarantee his salary for a year, ridiculed his instructions, and demanded that he be dismissed and that she be put in charge. If it had not been for Anita, she might have prevailed. "She knows she cannot manipulate you," Bentley said from the sidelines.

Further compromise seemed futile and a common family strategy had to be mapped out. If the three McCormicks stood together, Anita told Harold, "and refuse to have Dr. Kempf budge, I would have no idea that Katherine would let it go to court." She was wrong. In 1929, despite the mediation efforts of a small army of lawyers, the controversy did reach the California courts, Katherine having petitioned to become the administrator of Stanley's person and property. Shown the petition and lighting on the word "summons," Stanley thought it meant he had to appear in Chicago and started out of the Santa Barbara house for the railway station.

Most news accounts of the subsequent lawsuit pictured Katherine as a loving wife battling against malicious interference by the sick man's family, and Anita was sure that a public relations expert had been imported to sell Katherine's side of the story. Numerous doctors who had examined Stanley were put on the stand, along with his nurses, his brothers, and his sister. When the unpleasant ordeal came to an end, the only changes ordered by the judge were the dismissal of Dr. Kempf and the appointment of two additional trustees, neither related to the patient by blood or by marriage. Kempf was "perfectly splendid about it all," Anita said; "he wanted Harold and me to be with him and join in telling Stanley of the judge's decision, which we did." They also told Stanley they would "work in every possible way to bring Dr. Kempf back."

The weeks of trial had been grim, and yet in the midst of them Anita had taken time to describe for her daughter-in-law in Chicago the beauty of Santa Barbara on a "most wonderful morning after the rain yesterday. . . . The sea is near, the land is all wet and nice, and the most lovely clouds from white to very dark hanging over the ocean and mountains with that intense blue that I love so much back of everything and around it all. Gulls circle the land and little

---

pression of his love to become an artist, his mother's attachment of herself to him when he was a young man, making him believe she had heart disease, the resistance to his marriage, the deep sexual incompatibilities after marriage, despairing struggle with masturbation, and his unfortunate reticence and self-suppression when in conflict with the wishes of other people, have produced a condition of malignant compulsion neurosis."

ducks ride the waters in twos and in groups, and an airman has just passed, apparently enjoying a sun-ride."

Ahead, there would be jockeying for influence among Stanley's trustees; arguments over whether his care should be largely custodial or whether, as Anita wanted, there should be an aggressive program of therapy to bring him out of darkness; attempts to have Dr. Kempf reinstated; and countless conferences with lawyers and doctors. Through it all, Anita held fast to the hope that good would come of it for Stanley. No expense was spared. The budget for his personal care was a quarter of a million dollars in 1943. But he was never cured, and when his doctor telephoned Anita in 1947 to say that her brother had died peacefully, Anita could "not find it possible to wish that it was any other way." She then sat down and wrote Katherine: "I think of you so often. With a prayer that your steps may be helped. And that all the grief that has entered your life through Stanley may be translated into joy." Her responsibility for Stanley was over. She had no part in settling his $33,600,000 estate. That belonged to his widow.

In 1918, workmen had swarmed over the house at 101, inspecting the electrical wiring, fuse boxes, and switches, so that no sudden failure would endanger the functioning of Anita's week-old granddaughter's incubator. Nancy would be told long after how every clock had been regulated to prevent any time discrepancy from upsetting baby's schedule, and how, once the doctor's permission was obtained, select callers had been admitted—Nettie, uncles, aunts, cousins, butlers, maids, secretaries, all of whom entered the infant's room on tiptoe. In a leather-bound writing pad, Anita chronicled her granddaughter's every look, sound, gesture—("moving her arms different . . . mouth half smiles . . . expression of the most intense eagerness . . . pulled herself up").

Anita could have collected whatever rare objects she fancied, but all her passion to possess was centered on that child. A once lonely household which had revolved around one mistress suddenly in 1918 had three—Anita, Eleanor, and Nancy—and Anita desperately wanted to keep it that way.

It took Eleanor a year to admit that the arrangement could not last. She and her child had been looked after lavishly and lovingly, but twelve months under the same roof with her mother-in-law were sufficient to prove that Eleanor could no more make a life for herself and Nancy at 101 than the widowed Anita could have raised Em in Nettie's house. Eleanor could afford independence. She had been left a million dollars by her husband, and another million was waiting in trust for her daughter. But the prospect of separation, of losing them after the joy of having them to care for and to cuddle, was terrible to Anita. She tried resolutely to suppress "the selfish consideration," however, and when Eleanor proposed renting a house in Winnetka, walking distance from a Lake Michigan beach and a fifty-minute drive from downtown Chicago, the arrangement was wholeheartedly approved. But why pay rent? Anita bought the house as a gift.

After they had gone, Anita had second thoughts. Sunday lunches in Winnetka and their occasional visits to 101 were not the same as having Nancy in the nursery down the hall. Had she too readily relinquished her granddaughter? Em's spirit came to her, his presence seeming to sanction her yearning to raise his daughter herself. That she could have thought mother and child could be separated and that Eleanor might consent to so preposterous a request suggests a single-mindedness bordering on monomania. Eleanor was at first too stunned to respond; she could only say she would think it over. Unwilling to be estranged from one to whom she owed so much and of whom she was truly fond, Eleanor did not lose her temper, did not reply hastily, did not say that the proposal was outrageous. She simply said, finally, that she could not do it, and the two women parted unhappily.

But the rift could only be temporary. Their mutual affection was too strong, their interdependence too great, the child too important to them both, and as Anita became reconciled to Eleanor's refusal it was as if the quarrel had never occurred. Both widows recognized that they could neither live together nor go their separate, indifferent ways.

The idea of adopting a companion for Nancy came up two years later. Remembering her own pleasant childhood with her brother Freddy, Eleanor discussed with Anita the advantages of Nancy's having a playmate her own age. Adoption agencies were consulted and children inspected. The choice was narrowed to two small boys, the handsomer and healthier of whom was chosen, brought home to Winnetka and given the name John Blaine. Inexplicably, his adoption was never legalized.

Very early, John gave evidence of remarkable musical talent, which went along with reckless instability. He was an unsatisfac-

201

tory companion for Nancy, forever teasing. He defied discipline. No school would keep him for long. Resentment and rebellion grew with the years. He justifiably felt himself to be an outsider, unwanted —except by Anita (he always addressed her as Mrs. Blaine). She talked with him about his problems, paid his piano teachers, his debts, and later his psychiatrist. He thought she could do no wrong. She had, he said, "this humility of character and also this sort of general affection for humanity . . . and this was not a cultivated thing but was rather inborn and absolutely natural with any sort of pretense or phoneyness absolutely out of the question." Nothing went right for John. A first marriage broke up; he joined the army, went absent without leave; and only the intervention of Anita's lawyers kept him out of jail. The gifted and attractive boy became a frightened, bewildered man, unwelcome in Eleanor's home, a wanderer without work, a versatile pianist whom no one would employ. In his forties, he spent his days walking the streets or sitting in hotel lobbies until house detectives asked him to move on. He idled away hours in zoos—and drank. Periodic reports of his sessions with Dr. Kempf were sent to Anita, along with the bills.

Then he married a Chinese girl who had studied music in Paris, and the wedding, arranged by Nancy, brought him together with Eleanor for the first time in many years. He seemed more composed. They shook hands, but never saw each other again. Seven years later, he was shot in the back while running down a street in Harlem in the early morning hours. His murderer was not identified.

That tragic end was far in the future, however, when Eleanor, in 1927, confided to Anita that she planned to marry a husky architect whom she had met in the Adirondacks. Nine-year-old Nancy was to have a stepfather.

Clark Lawrence was living in Palm Beach, Florida, but came to Illinois to court Eleanor, causing some embarrassment when fire broke out in the Winnetka house and everyone, including "Larry," had to be routed out in the middle of the night by firemen. Shortly after the marriage he gave up his architectural practice in Florida and moved into Eleanor's home. Anita, embracing him warmly, as she would anyone Eleanor had chosen, helped establish him in Chicago, providing $75,000 for the expense of setting up an architectural office. But when the economy collapsed in 1929 and there were few commissions, Larry quit work and embarked on his permanent career as a gentleman of leisure.

A graduate of Cornell University with a commendable record as a captain of artillery in the First World War, Larry was a convivial

202

host and an excellent horseman, becoming master of the Long-meadow Hounds in Illinois. During World War II, he was given the rank of colonel, but a mental breakdown cut short his service. The gregarious manner was deceptive; a previous mental depression in the thirties had required his seclusion and psychiatric treatment. He had been a competent etcher, but gave that up also when he left architecture. He managed to keep occupied, however, with horses, estate management, and society. He liked to be among the rich, the well-born, or the well-known and had a discriminating eye for furniture, particularly early American. The historic house in Virginia, set amid 1,180 acres, which Anita bought for him and Eleanor after the Second World War, he transformed into a showplace.

But "the Colonel" (that was his preferred address) was not the ideal stepfather for two sensitive children. His rows with John led to the boy's being sent away from home. He was far more considerate of Nancy, particularly of her interest in riding, but his notion of humor made her squirm. She had inherited the prominent Blaine nose, and at an English boarding school where she and John had been placed for a year while Eleanor and Larry traveled, the children took to calling her "Parrot." Larry, thinking it quite a good joke, mailed her a postcard of a parrot and addressed her as "Dear Parrot." A tearful girl poured out her grief to her grandmother, her "Gurna," who took great pains to explain in an answering letter that teasing was a "beautiful thing that happens," for from it we learn that we could never inflict it on someone else—"not for anything! And that is a great pleasure to be thankful for."

That she was allowed to share her granddaughter's heartaches as well as enthusiasms seemed to Anita a gift of the gods. "Bumping around with you was great," she would write after one of their meetings; "grateful—thankful—the silent echo of love from my heart to yours, oh darling." How "awfully nice" it would be, she wrote on Nancy's twelfth birthday in England, "when radio reaches the point where everyone will carry one and just take it out of the pocket and speak to anyone on the other side of the world just as one might shout across the street. Well, I would shout to you today, have a happy birthday." If Anita had had her wish and had brought up her grandchild herself, the mutual adoration could not have been greater. "I wonder if you can have any idea," Anita wrote, "of the light you bring in."

Having inherited one-half of her father's estate, Nancy was no financial burden to the Lawrences. She paid her way. Moreover, the Lawrences could always rely on Anita's bounty, for she could deny her "dear beau fils" nothing, not after his "second telegram." Larry billed her for what he bought in her name, including presents for Nancy; notified her of exactly what she owed him for having the chimneys cleaned or for a motor boat, an oriental rug, theater tickets, or repairs at the Adirondacks camp. He was a precise bookkeeper. While some of Anita's causes and associations may have been thought odd in his circle, he took care not to say so. He did, however, draw the line at attending one New Year's Eve party at 101 which Nancy had arranged for her grandmother and to which she had invited several black guests. He would not have been at ease mixing socially either with them or with Nancy's white friends from the labor movement; so he and Eleanor went elsewhere. Nancy took it badly; Anita made light of it—"allow for everyone's point of view in opinion on all subjects." One Christmas, Anita wrote her shoemaker asking him to persuade the Colonel to order all the pairs of shoes he might want—"namely, streetwalking shoes, rough camp walking shoes, and evening shoes, and any other he might be able to use. And please send the bill completely to me."

There was one request which admittedly did trouble Anita. It was Larry's insistence that she give the Lawrences their own camp on Upper St. Regis Lake, rather than sharing hers. She didn't mind about the money, but she felt, as she wrote Roger Lee, that she had been "asked for something which in ways I think is not right." Larry kept after her, and she procrastinated, disturbed more by her seeming ungenerosity than by his persistence. Was she at fault? Was she thinking too little of others, too much of herself? "The thing that I am looking at inside now," she told Dr. Lee, "is not do they love me, but do I love them?" She did love them, and the Lawrences got their camp, bordered on one side by her land and on the other by the camp of an even wealthier woman, Mrs. Merriweather Post, whose luxurious hospitality ornamented many Lawrence summers. By then, Eleanor and Larry had a daughter of their own, Audrey, and had left Winnetka for "Castle Hill," their estate in Virginia.

Larry rode in the mornings, accompanied by a groom; entertained; traveled; went with Eleanor to meetings of the English Speaking Union; hunted and oversaw the Virginia property; and was commandant of the Upper St. Regis yacht club, to which no Jews, or half- or quarter-Jews, need apply for membership. Upper St. Regis Lake was not ready for that; nor was he.

He had long since washed his hands of John Lawrence (no longer John Blaine). It was Anita who tried to reconcile the forlorn young man to the wealth and position associated with his name and his own comparative poverty and anonymity. When John came to her with his anger, he was told that "one doesn't quarrel with one's life, one just handles it; so do not mind too much these strong feelings." She discreetly forbore telling him that she had had "very different ideas from the Lawrences" on how he should be handled. She had not let him know that when Nancy was old enough to have a car, she had offered to buy one for John and had advised the Lawrences "to let him have it that winter when he needed a pulling up," but that they had not "seen it that way." Then, when Nancy had come of age, Anita had suggested that John at last be told that he had never been adopted legally and therefore was not entitled to and should not expect to inherit any of the family wealth. But the Lawrences, she wrote Dr. Kempf, thought it "must not be spoken of to him, must not be alluded to in his presence," and it was not.

Whatever the tensions within the family or disorders in the wider world of the 1930s, they were not permitted to upset Anita's personal establishment, which, in her sixties, had become as fixed as the movement of the planets.

At seven-thirty each morning, one of two butlers arrived at the back door of 101 and greeted the other servants in their basement dining room, where eight places were set. After breakfast, the butler walked upstairs one flight to the pantry to prepare a tray for Mrs. Blaine, lowering the assembled dishes and silver on a dumbwaiter to the kitchen, where they were placed on a platewarmer. At about eight, Mrs. Blaine rang for her maid, who then buzzed the pantry and ordered the tray brought up. The order was relayed from pantry to kitchen, grapefruit or orange juice was set alongside a note giving the outside temperature, and the tray was carried in the elevator to the third floor and taken into a small study adjoining Mrs. Blaine's bedroom. A morning newspaper and notes from the secretaries were placed next to her chair, after which the butler announced that the room was ready and breakfast served. An hour later, the mail (would there be a letter from Nancy?) was left on a table outside the library, where Mrs. Blaine could pick it up at her convenience or have the secretaries do it for her. At ten o'clock, she rang for the butler to discuss meals for the day—for lunch an egg dish, a vegetable or salad, and a fresh fruit cup served in the library on two wooden trays put side-by-side on folding stands. At four in the afternoon, a tea tray with a few cookies and a small pitcher of orange juice was brought up. At five-thirty, the servants had supper. At seven, Mrs. Blaine's dinner was served in the same manner as lunch, with the addition of two shaded candles in silver holders. The menu was unvaried—a thermos of soup, a meat dish, potatoes and vegetables in hot-water dishes, hot rolls, a salad (if not served at lunch), and cooked fruit or pudding. At eight o'clock the night watchman arrived, and at ten a glass of hot milk in a thermos was left outside Mrs. Blaine's bedroom. The house was closed by checking all windows on the first floor and hall, locking the front door, and turning out all lights except in the stairways and the basement. The maid on duty closed up on the bedroom floor when her mistress retired for the night.

At informal luncheons, held in the library if business was to be transacted, each guest had a small table with pencil and writing pad by his chair. More formal dinners were given in the mahogany-paneled dining room and announced exactly fifteen minutes after the time of invitation (no cocktails), when Mrs. Blaine would lead the way to the table, press a bell to signal the pantry—one ring for one butler, two for two butlers, three to begin serving. No stronger drink than wine was offered. From early spring through the fall, fresh vegetables and flowers were brought each weekend from the House in the Woods that had been Nettie's and was now Anita's, and the excess flowers sent by taxi to the children's hospital.

There was no getting through the barricade of servants if Mrs. Blaine did not wish to be disturbed. "Really," Flora Cooke wrote, "I must talk to you about this 'stone wall' of yours." But when one did get through, the reception was an outstretched-arms welcome. She still tended to forget incidentals; for example, that others might be short of cash. For two years, she neglected to refund Katherine Taylor's travel expenses (Miss Taylor was a Parker School trustee), then woke up to the omission and reimbursed "K.T." with liberal interest added and no apology. Only the immediate family and very exceptional outsiders, Eleanor Roosevelt among them, were greeted at the front door by Anita in person, others being met by a butler, Olafson or Larsson, and escorted to a small, first-floor room where they waited to be announced. She would then sweep down the stairs in her rapid, free gait to receive them. If the guest was an old friend like Katharine Taylor, Anita would lean over the second floor balcony and call down in a clear voice, "Darling, I am so glad you have come! Come up." Friends were always introduced to whatever butler was on duty—"one of the many things," Tage Larsson remarked, "that gave the feeling you were of some value to her."

All sorts climbed those stairs for tea and talk and help. The rule she gave her granddaughter was one she herself followed: "Learn to know all kinds of people. Don't push away new experiences because you are afraid of what they might do to you. Learn to know them and love them and you will find out soon enough what kind of people they are and to deal with them accordingly." The door was always open to friends of Nancy's, who, in Anita's presence, found themselves saying things they never knew they knew and caught up in enthusiasms her attentiveness encouraged. One young car salesman whom Nancy brought to tea seemed to the granddaughter quite dull, though handsome; but for forty-five minutes he and her grandmother carried on a spirited conversation about automobile parts.

The typical caller had more momentous matters to discuss, of course, usually money. One of them was Salvador de Madariaga, to whom Anita had been introduced in 1936, shortly after brother Cyrus's death, by Quincy Wright, a professor of international law at the University of Chicago. Small, lively, whimsical, de Madariaga had been educated in France; had taught at Oxford; had written plays, novels, and poetry. Most exciting to Anita, he had served with the League of Nations from 1922 to 1927 as head of the Disarmament Section. Later, as Spanish ambassador to the United States and then France, he had kept closely in touch with the work of the League and had become increasingly skeptical of its effectiveness. The missing ingredient in international relations, he thought, was a consciousness in the minds of people everywhere that the world was one. He proposed to remedy this by organizing a World Association for the Advancement of World Citizenship—a foundation which would publish studies of political problems, scientific advances, and the arts, emphasizing their international applications.* He had already enlisted Thomas Mann, Jules Romains, Arnold Toynbee, Gilbert Murray, and Ray Lyman Wilbur as sponsors.

Anita picked up his idea so quickly that de Madariaga felt "he had solved the riddle of the universe." She gave him a thousand dollars at their initial meeting and offered to help him organize his World Association. Since he was unfamiliar with her previous volunteer organizing efforts on behalf of the League of Nations, he accepted the offer with pleasure and bid her Godspeed, whereupon

---

* One of de Madariaga's applause-provoking lines was, "It's going to take geologic time, so there's not a moment to lose."

she proceeded to introduce Chicagoans to de Madariaga's plan for peace. Finding a warm response, she telephoned him to say that she would now proceed to set up a local committee, mentioning casually that it would have complete autonomy. Oh yes, de Madariaga replied unthinkingly. It took a few weeks for both of them to understand that they had not understood each other. It was only after the Chicago group, that is to say Anita, had hired a "research officer" that de Madariaga woke up to the fact that this charming, generous lady had ideas of her own, and they might not be his. "In its essence," he wrote her, "the Foundation means a central perspective for all problems and therefore could ill brook a dispersion of initiative, which as a matter of fact is precisely the evil which it sets out to combat by its inception." He urged her to hold her fire "until a World Center is established in Geneva," for he did not see "how work can grow from the bottom upward rather than from the top downward; the main current will have to come from the trunk." If she wanted to be useful, why not raise at least a million dollars in Chicago to endow his Central Office?

That did not interest her. She went ahead and formed a small Chicago committee, and when it later met with de Madariaga it was to inform him that his central organization had too large a budget, was too dominated by "experts," in short, was "too pompous a structure." Chicagoans, Anita decided, must have their own office and name—World Citizens Association.

The Chicago committee was the only local group ever set up. Its mainstays were Anita, one of her attorneys—Edwin Cassels—Quincy Wright, Edwin Embree of the Rosenwald Foundation, and Wilbur, then president of Stanford University. Newspaper columnist Edgar Ansel Mowrer was hired part time to do some "scouting" for them in Europe; Adlai Stevenson occasionally showed up for meetings at 101; but by and large the World Citizens Association was four people who gathered every month or so in Mrs. Blaine's living room, where they were given apple pie and orange juice. Anita discouraged the idea of a dues-paying membership and the solicitation of outside contributions. The association was financed entirely by her. It worked as follows, according to Quincy Wright: "Mrs. Blaine would say, 'We are all equals here, everyone must express his views on what should be done to promote World Citizenship.' The majority should decide on a policy or action and then the treasurer would see whether funds were available. It never happened that funds were available except for projects vigorously supported by the treasurer."

What, one wonders, did these earnest, busy folk think they were accomplishing? Had the question been put, Anita might have answered by asking how effective any present group or government was in stemming the tide that was carrying the world toward global war? One had to pull the oar that was at hand. The reason for the work, Anita wrote Quincy Wright, was the extreme need in the world for man to look at world problems as a whole instead of sectionally, in order that the world may progress out of the stage of "sectionalism, pride, ambition and hatred, which lead to clashes of force between peoples, and into the stage in which the object of people is the good of the whole."

Confident of the basic decency of man and hopeful that rulers would do right if they could be shown the right, Anita perceived each new international crisis of the thirties as a personal challenge demanding a personal response. When Japan invaded Manchuria in 1931, she telegraphed the Japanese emperor that his nation has "so much to give to the world, shall she not give it in truth? Shall she adopt the method of falsehood? If she does, how great will be the darkness she spreads over the earth." A cable to Mahatma Ghandi, signed "A Seeker," suggested that he draft a statement on the wrongs of British rule in India, which she would pay to publicize. A wire to Franklin D. Roosevelt (copy to Nancy) praised his stand on reciprocal tariffs: "We wrecked something when we required foreign countries to repay us and then erected walls which would prevent their doing so." Italy's attack on Ethiopia in 1935 prompted a cablegram to Mussolini: "You surely do not want to send yourself down to history as a mass murderer and a public enemy, nor to send thousands of your countrymen and thousands from other countries to their graves for the purpose of conquest." Another went to the secretary of the League of Nations, urging that the Italian dictator be blocked in Ethiopia, for he was a "wild man and ought to be held in check by world action." Having been acquainted socially with the Hanfstaengels in Chicago, Anita wrote their eccentric offspring, Ernst (Putsy) Hanfstaengel, who had attached himself to Hitler's retinue in Berlin, "venturing from the association of family friendship" to ask whether he would feel it worthwhile and possible to relay her thoughts to Reichsführer Hitler. A week later, she cabled Hitler directly, pleading for international arbitration "in collaboration with other parts of the world."

Her once-prized League of Nations, weakened by Britain's and France's refusal to stand up to Mussolini in 1935 and now powerless four years after to influence Hitler, was bankrupt, and Anita faced that failure squarely. She told Quincy Wright that she could no longer in good conscience work for American membership in the League or single-handedly finance the League of Nations Association in Chicago. As the European powers prepared openly for war, she suggested to the director of the association in New York that the organization throw whatever weight it had behind amending the United States Neutrality Act, so that aid could be given to the threatened democracies, and that it should at the same time reexamine the conditions under which the United States might someday enter a reorganized and revitalized League.

The League had failed, she thought, because America "went home and pulled her skirts around her and said, 'it is nothing to me.' "[8] But that was history and unalterable. One's influence now must be thrown into checking the resurgent wave of isolationism in the United States. Anita could not begin to express "the sickness that is in me" when she heard politicians say that her country must think only of its own interests: "Our speakers, our argufiers think they have to use that argument in order to arouse us. You hear it on the radio and you see it and it strikes your ears and it hits your heart so that you can't bear it." The United States ought to be "entirely committed to helping Europe and to helping the world."[9]

Anita's next-to-last trip to Europe was made in 1937, when she was seventy-one, in the company of forty-three pieces of luggage, two maids, two butlers, a chauffeur, Dr. Roger Lee, his wife, and their three children. Her principal purpose in going was to talk with Sir Oliver Lodge, whom she had not seen since 1919. The time was ripe, she thought, for a spiritualist group in America dedicated to legitimate psychic research, and she wanted his guidance.

Lodge, nearly eighty-six, was overjoyed to have word from her after so many years and offered to send a car to Southampton to meet her and to arrange for sittings with a medium in London. She told him that, following his instructions, she had been filling hundreds of pages with automatic writing, starting "as you told me to do and no motion coming. I thought as to how I could make the process easily mechanical. I arranged a suspended rest for the wrist. Then motion began mechanically, and I have a record of all I received in this way." Lodge encouraged her to carry on her experiments, they exchanged ideas for furthering psychic research, and she came away from their talks grateful for what he had given her from his "great store of knowledge and thought, what you gave me of yourself from your present spirit. I love you so much."

Her gratitude seemed boundless. From Chicago, she sent him baskets of hyacinths, peaches packed by a French firm in Covent Garden, a fur cape, a cloth cape, an immense tub of azalias, followed by another box of fresh peaches, a basket of lilies of the valley, peach blossoms, carnations and hyacinths, a hand-carved chess set, and more flowers from Claridges.

They were to meet once more, two years later, at Lodge's country house, and out of those discussions about "the unseen world" came a suggestion that Anita bring to America an English medium whom Lodge respected. Anita, though receptive, thought a second opinion advisable and asked Dr. Lee to interview Mrs. Massingbird Rogers in London. His report to Anita was circumspect: no comment on the substance of the medium's work but no doubt of her sincerity. Mrs. Rogers was thereupon presented with a first-class ticket to America, given a secretary, installed in the Stevens Hotel in Chicago and then in the Copley-Plaza in Boston, where she lived on her benefactor's bounty for ten years. Anita rarely saw her in Boston but paid all her expenses, down to ten-cent tips, taxi fares, and hairdos.*

When Anita sailed for home from Liverpool in 1939 on that last voyage, the British were beginning to mobilize; war was declared the day her boat docked in Boston. The psychic research project was shelved. Everything now had second place to reelecting Franklin Roosevelt and persuading Congress to aid France and Britain. Anita bought a half-hour of radio network time over NBC to explain why she favored a third term. She joined the Committee to Defend America by Aiding the Allies. She sent telegrams to every congressman asking for repeal of the 1934 Johnston Act, which forbade private American loans to any nation which had defaulted on its World War I debts. At Adlai Stevenson's request, she paid for newspaper ads throughout the country, endorsing the pending Lend Lease bill.

A brief Adirondacks vacation in August of 1940 had a spectacular finale when her camp burned to the ground a day before her intended departure. She was off picnicking at the time, and when an excited messenger found her and broke the news, she said that she was sorry to have missed the fire. The camp was never rebuilt; the loss

---

* Anita's 1940 Christmas message was written, Mrs. Rogers alleged, by a "spirit guide"—Kian Chu. "I see," she wrote Anita, "the alterations Kian made in the prayer—and I like it much better."

seemed insignificant. After all, with Europe ablaze, her greatest worry was that the Germans might successfully invade Britain. If that happened, she wired Winston Churchill, the British and French governments must come to America, for "with Britain here, and Canada and us together taking care of Britain, and with South America absolutely holding unified, I am sure we can hold Hitler at arm's length over and across the water, and then try to teach Hitler something." It was 1917 all over again, and the "something" that had to be taught the aggressive enemy included charity: "We mustn't hate Hitler; we must hate what Hitler is doing."

Anything that might jeopardize an allied military victory had to be resisted, even the International Harvester Company, in which she was still a major stockholder. When a strike broke out at four plants in March 1941, and Anita's nephew Fowler (then vice president of International Harvester) refused to recognize the union or to raise wages, she defied company policy by asking FDR to impose a compulsory settlement, contributed to strike relief, and brought together Fowler and the Harvard-educated CIO leader, Powers Hapgood, but to no avail. Soon thereafter she was writing Congress recommending a declaration of war: "When we put our hands to a plow we do not turn back. We should now take our full responsibility." The traffic in telegrams was speeded up. She wired Sir Oliver Lodge in June, inviting him to bring his family to the United States. "Very touched," he replied, but he would stay in Cornwall. She cabled the owner of the *London Daily Sketch*, seeking space in his columns to rebut an article it had published by her cousin "Bertie" McCormick of the *Chicago Tribune*, whose notions about America's place in the world she termed "faulty" and "trivial." "Thank God!" she wired Churchill after the attack on Pearl Harbor: the Japanese had cleared the way for a triumphant march of *all* the democracies, including the United States.

Flags were flying, factories booming, Franklin Roosevelt was gloriously leading, and Anita was exhilarated, especially by "the unifying of the uniform and the thing it represents." On a wartime train trip to Colorado Springs, she had good conversation with a soldier from New Jersey and with another from the Bronx, and when she reached her destination, a GI who had been a dentist in Georgia gave her a lift. "I mean to look them up and have a party for them," she wrote Stanley. She was proud that her granddaughter Nancy, recently graduated from Vassar, had gone to Vermont to work on the land, taking the place of someone who could fight: "You have a lot of your father in you, he would be doing much thusly." Secretaries were reminded to send flowers to army and navy bases at Easter, telegrams were dispatched urging American intervention in the dispute between Britain and India, pamphlets published to prepare public opinion for a new League of Nations.

Anita had once described Nettie's Presbyterian missionaries in China as "a standing family joke." But in 1943, she wished to make some gesture in memory of her mother's interest in China, and the opportunity came on 20 March. Newspapermen had been alerted and were waiting in the hall of the Drake Hotel as Mrs. Blaine, wearing a long caracul coat and a purple toque topped by an ostrich feather, entered Madame Chiang Kai-shek's suite. In her briefcase, Anita carried International Harvester stock valued at $100,000. She pulled out the stock certificates, handed them to the lady seated on a sofa, and said, "You are to use this in any way you want." It was reported that Madame Chiang's eyes were moist; the money would be used for the war orphans of China, "perpetuating the spirit of China as it shines through the world." "Your words are just as beautiful as you are," Anita replied. And to Stanley she wrote that Madame Chiang was "deeply moved and grateful. It was a beautiful moment to me."

She prepared a statement to be inserted in a program for a Jewish benefit; she would do anything any Jew asked her, she wrote Nancy. She contributed a message to a pamphlet for a Russian fair being held in Chicago, her prayer that the world might find "the common path in our defense of liberty" and a harmony that would be "diverse in rich variety."[10] The words were not meant merely to stimulate contributions to war relief; they were her testament to the reality of brotherhood. "Dear Mr. Hitler," she had cabled the Reichsführer earlier that year, "it is our custom in civility to begin our communication so. It does not mean you are dear to me [for] you have given yourself to things that must be abhorrent. But in another sense you are dear to the Divine spirit which is all love. Thus I do not judge you. I am just one of the human beings here on earth as you are. I believe the great spirit will labor with you as with all people up to the furtherest possible point, to lead you to the light of love. Love lives and truth stands. . . . All else dies." (John Blaine Lawrence once asked her if she thought Hitler received the message: "She told me she didn't know, but she had tried to do something there, and she was dead serious about it.")

She would countenance no derogation of FDR or of his aims. Along with Frank McCulloch of the Union for Democratic Action, she drafted an attack on cousin "Bertie," accusing him of deliberate distortion and of being "divisive, obscuring, instead of unifying, throwing light and giving constructive help." And she wrote FDR that one should not "lose faith in democracy, however grossly the *Chicago Tribune* and such may dishonor it."

Looking beyond unconditional surrender, she proposed to the moribund World Citizens Association that under its auspices a conference be called in early 1941 of people "equipped to give weighty judgment on the next steps the world should take." De Madariaga was back in the picture. Grand, he responded; the conference would be "like a ray of light in the storm." Ray Lyman Wilbur agreed to chair a three-day gathering at the Onwentsia Country Club in Lake Forest, Illinois, all expenses paid, though he confessed that his expectations were more limited than Anita's or de Madariaga's; the conference might, he thought, "add to the present skeleton-like cobweb of world intercommunication, avoiding as many controversial subjects as possible."

That was much too modest an aim in Anita's opinion, and she took the floor to offer a set of grandiose goals. "Frankly," Wilbur said on the third day, glancing at his train schedule, "these generalizations, these sweetened preparations in sentences that catch their own tails at the end and just turn in a circle, I believe are out of date. We have got to get down to something tangible. I want to leave the resolutions and all the sweetness and light off to one side." Anita let that remark float away and then expressed her "strong feeling" that it would be wonderful if the conference passed a resolution approving the unification of religions. "The only resolution I would present," Wilbur answered, again looking at his watch, "would be that we buy you a beautiful bouquet for your kind hospitality," at which the conferees burst into applause. Wilbur made his escape and the conference was adjourned.[11]

There was one further use to be made of the World Citizens Association, to which Anita had already given more than $150,000. The United Nations preparatory conference was to open in San Francisco in the spring of 1945, and Anita suggested that the association issue a statement backing whatever came out of San Francisco, "in the feeling that however much the result might disappoint us, it will be our one anchor to a democratic world, and we must help our country to hang onto it."

When the League of Nations Association changed its name to the American Association for the United Nations, Anita took up where she had left off before the war, became a member of its board of directors and later a vice president, and represented the association

214

at a discussion in Washington of the new United Nations Relief and Rehabilitation Administration. "It was thrilling," she wrote Stanley, whom she always addressed as if he were competent to understand her letters, "to hear of their plans from officials of our government who have been working to prepare our part in the cooperative work. . . . Hope will begin to spring again in the stricken world." Quincy Wright was relied upon to keep her posted on the day-to-day progress in San Francisco; meanwhile, telegrams poured out of Chicago, cheering the delegates on, urging concessions where necessary, for it was better "to sacrifice a part than to sacrifice the whole; it matters vitally that this first chance for world agreement to prevent war, by substituting another process, must not be lost to mankind."

She saw the United Nations Charter as a prelude to world order: "As in traveling in the foothills in the heat of day, we catch glimpses of the snow-capped mountains and lose sight of them and catch them again, so in our ways, working through the underbrush, we may know that the heights are there to be reached." She dreamed of visiting every member nation of the United Nations, so that she could see "what the life of the children is." You are seventy-nine, Dr. Lee reminded her. She settled for writing an introduction to Quincy Wright's analysis of the UN Charter and had 150,000 free copies distributed: "Oh world of souls, look up! The next step is always higher than the last. The free world becomes a responsible world, the free press a responsible press. The free soul becomes a responsible soul and is his brother's keeper."

Anita thought highly of Roger Lee's judgment. She had taken him and his family with her on trips to Europe. She had discussed with him her schemes for psychic investigation, her relations with the Lawrences, her exasperation with Stanley's wife, and her concerns for her granddaughter's welfare. But the advice of the rotund, round-faced doctor that she slow down was dismissed. She meant to do more, not less. The causes and contributions multiplied—$15,000 for American colleges in the Near East, $50,000 to the American Veterans Committee in memory of her son, money for a five-year study of juvenile delinquency in Chicago, medical supplies and doctors for miners injured in a cave-in in Kentucky, anonymous gifts to day-care centers and to an orphanage in Turkey. The one commitment, the gift that always took precedence, however, was the gift of herself to her granddaughter, whose casual attitude toward possessions corresponded to her own.

When Nancy, in her teens, had confessed to embarrassment at the shape of her nose, "Gurna" made all the arrangements for a remedial operation; and when her granddaughter, shy of society, had had to face the painful ritual of coming out, Anita took over, organizing parties where group dances decreed a frequent change of partner. "Darling Nance," she wrote, "*so* thankful that we can both see and know that we can give our real thoughts to each other, that we can agree or disagree on them, see them alike or unalike, and agree on this: that one must live out what is in one of conviction. And of light." In the realm of the spirit, complete freedom. In the realm of the physical, however, Anita set limits. She made one firm request —that her granddaughter, who was devoted to horseback riding, not risk injury. That request led to voluminous correspondence when Nancy, then at Vassar, bought a horse. Scores of letters on the subject were exchanged between Anita, Nancy, Eleanor, and Roger Lee. Anita thought it dangerous to jump, Eleanor thought it a pity to oppose something in which her daughter excelled, Nancy was willing to go along with any decision they made. Finally, Dr. Lee was conscripted as referee and his judgment accepted; Nancy would not jump for one year.

Past, present, and future merged in the granddaughter. "This is the day," she wrote her on 26 September 1936, "that your grandfather and I started off to make a life together. He was so wonderful! I think you're a lot like him." She dreamed of her son, picturing him in a rocker, "sitting sort of crosswise with something in his arms. . . . I sat down on the floor to gaze at him. He opened his eyes and smiled. He was a child perhaps of six or seven. He said 'I am not up yet, you could put me in your bed.' I holding steady, not to overwhelm him. I could do that. I awoke." In Nancy, husband and son were flesh, not a dream but a young woman studying art history, having her own convictions about changing the world and letting "Gurna" share the pain and pleasure of her growing up.

From Nancy's birth, Anita had recorded in her journal every small step toward adulthood, watching for opportunities to smooth the child's way without diminishing Eleanor's authority. Eleanor had come into her life "in such a wonderful way; she is my very own." But Anita longed to pick up Nancy "and help her: What can I do: Be as near as the limits that are imposed will permit, use the chances I may have, to learn and to give. Make chances if none come accidentally." The light "goes out when you go," she wrote her granddaughter at Vassar, "only it doesn't really go out. It stays! Life bursts into radiance." When she sought words to express her feelings on Nancy's eighteenth birthday, "the day of your coming into womanhood by the laws of your state," there seemed "not to be any that would hold them." She was highly pleased by Nancy's work after the war as a textile labor organizer in North Carolina, for it was a means of "getting into the bare-bone essential facts of industry and of life of people."

When her granddaughter visited Chicago, there were gay, talkative dinners on trays in the upstairs library or evenings at the theater (Anita saw *Three Men on a Horse* eight times). She was held back from showering too many gifts on her grandchild by the knowledge that Nancy, who at one point seriously considered giving away the money inherited from her father, was made uneasy by luxury. Nevertheless, two days before an intimate celebration at 101 that had been planned for one of Nancy's birthdays, Anita telephoned to say that she had heard a "marvelous" chorus of ninety voices at Northwestern University and wouldn't it be lovely if they sang during the birthday dinner. She appreciated that Nancy desired a very modest party, but the singers wouldn't intrude; they would be invisible in her living room! The chorus was not invited, and "Gurna" was persuaded to settle for one pianist.

Of all the parties for Nancy at 101, the most unforgettable were those on New Year's Eve from 1936 to 1940, the coming of midnight signaled by a gong, lights extinguished, Anita appearing at the top of the stairs with a butler holding a lighted candle as she read Browning: "Grow old with me—the best is yet to be." The lights flashed on, champagne was poured, hats and noisemakers snatched from tables that had been mysteriously set up during the darkness, and hilarious young people would snake dance through the house from the basement kitchen to the garden. Each year, every guest received a favor a monogrammed matchbox, a silver-initialed moneyclip, or a silver bell with the New Year's date inscribed.

On her grandmother's eightieth birthday on 4 July 1946, Nancy took charge, organizing a festive evening reminiscent of the eightieth birthday party Anita had staged for Nettie more than thirty years earlier. The party could not be a surprise, for furniture had to be removed from 101 and stored temporarily in vans, charts of guests drawn up and hung in the dressing rooms, the list of invitees carefully gone over and typed in triplicate by Anita's secretaries. It was an eclectic gathering, McCormicks mingling with musicians and labor organizers. Family feuds were checked at the door. Even

"Bertie" paid tribute: "Cousin Anita and I have always been aiming at different targets ever since we were youngsters, but she has always been a straight shooter."

Anita had lost none of her fascination for the young. One awe-struck guest in his twenties* commented that "she managed without fuss or anything like condescension to suggest that Chicago was lucky to have me around." She loved to play four-hand piano with one of Nancy's friends, Paul Haggerty, or to accompany a group gathered around her in the living room, boisterously singing hymns. Best of all, she loved to waltz.

Shortly after her eightieth birthday, she had been introduced to Paul Draper and, entranced by his dancing, said nothing would do but to have a party in his honor.†[12] And if there was to be a party, why not include the cast of a play then running in Chicago, starring Constance Bennett. An invitation was extended to Miss Bennett, who sent word that she would be "too tired" to come. She had not reckoned on her hostess's resolution. Anita went to the theater, walked backstage after the performance, and, in the words of a by-stander, "completely undeterred, her arms outstretched, swept into Connie's drawing room, saying 'My Dear, I knew your father!'" Miss Bennett came.

The next morning, Anita was back at her desk, reading her mail, sorting out appeals, conferring with her secretaries, drafting a telegram prompted by some item in the newspaper, or dealing with the latest mischief of her errant niece Muriel.

Since the death of Harold and Edith, it had fallen to Anita and Muriel's brother Fowler to deal with an "unspeakable" situation in Muriel's household which had come to light. They would have preferred to stay out of it, or at least keep it out of the papers, for a public squabble within the family was abhorrent to them both. Since the safety of children was at stake, they felt obliged to act.

In fulfillment, she said, of her late husband's wish, Muriel in 1939 had adopted two orphans, and four years later, when she joined the

---

* Reuel Denney, who later wrote Nancy that "there was a very ancient indissoluble affinity between you and your grandmother that exceeded the usual terms of such a kinship."
† She was to do much more for Draper. In the fall of 1948, he and his partner Larry Adler sued a lady in Connecticut for libel, she having alleged that those who bought tickets to their concert would "indirectly make cash contributions to Moscow." Anita paid their court costs. The following year she gave Draper and Clark Foreman $10,000 to set up a "Cultural Center" for artists, irrespective of their political coloration.

Women's Army Corps, had appointed her housekeeper as their guardian. Following one of Muriel's visits home on furlough, the housekeeper had written Anita that she was "in terror" of her employer, and that during drunken bouts Muriel had physically and verbally abused her and the children. There were allusions to a lesbian relationship. Having passed this letter along to Fowler, Anita discussed it with Richard Bentley, her legal adviser since the death of his father Cyrus in 1930. Nothing was done until the companion-housekeeper came to Chicago for an operation, when she "let out things she had never told before," Anita wrote Nancy, revealing a "state of cruelty and terrorism on the part of Muriel hard to believe." Anita agonized over her duty to Muriel, to the children, to the McCormick name. She had a genuine affection for her niece, had once considered adopting her, and had given her a camp in the Adirondacks. "I think of your middle name as tolerance," Muriel had told her.

But could brutality be tolerated? If Muriel could be persuaded to give up the children without a legal fight, the sordid story might be kept private; that was the word Richard Bentley carried to an army camp in Georgia where Muriel was stationed. She would not hear of it. On her next furlough she brought the children with her to 101 to have it out with Anita. They went into the library after breakfast, and the next half hour convinced Anita that she and Fowler must act. One of the children had come into the room, "smiling, beautiful, gay." The child had taken no more than a few steps when Muriel asked why she had changed the position of a pin she was wearing: "I put it there, I never gave you permission to change it." The child was frightened, tears flowed. Muriel said, "you are a crybaby, go down to the front door and I will pick you up," and then, "I don't know whether I will pick you up or not."[13]

Anita and Fowler started proceedings in the courts; the court removed the children from Muriel's physical custody and named Fowler as their guardian; but hearings, appeals, and a sensational trial were to follow before the children were legally lodged with an Illinois family Anita deemed suitable.

By the end of that distasteful, five-year legal battle, Anita was eighty-one. She had managed to keep Fowler on course, counsel a frightened housekeeper, visit the adopted children as they were moved from camps to schools to foster homes, and brave the publicity. Muriel's admission that she had thrown the housekeeper to the floor and kicked her in the breasts had been played up in the Chicago papers, which reported in vivid detail Muriel's defense that the "friend had pulled her hair and scratched her face with her red nails."[14]

Brother and sister were never reconciled. But when it was all over, Anita had put her arms around Muriel, who wept gently on her aunt's shoulder.

While this miserable soap opera was being played out in the Chicago press, diverting readers from the casualty lists and battles in the Pacific, and Anita was following with rising excitement accounts of the new world organization being shaped by allied leaders, there came the shocking bulletin—Franklin D. Roosevelt was dead. "Oh the ache of it," she wrote Nancy, "and the puzzle as to what is ahead." During the 1936 campaign, she had done whatever she could to help reelect Roosevelt and swell his majority in Congress, and in 1944, she had written and paid for an open letter to the Republican convention, printed in the *Chicago Sun*, suggesting that the Republicans unite with Democrats to renominate Roosevelt, so that the nation would not be "subjected to the jar and question of a major change in leadership."[15] She had not been so naive as to think that the Republicans would take her advice; the idea had come to her "while I was feeling no other than a negative interest in the Republican Convention." But as she wrote Mr. Roosevelt, "I thought the voicing of it might have some benefit, certainly would do no harm."

FDR's popularity seemed the salvation of the country (though she voted for Herbert Hoover in 1932). "It almost takes my breath," she had remarked after the 1940 elections, "to think what would be the feeling of today if the result had been different and to realize what today is, leading as it does to great coordinated work for the human family everywhere." That Roosevelt was a Democrat was incidental. Indeed, she had suggested that he pick a Republican as his running mate in 1944. "It might be the long-awaited moment," she wrote the president, "to get rid of these terms which have come to mean so little that is real—Republican and Democrat—and in a junction of their forces begin to create terms of division which have real content in them to divide and unite men and women in the depths of their souls."[16] Her instinct was always to bring together, and in a crisis to follow the leader. "If it is the right way to hold a tight rein on the peoples to save them in the end for freedom," she

220

informed Roosevelt, "you will find a way to let the people know the meaning of that." The aura of Roosevelt illumined his associates —"Barkley with his patience, Philip Murray with his fine mind, McNutt with his good soldiership, Wallace with all he brings." When an Illinois senator dared criticize Admiral King and General Marshall, she could not understand how these "great leaders" of "wisdom and genius" could be subjected to such humiliation.

Now the commander-in-chief was dead, and it was up to everyone to "do his part." "There could be no word," she telegraphed Eleanor Roosevelt shortly after the San Francisco conference, "but one of triumph for his life work." The whole world must "stand in awe to think of the steps which he created to lead to the towering climax of today." At last, there might be an end to "the masquerading heroism [that] calls itself unlimited national sovereignty." But did Harry Truman accept that? Could one count on him? She was not sure.

The stateman who did inspire her trust was Henry Agard Wallace, whom she had admired from the moment he was elected vice president in 1940, when she had wired "how thankful" she was that he was at FDR's side. "Our mutual friend Dick Finnegan of the *Chicago Times* was in the other day," Wallace had replied, "telling me of the unusual service which you have rendered to the progressive cause in Chicago from time to time. . . . I hope to have the pleasure of meeting you." Four months later, he wrote to praise a letter she had mailed to Congress; he was especially struck by "that part where you say, 'we are the heirs of these objectives—Freedom for all; Opportunity for all; Education for all; Protection for all.'" He sent her copies of his speeches, one of which he said "required a lot of reading between the lines to be liked; your letter tells me that you were reading between the lines." That Wallace had been one of Roosevelt's top advisers was recommendation enough, but he was also a farmer, and her fortune derived from the dirt farmers of the Midwest. In Wallace, she discerned the uplifting imperative of the social gospel, "thoughts that will be a force to bring us to the place of our dreams." Had he not written that the world needed a revival of "those immaterial, intangible, unknowable forces which, by faith, we believe make for righteousness and which we customarily call God?" And that "this world was meant to be one world?"[17] Here was a man, she said, who "tells America to be good," while others "tell everyone else in the world to be good."

When he was forced to resign from President Truman's cabinet in 1946 and declared that he would "carry on the fight for peace,"

Anita volunteered her services and sent him a check for $10,000.* He replied that he hoped "to encourage men and women in every town in America to organize and work for a lasting peace," and that in order to have the work done "as efficiently as possible," he had rented an office in Washington. With a small paid staff and volunteers on weekends he would try to "answer the mass of mail I am receiving, in addition to distributing literature to the people all over America," and would use her "generous contribution in following out this plan." He intended calling together "about one hundred sincere leaders who are anxious to take concerted action for peace," possibly the following January, and hoped she would be among them. "Any plan that you would choose would be right for me," Anita answered.

During the ensuing months, Anita read Wallace's speeches, sent him encouraging words, and met the advisers who were to be the core of Wallace's third-party campaign for the presidency in 1948. She already knew Sidney Hillman of the CIO, a labor leader reputed to have "a good nose for money" and father of the National Citizens Political Action Committee.[18] Although distrusted by traditional politicians, the NCPAC by 1944 had attracted eighteen thousand members, Anita among them. At a luncheon in Chicago, Hillman had asked her to help start a local branch, of which she became temporary chairman; thereafter, she went on the national executive committee, primarily to work for a fourth term for Roosevelt.

At first she was not altogether at ease with certain members of the Political Action Committee and sometimes felt as if she had mistakenly showed up at the wrong party. Her co-workers here were not of the class to which she was accustomed—high-minded citizens of independent means or unimpeachable professional connections— but amateurs in the rough and tumble of politics. She found herself sitting beside working-class organizers and radical intellectuals who used inflammatory language and didn't mind throwing mud at the

* Before accepting the check, Wallace had written, "I believe we should have a good talk on purposes and methods." Two months went by, and no talk. Instead, Wallace had asked Harold Young of his staff to telephone Anita. "I have waited with entire patience," Anita then wrote Wallace, "for the moment for conferring as you at once suggested. . . . I couldn't just assent to the mechanical suggestions made by Mr. Young by telephone without your direct word. So the little nugget and the great need are waiting on your wish for our joint thought about its use." Wallace promptly wrote her at length about his plans, and she telegraphed that she was "thrilled. . . . Please go forward and use the little nugget just as you may wish."

opposition. It was a strange experience, though rather intoxicating to a woman who, sixty-six years before, had thought the nomination of James Garfield for the presidency "the most exciting thing that mine eyes beheld."

When some Chicago NCPAC members suggested in 1944 that they drop the PAC label, she threatened to withdraw as temporary chairman. "I assume," she told them, that the purpose "is to avoid the knocking which PAC is receiving," but if they were "a branch of national PAC and wish to be so, is this not a subterfuge?" Assured that the local committee would frankly acknowledge its collaboration with the national organization, she eventually went along with a new name—the Illinois Progressive Voters Council; any name would do if they would all "pitch in."

In Anita's judgment (and she had so wired the entire United States Senate when the nomination of Wallace as secretary of commerce was under fire in 1945), Wallace was "conservative, not radical—conservative of the interests, the rights, the lives of all people and of the essential responsibility of those who do the people's work." The government should give him "more responsibility, not less." Simultaneously, she was entreating Wallace not to decline the cabinet post, even if the department was stripped of some of its jurisdiction. Stay near the source of power, she wrote him; "you made the Vice Presidency a different matter, why not also the Secretaryship of Commerce?" He was grateful for her loyalty; they would have "many things to talk about the next time we see each other." But when Truman asked for the secretary's resignation in 1946, after Wallace's public attack on the president's foreign policy, Anita reversed her field. It was better to be out than in: "At last you are where the world needs you to be, free and on your own platform." As an independent, he would be rid of "elements in the Democratic Party who do not care what happens to the world nor to the honor of the United States under its commitments to the world." By his dismissal, he had become "a symbol of all the Atlantic Charter contains and of more to come." The fog had lifted, revealing Wallace on top of the mountain, "facing the skies with every man and woman who wants what we fought for. It feels like the dawn of achievement."

Shortly after his departure from the cabinet, Anita suggested forming a third party. It was not a sudden inspiration. She had written Woodrow Wilson in 1912 that "the two parties have not had an intellectual line clearly drawn between them." And on the day Franklin Roosevelt died, she had remarked that she "would like to see a

Progressive Party now arise from this catastrophe so that the forces would fall where they belong . . . but the time may not be ripe." Now, with Wallace dismissed and a Cold War frustrating FDR's wartime promise of big-power collaboration for peace, she was convinced the time had come, despite the opposite view of her granddaughter, who now worked for the CIO in Illinois, belonged to Americans for Democratic Action, and would campaign to elect Adlai Stevenson as governor and a relatively unknown young Democrat, Sidney Yates, as representative from her Chicago district.

Anita joined the national board of the Progressive party. Through Hillman she met Calvin Benham Baldwin, "Beanie," who was to become the go-between whenever Mrs. Blaine was to be asked for additional money for the party. It was Hillman, also, who introduced her to Wallace's friends Clark Foreman, president of the Southern Congress for Human Welfare, and Frieda Kirchway, editor of *The Nation*.

She gave Wallace workers for the Progressive Citizens of America the use of two rooms she had leased in the Farwell Building in Chicago, and when the building agents removed the committee's name from the door (an "undesirable tenant"), Anita demanded and got "an apology to myself as hostess." She subsequently served on the national Wallace for President Committee, along with "Beanie" Baldwin, Paul Robeson, Rexford Guy Tugwell, the sculptor Joe Davidson, and Angus Cameron, editor-in-chief of Little, Brown publishing company. She provided hotel suites, meals, and transportation for the candidate and his colleagues when they were in Chicago, put on a party at 101 for a foreign admirer of Wallace, Konni Zilliacus, a left-wing member of the British Labour party, to which she invited her bemused, more conservative Chicago friends. She even tried to heal the breach between Wallace and Paul Douglas, the 1948 Democratic candidate from Illinois for the United States Senate, former socialist, marine, and a passionate anticommunist, though Wallace wrote her it was "impossible to get together with Douglas as long as I believe that peace is the all-important issue, and as long as he believes that hatred of Russia and communism is all-important."

As to "disavowing Communist objectives and methods," Wallace continued in the same letter, "I have no hesitancy in saying that I personally believe in progressive capitalism, that I do not believe in the materialistic dialectic, that I do believe in God, that I do not believe that force ever settles anything ultimately. But I utterly refuse to engage in the only kind of red-baiting and Russia denunciation which would momentarily satisfy a Douglas. These people live by hate of Communism and Russia to an extent which governs their whole lives. I utterly and completely refuse to be infected by their fears and hates." Wallace went on to say he was against any foreign aid which had "political strings attached," was "in favor of World Federation, with world law and a world police force stronger than the military might of either the United States or Russia," and favored "internationalization of the Dardanelles, the Panama Canal, the Suez Canal and all strategic air bases, like Greenland, Iceland, Okinawa, etc." Nevertheless, he would be "glad to meet Paul Douglas on April 11 for old-times sake." Douglas countered that he had no objection to their meeting, if the discussion centered on "support of the Marshall Plan, support of collective security and the use of force to check aggression, disavowal of Communist aims and methods." Once Wallace subscribed to these three points, "the distance between them would be lessened." Anita's mediating initiative went no further.

The contribution from Anita which Wallace's managers undoubtedly valued most was money. In July, Wallace sent her a four-page letter, responding to her offer "to contribute throughout the remainder of the campaign a total of $500,000.00, of which $150,000 can be made available immediately." In it, he listed the state organizations "which I feel should be given immediate assistance; and the amounts which were to go to each." He had had his attorneys "check the legal authority for these contributions and they have advised me that these gifts are in conformity with the law." He suggested the checks be turned over to "Beanie" Baldwin. Three of the checks were returned by Wallace, who asked that she "re-write them so that there will be no violation of the laws on political contributions; the total amount which any individual can give to a national committee is $5,000." By the end of 1948, she had become the largest single contributor to the Progressive party, supplying it with nearly $800,000 and, at Wallace's suggestion, additionally contributing to auxiliary endeavors such as "People's Songs." Her help was sought for other projects as well. In August of 1948, Wallace recommended that she underwrite publication of a pamphlet by Frederick Schumann, *The United States and the USSR*. "At the moment," he wrote, "we can't print anything because we are about $120,000 in arrears on our account with the printer."

Ironically, her subsidies were to prove embarrassing to the candidate. Her checks had been distributed among state party headquarters, as Wallace requested, but on her income tax return for 1948

Anita reported giving $753,000 to Wallace himself, and the Internal Revenue Service wanted to know why Wallace had not acknowledged that income on his own return. Anita's lawyers were slow in correcting the error; so Wallace had some uncomfortable months before the IRS was convinced that he had done nothing wrong. It was noted, however, that in a letter to her dated 29 November 1948, Wallace had proposed that a contribution "take the form of a gift to me. I will then deposit the money in a special account, to be used to defray the expenses of that part of my own work which cannot be borne by the regular budget of the Party." He had said that he would be grateful if she could send a check "payable to myself in the sum of $50,000."

Most McCormick and Blaine nieces and nephews were inured to "Aunt Anita's" political unconventionality and respected it, but cousin Bertie's *Tribune* could never resist exposing the latest example of "radicalism" within the citadel of privilege. On 6 May 1948, it carried a story that twelve Wallace supporters were either communists or communist sympathizers, so identified by the House Un-American Activities Committee, with Anita one of the Terrible Twelve. The *Tribune* report was based on a speech by Senator Karl E. Mundt, who had said in Chicago that a dozen and a half three-by-five cards in FBI files confirmed Anita's subversive connections. The FBI cards, it turned out, revealed nothing more subversive than her open support of Wallace.

She read the *Tribune* story with amusement, had it filed, and went back to drafting a statement to the Women of Illinois, giving her reasons for backing a third party. As in her endorsement of Cox in 1920, the presidential candidate's name was not mentioned, nor was politics: "When you stand at night under the sky and look at the myriad of little balls which shine down on you, even with as little as we know about them, it seems an amazing thing that anyone on this, our little globe, would be obliged to make efforts to persuade his fellow men to think about this little globe of ours as 'one world.' "

She was never heard to comment on Wallace's specific programs, or on Soviet foreign policy, or on the alleged infiltration of the Progressive party by communists. It never occurred to her that Anita McCormick Blaine's loyalty to her country and its institutions could be in doubt. When the American Communist party, echoing the Kremlin line, had propagandized in 1942 for an immediate allied military landing in Europe to relieve the hard-pressed Russians, she had telegraphed FDR that it pained her "to have this one and that one trying to tell what the United States should do in regard to the war in Russia, in regard to the second front. And if I thought it would sway you in itself, it would frighten me. But it does not, for you are the commander and the inflexible leader."

Her remoteness from the practicalities of politics was illustrated by a letter to "Dear Henry" one month before the 1948 election, picking up his warning of a third world war. She wrote that "something might happen that is *not* planned or expected, something might just go off"—an unanticipated explosion somewhere. She therefore proposed that "the three candidates for President . . . meet at once and act together to stop instantly any move toward war." She championed Henry Wallace because he was a sensitive man of good will, a man of peace—that was the politics of it, and the remonstrances of Nancy, who had some knowledge of left-wing political intrigue and of the Communist party's hidden agenda, did not sway her.

When Wallace called at 101, their conversations were not limited to donations; they had in common also an interest in psychic phenomena. "Last night after bidding you goodnight," he wrote, "I read Eileen Garrett [the medium]. Perhaps she sees, but I would say 'as through a glass darkly.'" There had been one "unforgettable Saturday afternoon" at 101, he recalled, when Anita had spoken to him of "the spiritual urge" which had kept her "seeking for reality over such long years." He thought he understood much of it, because of the impact on him of his father's death in 1924: "Perhaps there is something for science to look into here. Perhaps also I should not make a statement because I have never had any personal experience with mediums. But I do understand your earnest, inmost desire, and I therefore hope you will forgive me when I say that your dear ones are much more definitely and constructively and joyously with you when there is no third person to intervene. The constructive path is quite different and I am sure you know what it is in your inmost heart of hearts. You, yourself are the key to reality, not some medium. You, yourself can have access to the reality you seek. A medium will hurt, not help something which is very precious. And you, yourself have within you a reality which is most extraordinary indeed. And you can cherish this reality every day of the year and every minute of the day."

After the election and his defeat, Wallace put before Anita his vision of a World Peace Center near the United Nations building in New York, where foreign delegates could meet unofficially. Would she like to invest $856,000 in that? He was likewise thinking of starting a publishing company, and of calling a "People's Convention" in 1950 to draft a world constitution. To any ambition he might have, she was responsive, and when the Progressive party failed to carry a single state in 1948, she did not give up. She sent President Truman a letter, to be handed him personally by her butler, asking him to "introduce Mr. Henry Wallace into his counsels." When the first emissary had to be recalled to Chicago because of sickness in his family, Anita sent a second butler, asking Matthew Connelly of the White House staff to allow her "messenger to hand the letter personally to the President." The letter was undelivered; that was not the way to reach the president of the United States, Rex Tugwell told her. And when the Progressive party honored Wallace the following April, Anita telegraphed thanks for his "years long of constant work to bring men to the measures of Democracy and the essence of it to the minds of men," and called on him to continue leading: "Henry Wallace, we ask you for the high sign of advance."

"For me," Anita had written her granddaughter in 1942, "the thing to work for was always the world as a whole." The character of different societies in the variety of their histories, customs, needs and governments was of secondary concern; the human family was one. For a woman of her means and interests she had traveled little. Much of her own country, all of Asia, Africa, the Middle East, Latin America were unfamiliar. She did not anticipate how fiercely the winds of nationalism and of ideological, sectional, and racial rivalry would blow through the postwar world. And if she had forecast that stormy future, her belief in the urgency of education for world citizenship would simply have been reinforced.

The United Nations was a long step forward, but could any organization limited by the sovereignty of nation states prevent war? The lesson of her generation, it seemed to her, was that it could not. Lasting peace could only be assured by a universal allegiance above and beyond governments, based on the people themselves. But how was the foundation to be laid? She was waiting for the word, "the high sign." It came in 1948 through Harris Wofford, Jr., à twenty-two-year-old University of Chicago student who was organizing for the Student World Federalists and would, two decades later, become president of Bryn Mawr College.

Henry C. Usborne and a hundred other members of the British House of Commons had issued a call for a World Constituent Assembly to be held in Geneva in 1950 for the purpose of writing a World Constitution, to be preceded by an unofficial "election" of people's delegates in as many countries as possible. In May 1948, Wofford and a young federalist friend, Stephen Benedict, had gone to New York to persuade Stringfellow Barr, professor of history and former president of St. John's College in Maryland, to take the lead in the United States in preparing for that assembly. When Barr remarked in an offhand way that such an election would cost as much as $20 million, Wofford said that he knew someone who might consider giving the first million. That caught Barr's attention.

Three months later, Barr, Usborne, and Wofford flew to Chicago, where they cooled their heels at the Drake Hotel for twenty-four hours and were then bidden to come to 101 the next evening, July Fourth. Celebrating her eighty-second birthday, Mrs. Blaine waltzed with collegian Wofford, after which she interrupted the merrymaking and asked her guests to gather under a large tree in the garden lit by Japanese lanterns to hear a message from the spokesmen for world government. It was not an auspicious setting for serious talk, but the evening passed pleasantly and the guests from the East returned for a more businesslike discussion the following day.

Anita's first question was why Professor Barr cared about world peace? He thought for a moment, threw away his prepared script, and began speaking of friends and family he had lost in two wars. Tears came to his eyes, and to Anita's. There was silence. She then asked what she could do. Barr, having been cautioned by Usborne to ask for no more than $50,000, replied that if she was willing to put up the first million, he would postpone his return to teaching and devote full time to their project, but she would have to give him her answer within four days. Before that deadline, she asked, would he go to Boston to talk it over with Dr. Roger Lee, so that she might have Lee's opinion? Barr would.

Four days later, at one o'clock in the morning, the telephone rang in Barr's New York apartment. It was Mrs. Blaine to say she would give the million dollars. And could she call him "Winkie." He was amenable to both. She then suggested that he, his lawyer, and his academic colleague Scott Buchanan meet with her and Henry Wallace in Chicago on 31 July to set up a trust fund. That, too, was acceptable.

Wallace did not attend the meeting on the 31st, but Anita had kept him informed and he had written her on 10 July that "the greatest effort must be made to see that this new venture and New Party are obverse and reverse sides of the same coin. One must strengthen the other, not weaken the other. To this end, I would like very much to be in an influential position in the new movement." As he had emphasized during the 1948 campaign, however, he wanted no part of any organization that would stir up the distrust of Eastern powers. Nor had he much faith in the World Federalists. "Where the ground is holiest," he wrote, "the danger is often the greatest. Or in the words of Scott Buchanan when the three of us were together, 'Toynbee the English historian fears that the greatest danger is that One World may be brought too soon in the wrong way by the wrong people.'"

In addition to seeing Dr. Lee, who interposed no objection to the plan, Barr and Buchanan conferred with Wallace, for Anita wanted his consent before they went any further. Afterward Wallace telephoned his approval of a People's Convention and said that Anita ought to feel "very thankful and prayerful to reflect that your efforts and your efforts alone may result in 1950 going down in history as having the same significance for a World Constitution as 1787 had for the U.S. Constitution." She promptly wired Barr that Wallace had sent "gladness and offers himself for a place in the Council."

The offer was not unreservedly welcome to Barr, or to Usborne, who was apprehensive that the People's Convention might become compromised by too close an association with the Progressive party. For the same reason, Usborne preferred that Barr's friend Scott Buchanan not be a trustee. But Anita at this late date was not to be deterred by any fear of what people might say; she wanted Buchanan because he *was* an associate of Wallace.

Negotiations on the million dollar trust fund opened at 101, with an agreement that all the money would be spent by 31 December 1958 unless the trustees voted unanimously to extend the life of the foundation for an additional ten years. Anita then telephoned an official of the Continental Bank of Chicago, instructing him to hand deliver that afternoon certificates evidencing her holdings in the International Harvester Company, since she was not sure what she was worth. When the certificates arrived, Barr's lawyer was "rather staggered" to learn that she owned 700,000 shares of Harvester stock, then selling for just over $30 a share. She asked the bank's representative to split the certificates to produce $1 million in cash. The meeting ended; Barr returned to New York and several days later received by express mail 33,334 shares of Harvester stock, enclosed in a silver Georgian tea caddy, which he had admired at 101. There was also a note: "My gratitude goes to you for the chance to work with you and all those in the great conclave, to bring the world to its whole world of government."[19] Before the stock could be sold, its market value slipped more than one point, whereupon Anita mailed a check for $70,439.90 to make up the loss.

The charter of the Foundation for World Government read in part: "WHEREAS, world peace and human progress depend upon the establishment of a federal world government representing all mankind; and WHEREAS, this goal can only be achieved if, through a moral and political regeneration, people everywhere desire a new and higher level; it [is] the intent of the parties that such fund shall be used particularly to educate the public to understand what it would mean to each individual's freedom, security and prosperity and to the cause of peace to accomplish the purposes set forth." The language was designed to qualify the foundation for tax exemption. Anita, Wofford, Barr, and Buchanan were the foundation's directors, and all except Anita were "working trustees," that is to say, paid. The Emergency Committee of Atomic Scientists immediately earmarked a thousand dollars for its work.

Within a month, this "gay and timeless affair,"[20] as Anita referred to the Foundation for World Government, had become a shooting target. In a newspaper interview she had let slip the name of Henry Wallace, saying that "his philosophy and that of the Foundation are similar" and that she could not "imagine that he wouldn't be active, it seems very natural that he would be a trustee." The interviewer, Frederick Woltman, discerned in that statement a sinister plot to provide Wallace "with a million-dollar kitty to work with and a world-wide sounding board."[21]

Federalist groups quickly repudiated the foundation. Henry Wallace, said Cord Myer, Jr., head of the World Federalists, was "anathema." The bridge expert Ely Culbertson, who was chairman of the Citizens Committee for U.N. Reform, told Woltman that Wallace was "completely controlled by the Communists," and a foundation "controlled by Communist-Wallaceites could only mean added income for Moscow propaganda." The Emergency Committee of Atomic Scientists withdrew its offer of office space. The Internal Revenue Service sent its agents to investigate. They must not let this hysteria engulf them, Barr nervously wrote Anita; their work required "calm thought and steady nerves." It was not she who needed to be reassured; the gift, she replied, had given her a "cleared, freed feeling."

It took the foundation seven years to get through the million dollars, leaving few traces of its passage through many hands. After

231

protracted negotiation between Anita's lawyers and the IRS, the government ruled against recognizing the foundation as a charitable enterprise and imposed a gift tax of over half a million dollars. The original idea of a World Assembly was dropped. There were no people's elections, no assembly in Geneva. They had tried, Barr insisted, "to rally men and women of several continents whose thinking could help and put them in touch with each other," but as Barr's attorney* later observed, the money had not been used "as trenchantly as some of us hoped. It produced several books and paid for trips to exotic areas, but it made few converts to the world government concept. The crop of vain regrets was large." Still, he added philosophically, Mrs. Blaine's was not "the first million dollars to be spent non-constructively."

Anita was no readier at eighty-three to quit than she had been fifty years earlier when she had underwritten the Francis Parker School. "There are natures," she had noted in her diary in 1888, "whose love is like a perpetual fountain, continually overflowing and gladdening the hearts of all who pass"; the source which fed and freshened the fountain seemed inexhaustible. Dr. Lee urged her to let up, but while there was time left to do and give what she had she would use it. Those to whom she was closest had been provided for in her will, and she had arranged that two-thirds of her estate go into the setting up of a New World Foundation, a primary objective of which would be "the right education of children." But she was not finished yet.

A new interest—journalism—was to be her last. Like her father and cousin Bertie McCormick, she had always been fascinated by the power of the press and had developed some distinct notions about newspapers. They should avoid sensational headlines, bias, repetitious reporting, and trashy stories; they should show "due respect for the reader's intelligence," not coloring the news to cheat him, "nor inventing it to interest and allure him, but treating him as we would be treated—giving news as news, opinions as opinions, arguments and persuasions frankly as such and imaginings and inventions as such—not under the guise of facts." In 1899, she had thought of buying a Chicago paper that was about to go under, "tak-

* A. J. G. Priest, then a partner of Reed and Priest in New York and later a member of the law faculty at the University of Virginia.

ing it and running it," keeping it small and in touch with its sub-
scribers by asking their opinions and giving them "tables of all laws
passed and a clear analysis of them." She had not gone through with
the purchase, "but at least I have the satisfaction of imagining myself doing some work," she had written Missy, "and giving you, I
believe a real scare." During the Second World War, press animosity
toward FDR, especially the *Chicago Tribune's*, had so provoked her
that she had gone to the extreme of advocating the shutting down of
papers which "act to oppose and seek to undermine our total effort,"
the deporting of their owners, and the setting up of a committee of
"self-appointed censors" to monitor the news. When Marshall Field
in 1941 launched his morning paper, the *Chicago Sun*, she hailed its
promise to maintain "freedom in thought, freedom in speech on the
basis of truth—the only foundation on which Democracy can exist."

Now, in 1949, her chance had come. Billing itself as independent,
the *Weekly National Guardian* had been founded to publicize the
principles of Henry Wallace and the Progressive party. Its first issue
of 18 October 1948 carried an article by Wallace himself. Its editors
—James Aronson, formerly of the *New York Times;* Cedric Bel-
frage, once film and theater critic of the London *Daily Express;* and
John T. McManus, who had worked on the *New York Times* and
Time magazine—had set out to give "the inheritors of Franklin
Roosevelt's America an uninterrupted flow of facts to fight with in
the continuing battle for a better world."[22] Three months after its
first issue, the paper was tottering on the edge of bankruptcy, and
on 7 February 1949 the editors warned in bold type that they could
not go on publishing without outside help. The collapse of the
Guardian, they warned, "would not only leave the Wallace-Progres-
sive Movement without a single sympathetic publication," but force
upon the American people a choice between "only the Communist
Party press on the left and the commercial press overwhelmingly
hostile to liberal American tradition—on the right." The editors did
not "propose to let this happen without a fight and without inviting
our readers to join that fight."

The editorial caught Anita's eye. She telephoned the *Guardian* in
New York asking to speak with a representative of the paper, following up with a letter requesting the editors to send her "telegraph
collect some information I greatly want." She had two questions:
who was responsible for the paper, and did the *Guardian* have "a
plan for future publication in harmony with the principles of its
page one, February 7?" On 11 February, she wrote McManus that
she had been "suffering with Henry Wallace and his helpers over

233

the possibilities of avenues of light going out" and wanted to be of assistance. Since her traveling days were over, could he come to Chicago? A copy of the letter went to Wallace. The editors came within the week, bringing along "their problem and their suggestion of a solution to save their organ and keep their paper going," Anita wrote Wallace on 16 February. "It all feels to me very good, I hope it does to you."

Learning of this latest enthusiasm, Nancy once again tried to restrain her grandmother, pointing out that the *Guardian* was financially unsound and, worse, had a "very distasteful" editorial policy. Of course it was financially unsound, Anita admitted, why else would she be needed? The opportunity to send "real light" was not to be spurned. She was soon giving the *Guardian* $5,000 a month, lending McManus more than $200,000, and discussing with him the purchase of a second paper.

Henry Wallace then had a further thought. His good friend Anita ought to get together with Ted Thackrey, former editor and publisher of the *New York Post*, who had in mind launching a liberal daily in New York City. She sent her lawyer East to investigate. He reported back that Thackrey seemed honest, though the investigator admitted not being in complete sympathy with his views. A pilgrimage to Chicago was duly arranged, and after meeting with Thackrey and his attorneys and praying for "mutual understanding and harmonious association," Anita gave him $300,000, half the capital he said he needed.[23]

Thackrey was received at 101 in much the same way as Barr. He arrived during a dinner party; his hostess introduced him around, after which the company gaily linked arms for the procession to the dining room. It had "more the appearance and feel of a congo line than a formal rite," Thackrey recalled. There was no opportunity to mention his mission during dinner or the square dancing which followed, but, like Barr, he returned the next day to outline his proposal. He was prepared to go on at some length with his explanation of the role of the *Daily Compass*. Before he had finished his presentation, however, Anita excused herself for a few moments of private meditation.* When she rejoined Thackrey, she told him she was eager to "join the effort now starting to elevate, and in fact, to save the press and the people," as she later reported to Wallace. Thack-

---

* "This was done with such obvious reliance on the Creator, and with such simplicity and sincerity," Thackrey told Anita's granddaughter in 1968, "that it had a lasting influence on our relationship."

rey could hardly believe it; "What a blithe spirit . . . one of the few gentlewomen I ever knew."

The *Daily Compass* proved a greater drain than the *National Guardian*. Within a month, Thackrey was back for an additional $300,000, and also to pick up copy, for Anita had promised to contribute a column to the paper titled "The Open Door," filled with religious and philosophical quotations. Four weeks later, he reappeared to announce that the *Compass* was losing $14,000 a week and that it was "unlikely that we could bring the newspaper through to a profitable basis without at least $1 million more of capital." Money must not stand in their way, she replied; the *Daily Compass* must survive at least until 1952, so that it might help swell the vote for Henry Wallace, should he again run for the presidency. Moreover, the voices that were being raised against "reliance on arms as opposed to negotiation for peace" must not be stilled. In the midst of this conversation, Anita again left him alone for several minutes while she sought inspiration, returning to say that if he was willing to carry on, she was prepared "to risk up to an additional million dollars in the hope of establishing the newspaper on a self-sustaining basis."[24] Before she could fulfill her pledge, illness put her beyond reach of any supplicant, but she had already given him $150,000 more.

The "gay and timeless affair" was nearly finished. Her granddaughter was to marry in 1951 and two years later give birth to a son, Anita's great-grandchild; she, speechless, was to hold that infant in her arms but without any sign of recognition. For five silent years, her secretaries and servants quietly carried on without her knowing who they were. Commercial Chicago had by then encircled 101, throwing up high-rise apartments and office buildings. A McCormick residence behind Anita's was now a Swedish restaurant. A block away, Michigan Avenue hummed with cars and buses, and elegant shops crowded each other. But apart from the removal of the tennis court in the backyard, Anita's home appeared as unchanged as its owner. She wore the same ankle-length, full-skirted dresses with a bit of lace at the neck, and her gray hair was pulled back in a bun, topped by a black velvet bow and a tortoiseshell pin. She was allowed few callers; there were few left to call. Harold's daughter Mathilde had died in 1947, the same year as Stanley and

Anita's sister-in-law Margaret Damrosch. Anita had outlived her brothers and sister, Walter Damrosch, Cousin Carrie, Missy, Grace Walker, Flora Cooke. Old friends like Katherine Taylor wrote her fond notes which she could not read: "Dear, your power to recognize *life* and to identify yourself with it, in all things you touch, is one of the great things about you." There was no answer.

Shortly after her final meeting with Thackrey in 1949, Anita had gone into the hospital for an intestinal operation which was probably unnecessary. Brought back to 101, she never again left it. She had always been vigorous and still strode briskly from room to room, supported by nurses, but her mental faculties had faded. Attendants were with her day and night. No telephone calls were put through, no letters or telegrams. She was completely cut off from her one world, unaware of a war in Korea—the fifth to be fought by the United States in her lifetime. Her last letter before entering the hospital was to the National Association for the Advancement of Colored People, pleading for the reinstatement of W. E. B. DuBois, who had lost favor because he had campaigned for Henry Wallace. "If you deprive by your rules a member of your society of this freedom of speech," she wrote, "what have you left him of freedom?"

The old hymn runs, "Teach me to live that I may dread the grave as little as my bed." In the Adirondacks the autumn of 1929, she had penciled the words: "October flings the glory of life abroad and some think the premonition of death, but there is no such thing. Change but not death. Life cannot die." She had seen death on the faces of her parents, her husband, her son, her beloved Henry Favill, her three brothers, and her sister and was sure "that it is not dark but light—and oh so beautiful." Her philanthropies had been abundant, some thought foolish, but as she had counseled John Blaine Lawrence, a full life begins "with the realization of other people's needs and woes. . . . Into this life could come experiences of mistake, and even bitter mistake, but all could turn to blessing and the use of them to swell the tide of enlightenment and of understanding and of helpfulness in the world—so needing it."

It had been an American story, the Middle Western woman of wealth and character, vital, venturesome, led by the inner light— "Follow follow / follow the gleam / banners unfurled / over the world." In the dark hours of loss, Anita might have withdrawn into sorrowing solitude, feeling cheated and shutting herself off from an unjust society. Or, she might have bought power and prestige, commissioned concrete monuments to her beneficence, sought fame or social distinction as the reflected glory of grand possessions. All these avenues were open, and she chose none of them, going her own straight way without looking down on those who chose a different route. She gambled on goodness without calculating the odds. That was her folly. She could not be crafty, because it would have violated her deepest sense of self. That was her strength. And if she had not been certain of personal immortality, all hope and effort would have seemed futile. The voices which spoke to life from beyond life spoke truly, confirming the infinite sovereignty of love, in whose service we are rewarded by grace.

She died on Lincoln's birthday, 12 February 1954, having long since lost the power of coherent speech. But she had said it all before: "The sun is shining over the mountain in blinding intensity soon to disappear. A bird sings his evening song. The wings on the water grow quiet. And the water is quietly rippled and reflective. In this moment of intensity and serenity, I would pass into the thought of the earth and all that it holds, all that it gives. While nature sings her song of lullaby, I would pass peacefully, thrillingly, into the wonders of the night and reach out with longing mind to ask questions and to await answers that await me at the appointed hours."

SOURCES

Most of the quoted material is drawn from letters, diaries, and papers in the files of Anita McCormick Blaine at the State Historical Society of Wisconsin, in Madison. Material is also drawn from papers at the Chicago Historical Society, at the Library of Congress, or in the author's possession (see also Acknowledgments, p. ix).

I

PRIMARY SOURCES

Anita McCormick Blaine. To Nettie, 20 July 1878; 21 July 1878; 8 August 1878; 29 October 1882. To Mary Virginia, 6 February 1881. To Harriot Hammond ("Missy"), 18 May 1884; 28 January 1888. Journals, 22 October 1878; 26 May 1884; 15 June 1884.

Cyrus Hall McCormick. To Nettie, 6 July 1866; to Dun, Wyman and Co., New York, 7 December 1880.

Nettie Fowler McCormick. To Cyrus, 28 August 1878. To Anita, 7 March 1879. To "My dear Uncle," Eldridge O. Merick, 31 October 1871. To Helen Hard, 13 April 1861. To Helen Hard Potts, 17 September 1867. To "Dear Sir," n.d. Journals (Nettie kept journals intermittently from 1850 to 1896): 31 October 1852; 3 November 1854; 8 February 1855; 27 October 1855; 21 December 1855; 1 January 1856; 1 April 1856; 14 April 1856; 15 February 1862; 30 July 1863; 21 January 1864; 16 March 1866; 19 November 1866; 5 June 1868; 29 June 1872.

Stella Virginia Roderick. Interviews with Cyrus Hall McCormick, Jr., 21 January 1933; with Anita, 4 July 1943; with Harold Fowler McCormick, 21 February 1933.

NOTES (PAGES 4–31)

1. *Richfield Springs . . . Its Attractions as a Summer Resort* (pamphlet published for T. R. Proctor, New York: William M. Clarke, 1883).
2. Quoted in Stella Virginia Roderick, *Nettie Fowler McCormick* (Peterborough, N.H.: Peter R. Smith, 1956).
3. Quoted in Harold M. Mayer and Richard C. Wade, *Chicago: The Growth of a Metropolis* (Chicago, 1969), p. 117. See also Bessie Louise Pierce, *A History of Chicago, 1848–1871* (New York, 1940), pp. 476–78.
4. Jonas Hutchinson, lawyer and notary public with an office at 86 Washington Street, to his mother in New Hampshire, in *The Great Chicago Fire* (Chicago, 1946), pp. 17–20.
5. William T. Hutchinson, *Cyrus Hall McCormick* (New York, 1930), vol. 1, p. 90.
6. Ibid., vol. 2, p. 751.
7. Quoted in Roderick, *Nettie Fowler McCormick*, p. 48.
8. Ibid., p. 50.
9. Cyrus Hall McCormick to his brother William, quoted in ibid., p. 49.
10. Quoted in Roderick, *Nettie Fowler McCormick*, p. 75.
11. *Daily Inter Ocean*, 14 May 1884.
12. *New York World*, 10 July 1864.
13. Quoted in Roderick, *Nettie Fowler McCormick*, p. 83.
14. *Aunt Bet: The Story of a Long Life*, privately published by Mary Mildred Sullivan and George Hammond Sullivan (Virginia, 1900), p. 30.
15. Anita's remarks at the International Harvester centennial luncheon, 17 October 1947.

II

PRIMARY SOURCES

Anita McCormick Blaine. To Nettie, 31 August 1879; 7 May 1885; 12 August 1887; 28 September 1889; 29 September 1889; 17 January 1890; 27 January 1890; 12 May 1891; 30 August 1891; undated. To Cyrus, Jr., undated (1888). To Virginia, 10 June 1880; 1 April 1881; 4 July 1881. To "Missy," 19 October 1885; 3 December 1885; 27 September 1886; 28 January 1888; 28 February 1888; 25 May 1888; 24 November 1888; 4 February 1889; 16 February 1889; 25 June 1890; undated (spring 1892). To Emmons Blaine, 26 June 1889; 30 July 1889; 8 August 1889; 12 September 1889; 13 September 1889; 28 September 1889. To Nancy Blaine, two letters, undated. Journals, 31 August 1879; 5 January 1881; 10 March 1883; 31 March 1885; 16 May 1889; 27 May 1889; 9 June 1889. Composition, "The Disadvantages of Being a School Girl," 26 March 1881. Composition, "Ten Ways of Showing Selfishness," 28 November 1882. Penciled note, "Bad Habits of a Good Society," 18 January 1889. Two penciled notes, 22 April 1892, and undated (but before June 1892). Address to Friday Club, 5 November 1937.

Nettie Fowler McCormick. To Cyrus, Jr., 13 April 1885. To Anita, 23 August 1890. Notes, 7 and 8 May 1889; 14 June 1889; 13 and 15 June 1892.

Harriot Hammond ("Missy"). To Anita, 28 October 1885; 30 June 1889. To Nettie, 29 August 1890; 8 September 1890. Notes of a conversation with Emmons Blaine, 1883.

Emmons Blaine. To Harriet Blaine, 25 October 1886. To Nettie, 29 September 1889.

James G. Blaine and Harriet Blaine. To Anita, 15 June 1889; 20 June 1889. To Emmons, 7 September 1890.

Harriet Blaine Beale. To her family, 1 September 1889.

John A. Ryerson. Journal, 5 February 1887 (on Anita's coming-out ball).

NOTES (PAGES 38–70)

1. Henry B. Fuller, *With the Procession* (Chicago, 1965), p. 57.
2. Stephen Longstreet, *Chicago: An Intimate Portrait of People, Pleasures, and Power, 1860–1919* (New York, 1973), pp. 246–54; Finis Farr, *Chicago* (New York, 1973), pp. 144–52; Robert Ozanne, *A Century of Labor-Management Relations at McCormick and International Harvester* (Wisconsin, 1967), pp. 20–28; Harry Bernard, *Eagle Forgotten: The Life of John Peter Altgeld* (New York, 1938), pp. 96–114.
3. Henry F. Pringle, *Theodore Roosevelt* (New York, 1931), p. 589.
4. Ozanne, *A Century of Labor-Management Relations*, pp. 13, 20–28.
5. This letter from Anita to Nettie, undated but written in 1886, was never sent.
6. *The Manners That Win* (Minnesota, 1879).
7. Harriet (Mrs. James G.) Blaine to Abigail Dodge, 3 December 1880, in *Letters of Mrs. James G. Blaine* (New York, 1908), vol. 1, p. 185.
8. Ibid., vol. 2, p. 109.
9. *Chicago Herald*, 19 June 1892.

III

PRIMARY SOURCES

Anita McCormick Blaine. To Cyrus, Jr., 23 July 1901. To Harriet (Mrs. Cyrus, Jr.), 6 January 1893; 31 January 1893. To Emmons, Jr., 14 July 1907; 11 August 1914. To "Missy," 16 February 1901; 3 March 1901; March 1902; 21 October 1903; various undated letters (probably 1894 and 1900–1901). To Cyrus Bentley, 18 May 1900; undated (July 1899?). To Fred A. Busse, 18 December 1907. To John A. Chapman, 8 April 1908. To Flora J. Cooke, 8 December 1909. To "Edward," 11 March 1908. To Miss Fleming, 29 October 1903. To William Rainey Harper, 15 June 1905. To the trustees and principal of the Francis W. Parker School, undated (May–June 1908?). To Dr. Edward J. Kempf (memorandum), undated. To Louis F. Post, 18 February 1908; 1 July 1908. To Byron L. Smith, 10 December 1901. To A. S. Trude, rough draft, January–June 1898. Journals,

10 April 1898; undated (1898); 19 August 1900. Notes and memoranda to herself, 9 August 1892; 22 November 1892; 18 August 1900; 14 May 1901; 9 May 1906. Penciled note, "Prospectus Slum School," undated (early 1899?). Draft attached to special report of the Board of Education on promotion and marking of teachers, undated (1907?). Fifty-page report, "Recommendations," June 1908. Talk to Francis W. Parker School, 31 May 1902. Remarks at Truancy Conference, December 1906. Talk to Francis W. Parker Club, 1 November 1913. Talk to Parents' Association of the School of Education, University of Chicago, 5 June 1911.

Harriot Hammond ("Missy"). To Anita, 2 December 1896; March 1902.

Owen Aldis. To Anita, 9 November 1899.

Harriet Blaine Beale. To Anita, 26 January 1893; undated (1912).

Cyrus Bentley. To Anita, 1 June 1899; 3 April 1900; undated (1900?); 20 April 1901; 8 November 1901; May 1905; 14 July 1909. Report to trustees of Francis W. Parker School, 28 December 1900.

Flora J. Cooke. To Anita, 1 August 1904; 6 March 1908; 2 February 1913.

William W. Cutler III. Interview with Katharine Taylor, 28 June 1966.

John Dewey. To Anita, 30 April 1903.

Alan Eaton. "Report on Work of the Tenth Grade," 23 November 1905.

Sherwood Eddy. To Anita, 16 August 1922.

Henry B. Favill. To Anita, 23 August 1898; 6 September 1902; 13 September 1906; 25 December 1906. To Flora J. Cooke, 26 May 1908.

Wilbur Jackman. To Cyrus Bentley, 20 June 1900. To Anita, 13 April 1903. To William Rainey Harper, 4 May 1903.

William Lusk. To Anita, 11 October 1903; 29 June 1904 ("William" to "Jane"); 10 August 1904; 25 April 1905; 1 September 1945 (in unpublished manuscript, p. 129).

Francis W. Parker. To Zonia Baber, 8 January 1897. To Anita, 4 June 1898; 29 June 1898; 15 December 1898. To John Dewey, 9 February 1901.

Raymond Robins. To Anita, 1 April 1904; 3 April 1904; 3 March 1905; 10 March 1905.

James Gamble Rogers (architect). To Anita, 12 July 1899.

Caroline Slade ("Carrie"). To Anita, 9 August 1902; 6 May 1904; 18 November 1904; 22 May 1905; 17 January 1906; 1 July 1907.

NOTES (PAGES 76–127)

1. Nettie Fowler McCormick, notes, quoted in Roderick, *Nettie Fowler McCormick*, pp. 184–85.
2. *Chicago Record*, 30 December 1893.
3. Quoted in Roderick, *Nettie Fowler McCormick*, p. 189.
4. John Dewey's *The School and Society* was published by the University of Chicago Press in 1899.

5. *Chicago Times-Herald,* 21 August 1898.

6. Dr. George W. Myers, 18 January 1927, University of Chicago, Presidents' Papers.

7. "Proposal of Chicago Institute Trustees to University of Chicago," 21 February 1901.

8. Quoted in Roderick, *Nettie Fowler McCormick,* p. 225.

9. Undated letter from Anita to Em to be opened only after her death.

10. Allen B. Pond, president of the City Club of Chicago, 21 February 1916.

11. Henry B. Favill's speech to the graduating class of St. Luke's Hospital Training School for Nurses (*The Alumnae,* July 1904).

12. See note 9.

13. See "Raymond Robins," in *The National Cyclopedia of American Biography,* pp. 11–12.

14. *Chicago Tribune,* 17 June 1905.

15. Ibid., 19 July 1906; *Chicago Record-Herald,* 5 July 1906.

16. According to Harold Ickes, in *The Autobiography of a Curmudgeon* (New York, 1969).

17. *Chicago Tribune,* 18 May 1907.

18. Minutes of Chicago Board of Education meeting, 22 May 1907.

See also Robert L. McCaul's scholarly account of the Parker-Dewey school merger in "Dewey and the University of Chicago," *School and Society,* vol. 89, pp. 152–57, 179–83, 202–6.

IV

PRIMARY SOURCES

Anita McCormick Blaine. To Nettie, 24 August 1898; 15 September 1905; 21 October 1917. To Nettie and Harold, 20 August 1908. To Cyrus, Jr., 27 April 1926. To Stanley, 5 June 1902. To Emmons, Jr., 11 May 1911; 20 September 1911; 9 January 1912; 7 March 1913; 17 March 1914; 30 May 1914; 2 December 1914; 9 April 1916; 16 June 1918. To Hall McCormick, 14 November 1910. To Leander McCormick, 4 May 1895. To "Missy," 12 July 1898; 14 January 1900. To Jane Addams, 26 June 1912. To Cyrus Bentley, undated (1908). To Ruth Campbell (the "young cousin"), 17 July 1913. To Burt J. Fitzgerald (on street names), 17 February 1906. To Mr. Heckman (accompanying check to University of Chicago), 2 April 1907. To David Howton (secretary of agriculture), 8 April 1916. To Emita Jewett (on "receiver's right"), 8 November 1914. To Dr. Edward J. Kempf, 11 July 1929. To Mrs. John Logan (declining autobiographical information), 26 July 1911. To Dr. James G. K. McClure (of McCormick Theological Seminary), 18 April 1926. To Warren Manning (architect for Virginia), 7 August 1913. To Dr. Adolf Meyer, 4 April 1919. To Allen Miller (attorney who borrowed from Anita), 26 July 1911; 12 December 1914. To Josephine Moriarity (dressmaker), 23 June 1911. To Dr. Timothy Stone (of McCormick Theological Seminary), 26 April 1926. To Nellie Swarz, 28 May 1908. To R. J. Tomkins (waiter at Blackstone Hotel), 24 July 1917. To Mr. Wells (on Emmons, Jr., as Harvard student), undated (1 October 1910?). Journals, undated (1898), and various entries between 1 September 1899 through 1 April 1900. Memorandum, marked "Private," on Stanley. Penciled note, "A Dream," undated (1901?). "Family History and Supporting Papers," 1910. "Family and Personal History; History of Courtship and Marriage and Onset of Present Illness," undated. Interview with Dr. Lewis Pollock (concerning Stanley), 29 September 1932, pp. 7–9, 24–26, 45–46; 3 October 1932, pp. 61–64.

Nettie Fowler McCormick. To Dr. G. V. T. Hamilton (on Stanley), undated (October 1907?).

Cyrus Hall McCormick, Jr. To Anita, 22 December 1920. To Cyrus Hall McCormick III, 12 February 1913.

Harold Fowler McCormick. To Anita, 30 September 1898.

Emmons Blaine, Jr. To Anita, 11 August 1908; 27 May 1912; 13 March 1916; 13 May 1916; 2 March 1918. To Anne Thorpe ("young lady at Vassar"), 29 February 1916. "Supplementary Statement" to Draft Board, 14 January 1918.

Harriot Hammond ("Missy"). To Anita, 17 February 1894.

Harriet Blaine Beale. To Anita, August 1914; 2 April 1900.

Cyrus Bentley. To Anita, 11 November 1906; 10 July 1913.

Blanche Booth (secretary to Anita). To Alan Eaton, 18 August 1906.

Dr. Bacon (attending Eleanor Blaine). To Dr. Whitredge Williams, 19 November 1918.

Margaret Blaine Damrosch. To Anita, 22 September 1916. To Alice Damrosch, 8 December 1917; 9 November 1918.

Katherine Dexter McCormick. To Anita, 10 December 1906.

Henry B. Favill. To Anita, undated (13 June 1908?).

Lucy McCormick Jewett. To Anita, undated (1910).

Edward J. Kempf. To Anita, 24 February 1928.

Alfred Olafson (butler). To Nancy Blaine Harrison, 30 May 1968.

Emil Sundeen. To Nancy (on Nancy's leaving hospital as infant), 24 February 1954.

Miscellaneous. Memorandum of conversation between Georgiana Ceder (secretary) and Cyrus Bentley, undated (July–November 1929). Minutes of conference among Anita, Harold, and Cyrus Adams, 10 June 1911.

NOTES (PAGES 132–63)

1. Undated report on Stanley McCormick, in "Family and Personal History," vol. 1, pp. 26–28.
2. Quoted in Longstreet, *Chicago*, p. 377.
3. Carter H. Harrison, *Stormy Years: The Autobiography of Carter H. Harrison, Five Times Mayor of Chicago* (Indianapolis, 1935), p. 79.
4. Francis Hackett, *American Rainbow* (New York, 1971), p. 145.

5. Lloyd Lewis and Henry Justin Smith, *Chicago: The History of Its Reputation* (New York, 1929), p. 257.

6. Lincoln Steffens, *The Shame of the Cities* (1904; reprinted New York, 1948), p. 234.

7. N. C. Chatfield-Taylor, *Chicago* (New York, 1917), p. 118.

8. Richard Hofstadter, *The Age of Reform: From Bryan to F.D.R.* (New York, 1960), p. 137.

9. A speech by Anita, "The Need of a Children's Bureau: An Episode," spring 1913, pp. 33–37.

10. A speech by Anita to the graduating class of the School of Civics and Philanthropy, June 1910, p. 7.

11. *Chicago Inter Ocean*, 18 June 1899.

12. *Milwaukee Journal*, 23 June 1899.

13. *Chicago Post*, 15 March 1900.

14. Ibid., 17 March 1900; *Chicago Times-Herald*, 18 March 1900.

15. William James, *The Varieties of Religious Experience* (New York, 1913), p. 91.

16. Quoted in Roderick, *Nettie Fowler McCormick*, p. 193.

17. Emmett Dedmon, *Fabulous Chicago* (New York, 1953), p. 251.

V

PRIMARY SOURCES

Anita McCormick Blaine. To Nettie, undated (10 July 1915?). To Cyrus, Jr., 25 November 1921; 13 June 1935. To Harold, undated (October 1912). To Ganna Walska and Harold, 6 June 1921; 22 August 1922; 24 January 1923. To Harold and Adah McCormick, 31 May 1938. To Stanley, 14 January 1924; 21 March 1943; 16 August 1943; 2 November 1943. To Emmons, Jr., 5 November 1908; 12 February 1912; 15 October 1912; 11 August 1914. To Nancy, 7 June 1930; 17 September 1936; undated (1944); 23 April 1945; undated. To "Missy," 12 July 1898. To Winston Churchill, 15 March 1942. To Winston Churchill and Paul Reynaud, 16 June 1940. To Matthew Connelly, 8 December 1948. To "The Emperor of Japan and His Ministers," 7 November 1931. To Richard J. Finnegan (journalist), 6 November 1940. To Ernst Hanfstaengel, 14 March 1936. To Sidney Hillman and others, 21 August 1944. To Hitler, 18 July 1943. To John Blaine Lawrence, undated. To Dr. Roger Lee, undated (after 1933). To Sir Oliver Lodge, 1 February 1920; 10 April 1937; 26 September 1937. To Katherine McCormick, 27 April 1947. To Frank McCulloch, 11 September 1942. To Dr. Adolf Meyer, 10 June 1930. To Benito Mussolini, 19 September 1935. To the NAACP, 8 March 1949 (copy to W. E. B. Du Bois, 7 April 1949). To the *National Guardian*, 9 February 1949. To Max Oser, 1 March 1922. To Eleanor Roosevelt, 16 August 1945. To Franklin D. Roosevelt, 10 March 1934; 20 June 1940; 18 July 1942 (telegram); 12 July 1944; undated (July 1944); 15 January 1945 (penciled draft). To Louis Slade, 8 March 1923. To United Nations Preparatory Conference, 3 June 1945. To the United States Congress, 5 May 1941. To all United States senators, 27 January 1945. To Henry A. Wallace, 30 January 1945; 21 September 1946; 22 September 1946; 15 November 1946; 23 November 1946; 11

August 1948; 6 October 1948; 3 April 1949 (message); 2 May 1949. To Ray Lyman Wilbur, 12 March 1939. To Woodrow Wilson, 2 June 1915; 26 March 1916; 11 July 1917; 13 December 1918; 2 March 1921 (draft); undated (draft). To "Dear Member of the World Citizens Association," 13 June 1945. Journals, 6 April 1898. Statement, 30 April 1917. Statement, "Vote for Cox," 27 October 1920. Handwritten draft of marriage service, 13 February 1923. Notes on Nettie's death, undated (August 1923?). Notes on Clark Lawrence, 13 February 1947. "Notes of Information—John Lawrence," marked "Private," 3 June 1939. Note, "A Dream," 20 February 1936. Note, "Easter 1946," 21 April 1946 (see the quotation with which the text closes, above). Penciled note, 15 August 1948. "Rough Draft of Possible Statement about Subversive Attitudes of the Press," 3 May 1942, 30 January 1945. Memorandum of talk with Paul Douglas, 23 March 1948. Interview with Dr. Lewis Pollock, 10 October 1932.

Anita McCormick Blaine and Chauncey McCormick. To "The Council of the League of Nations non-Partisan Association," 25 February 1924.

Cyrus Hall McCormick, Jr. To Woodrow Wilson, 2 April 1898. To Anita, 26 October 1932; 27 June 1934.

Harold Fowler McCormick. To Nettie, 16 September 1912; 2 December 1921. To Cyrus, Jr., and Anita, 21 April 1933.

Nancy Blaine Harrison. Talk at Francis W. Parker School, 22 April 1955.

Stringfellow Barr. To Anita, 21 September 1948. To Nancy, 8 October 1968.

Phelan Beale. To Anita, 12 July 1922.

Cyrus Bentley. To Flora J. Cooke, 26 May 1918. To Dr. Nathaniel Brush, 3 March 1924. Typescript, "The Francis W. Parker School and the War," undated (May 1918?).

Richard Bentley. To Anita, 28 July 1949.

Portia Cheal (secretary to Mrs. Massingbird Rogers). To Nancy, 27 April 1969.

Everett Colby. To Anita (on world citizens organization), 17 December 1924.

Everett Colby and Hamilton Holt. To Anita, 6 February 1924.

Walter Damrosch. To Anita, 16 October 1923.

Barbara Davis. Interviews with Nancy, 7 July 1972, 5 July 1973; with Katharine Taylor, 24–25 April 1973.

Reuel Denney. To Nancy, undated.

Rosalind Greene (of World Citizens Association). To Anita, 2 May 1937; 22 March 1939.
Muriel McCormick Hubbard. To Anita, 7 November 1935.

Edward J. Kempf. To Anita, 9 December 1927.

Tage Larsson (butler). To Nancy, 4 July 1968.

John Blaine Lawrence. To Nancy, 27 May 1968.

Sir Oliver Lodge. To Anita, 6 March 1920; 11 March 1920; 6 May 1920; 27 February 1921; 21 October 1939.

Chauncey McCormick. To Anita, 18 October 1920; 12 February 1923.

Salvador de Madariaga. To Anita, 14 May 1937.

A. J. G. Priest. To Nancy, undated.

Adlai Stevenson. To Anita, 11 March 1941.

T. O. Thackrey. To Nancy, 25 June 1968.

Grace Walker. Memoranda to Anita, 18 January 1930; 24 May 1942.

Henry A. Wallace. To Anita, 25 January 1941; 13 May 1941; 5 February 1945; 24 September 1946; 2 April 1948; 10 July 1948; 13 July 1948; 21 July 1948; 12 August 1948; 17 August 1948.

Ganna Walska. To Anita, undated (17 September 1924?).

Ray Lyman Wilbur. To Anita, 24 May 1939.

Woodrow Wilson. To Anita, 30 November 1912; 22 April 1918; 1 May 1918.

Harris Wofford. To Nancy, 18 February 1954.

Louise (Mrs. Quincy) Wright. To Nancy, 15 April 1954.

NOTES (PAGES 179–235)

1. Paul Wooley, "My Duty in War Time," *The Recorder*, vol. 14, no. 2 (1918), p. 35.
2. *Omaha Morning World-Telegram*, 23 October 1920.
3. Sir Oliver Lodge, *Raymond* (New York, 1916).
4. Charles A. Mercier, *Spiritualism and Sir Oliver Lodge* (London, n.d.).
5. *New York Times*, 15 January 1922.
6. Ibid., 18 June 1922.
7. Ganna Walska, *Always Room at the Top* (New York, 1943), extensively quoted by Effie Alleyson in the *Chicago Herald-American Pictorial Review*, 10 October 1943.
8. *Proceedings of the Onwentsia Conference*, Lake Forest, Illinois, 4–6 April 1941, p. 52.
9. Article by Anita, "Help England While We Arm," *Chicago Herald-American*, 21 January 1941.
10. "Program of Russian Fair and Cabaret," Hotel Sherman, Chicago, 30 September to 1 October 1942.
11. *Proceedings of the Onwentsia Conference*, pp. 404, 410–11.
12. E. J. Kahn, Jr., "A Wayward Press," *The New Yorker*, 15 April 1950.
13. *Chicago Tribune*, 4 November 1947.
14. *Chicago Herald-American*, 14 February 1948.
15. *Chicago Sun*, 28 June 1944.
16. Ibid.

17. Henry A. Wallace, *Statesmanship and Religion* (New York, 1934), p. 96.

18. Curtis D. MacDougall, *Gideon's Army* (New York, 1965), vol. 1, p. 297.

19. Harris Wofford, "A Cold War Odyssey: Story of the Foundation for World Government" (unpublished study, undated; in author's files).

20. Quoted in a letter from Harris Wofford to Nancy, 18 February 1954.

21. *New York World-Telegram*, 14 September 1948 ("Angel's Million Assures Wallace Post-Election Job").

22. *National Guardian*, 18 October 1948.

23. T. O. Thackrey, "The Compass Story: Some Lessons Learned in Failure," *Editor and Publisher*, 26 December 1953, pp. 9, 50–51.

24. Ibid.

INDEX